CHINA IN AN ERA OF TRANSITION

China in an Era of Transition

Understanding Contemporary State and Society Actors

Edited by
Reza Hasmath and Jennifer Hsu

palgrave
macmillan

CHINA IN AN ERA OF TRANSITION
Copyright © Reza Hasmath and Jennifer Hsu, 2009.

All rights reserved.

First published in 2009 by
PALGRAVE MACMILLAN®
in the United States—a division of St. Martin's Press LLC,
175 Fifth Avenue, New York, NY 10010.

Where this book is distributed in the UK, Europe and the rest of the world,
this is by Palgrave Macmillan, a division of Macmillan Publishers Limited,
registered in England, company number 785998, of Houndmills,
Basingstoke, Hampshire RG21 6XS.

Palgrave Macmillan is the global academic imprint of the above companies
and has companies and representatives throughout the world.

Palgrave® and Macmillan® are registered trademarks in the United States,
the United Kingdom, Europe and other countries.

ISBN-13: 978–0–230–61350–8
ISBN-10: 0–230–61350–0

Library of Congress Cataloging-in-Publication Data

China in an era of transition: understanding contemporary state and
society actors / [edited by] Reza Hasmath and Jennifer Hsu.
    p. cm.
Includes bibliographical references and index.
ISBN 0–230–61350–0
    1. China—Social conditions—2000– 2. China—Economic conditions—
2000– 3. China—Politics and government—2002– I. Hasmath, Reza.
II. Hsu, Jennifer.

HN733.5.C4295 2008
306.0951—dc22   2008035082

A catalogue record of the book is available from the British Library.

Design by Newgen Imaging Systems (P) Ltd., Chennai, India.

First edition: April 2009

10 9 8 7 6 5 4 3 2 1

Printed in the United States of America.

Contents

Figures and Tables

Abbreviations

ACFTU	All-China Federation of Trade Unions
ACWF	All-China Women's Federation
BBS	Bulletin Board Site
BLAOMW	Beijing Legal Aid Office for Migrant Workers
CBD	Central Business District
CCI	Conspicuous Consumption Index
CCYL	Chinese Communist Youth League
CEA	Chinese Ecological Agriculture Movement
CMC	Compassion for Migrant Children
CPC	Communist Party of China
CSO	Civil Society Organization
EDI	Expenditures Disparity Index
FUSVA	Fudan University Student Volunteers Association
GMO	Genetically modified organism
GONGO	Government-organized Nongovernmental Organization
GYZJ	Gongyou Zhijia
HWEI	High-wage, education-intensive
IFOAM	International Federation of Organic Agriculture Movements
IOE	Individually Owned Enterprises
LHA	Loving Heart Association
MOA	Ministry of Agriculture
NGO	Nongovernmental Organization
NIES	Nanjing Institute of Environmental Sciences
OCIA	Organic Crop Improvement Association
OFDC	Organic Food Development Center
PRC	People's Republic of China
RAJY	Reai Jiayuan
RBF	Rockefeller Brothers Fund
SEPA	State Environmental Protection Agency
SEZ	Special Economic Zone
SOE	State-owned Enterprise

SPEEC	Survey on Private Enterprises and Entrepreneurs in China
SSC	Shining Stone Community
TBC	Taiwanese business community
TVE	Township and village enterprise
TXXW	Tongxin Xiwang
XSTX	Xishou Tongxin
XXN	Xiaoxiao Niao

INTRODUCTION

Reza Hasmath and Jennifer Hsu

China's recent rise to prominence has resulted in constant media attention and academic enquiries; its successes and scandals are swiftly brought to the forefront of the public's consciousness. However, the nation's achievements and failures are often viewed in a vacuum, where little thought is given to the interrelatedness of social issues from both state and society perspectives. Given the continued dominance of the Chinese state in many aspects of society, yet, bearing in mind the growing role of social actors in shaping China's development, the contributors of this collection resituate our understanding of the challenges facing the nation by presenting a nuanced view of Chinese state-society relationship.

Thirty years of unrelenting economic development has created a range of social issues that China needs to contend with to ensure it does not hamper future growth. Factors such as urbanization, the marginalization of social groups, the emergence and influence of the business elites, and the potential for dissent by Internet users, present interesting challenges and insights into the workings between state and society. The pressing nature of these issues has given rise to new social actors. The cumbersome state has meant social actors, such as entrepreneurs and migrant workers, are increasingly relying on themselves, rather than waiting for solutions directed by the government. Nonetheless, the state is still dominant and far from retreating from the social realm—it is presently reconfiguring itself to "better manage" society. What we see is the beginning of an era of transition where the Chinese state no longer has a monopoly on managing social development.

Social actors are demonstrating their activeness in managing their own affairs, but at the same time negotiating with the state to increase the space afforded to them to further advance their causes. Rather than treating social actors as victims of the state's persistent drive for economic growth,

Jennifer Hubbert examines the role of retired intellectuals and their relationship with the state. Her chapter suggests intellectuals who emerged from Mao's period have had varied experiences due to economic liberalization. Nevertheless, intellectuals have been able to utilize their narrative of suffering from the Maoist period, where they were under-appreciated for their skills and marginalized for the sake of national development. As a result of their sufferings, they now use their experiences to lay moral claim on contemporary China. That is, they have deployed their sufferings to legitimate their moral authority to represent the nation.

The relationship between women and the state have also seen dramatic shifts since the start of economic reforms. Carrie Liu Currier's chapter illustrates that unlike intellectuals, women workers in present day China have become increasingly marginalized at the hands of the state, where they are encouraged to return to more traditional household roles. Currier argues the Chinese state has effectively adopted policies favoring a more flexible female workforce to appease the more volatile male workforce. She demonstrates if the state continues to negatively intervene against female workforce, there is great potential for dissatisfaction that may evolve into more overt forms of activism. Overall, Currier's chapter suggests the need to be aware of the possibility for social action against the state, especially if further state failures continue for various social groups.

The tension between the state and ethnic groups is another issue deserving significant attention. Reza Hasmath's chapter on ethnic minorities in Beijing depicts the importance of the integration of ethnic minorities to the development of the city. However, for a variety of policy and sociological reasons discussed in the chapter, despite having higher levels of education than the majority Han, ethnic minorities are poorly represented in high wage, education-intensive occupational sectors. What we see in Hasmath's assessment of Beijing's ethnic minorities is again inequity in the employment situation, similar to Currier's observations on the female workforce.

Ian Morley's chapter on the management of urbanization across China demonstrates this desire on the part of the state to reinforce the developmental ideal, but within a discourse shaped by the elites. The spatial transformation that is taking place in Chinese cities shows that while the urban elites are attempting to speak of shared values of "modernization" to benefit all, owing to an unequal distribution of wealth from China's tremendous economic development, urban restructuring has had different meanings for various urban actors. Seemingly, urban elites have negotiated the terrains of economic development and have translated the abstract into reality, as evidenced by the high rises erected across the China's urban landscapes.

The mechanism behind the spatial transformations outlined in Morley's chapter is the focus for Xiaogang Deng, Lening Zhang, and Andrea Leverntz. Their chapter focuses on the dual land use policy that is prevalent in China, especially examining the state's acquisition of land for "public interests" with little or no compensation. Deng et al. reveal that the convergence of interests by developers and government officials has essentially marginalized those who are most dependent on their land for a livelihood. The decentralization of the power structure has given local governments greater autonomy to design and enforce policies, and what is occurring is a state structure that is failing to protect its citizens.

Spatial transformation of the urban areas is not only occurring under the direction of urban elites, but also at the hands of migrant workers. Li Zhang's study of *chengzhongcun* literally meaning "village within a city," maps the dynamic relationship between the state and migrants and indigenous villagers of *chengzhongcun*. Far from victims of the state's ideal of development and modernization, villagers and migrants have defied government attempts to bring order to the chaotic development of these *chengzhongcun*. Where there is demand for housing from migrant workers moving into the cities, there will be attempts by villagers to subvert the authorities to supplement their income.

The theme of migrant workers is further developed in Jennifer Hsu's chapter, focusing on the role of the state in the development of civil society organizations representing migrant workers in Beijing and Shanghai. The surfacing of these organizations is indicative that the room for new social actors to participate in the development of the nation is certainly larger than prereform times and it is in part, attributable to the state's decreasing capacity. What we see in Hsu's chapter is the savvy nature of these organizations to work within the confines of government boundaries to gradually push for change for migrant workers and also extending the borders of their work.

Similarly in Jing Yang's chapter on entrepreneurs in China, is their adaptation strategy to the political environment to advance their own agenda. While Yang shows that new and young entrepreneurs are increasingly active in the realm of economic policies, it is not for the purpose of sociopolitical change. Thus, the role and intentions of these new social actors is juxtaposed against the backdrop of continuing economic change and expectation for political transformation.

This is further supported by Joshua Su-Ya Wu's chapter on the Taiwanese business community (TBC) in China. The presence of the TBC in China has reshaped not only the economic landscape, but also the social and cultural ones, where they are most active. The closeness of their relationship with the state as suggested by Wu, fosters a culture of collusion and corruption. However, such a relationship is profit driven and rarely is it used in such a sense where it positively affects sociopolitical development. The style of doing business and the lifestyle and norms that the Taiwanese bring to their new Chinese environment is threatening the social harmony of the existing community. Therefore, instead of seeing the state as the exploitative factor in the state-society relationship, both cases of entrepreneurs have utilized their position as new and wealthy social actors to advocate the state to expand their areas of economic operation.

One of the main observations that emerge from the chapters thus far is that the Chinese state is not as homogenized as it first appears. Paul Thiers' chapter focuses on the emergence of nongovernmental organizations (NGOs) and the dual identity of the state in its dealings with various stakeholders. Economic reforms have given or necessitated the need for government institutions to find new sources of income and as a consequence, the formation of corporations has increased the possibility of state fragmentation. Thiers therefore highlights the need to consider the relationship between state and semi-state institutions, suggesting a view for potential political pluralism.

The state-society relationship emerging from online public communities and its relationship with China's foreign relations is explored in the final chapter. Junhao Hong examines the development of patriotic online forums that emerge out of foreign disputes, and assess whether these new social actors can pave the way for greater political participation. In particular, Hong ponders whether the increasing rate of Internet availability and usage across China will unavoidably lead toward political liberalization. Regardless of whether this eventuates in the near future, it does illustrate the importance of nonstate actors in the process of social change.

The range of social actors that have emerged during this era of transition exhibits varying levels of relationships with the state. The Chinese state may still be dominant, but it is clearly no longer the only visible stakeholder in the country's social development. As will be seen in various cases throughout the chapters, economic development has created vastly different experiences across the society, where those affected have become more proactive in resolving the issues confronting them. The space for their growth will expand. It is clear that the state needs to acknowledge their existence and contribution to China if it is to avoid social instability. Which begs the question, how will the state reposition itself? What appears to be emerging is a state that is adapting to the needs of society, but simultaneously reasserting itself through social actors to maintain legitimacy and reassert its usefulness to its citizenry.

CHAPTER ONE

RECLAIMING AUTHORITY: THE NARRATIVE POLITICS OF LOST PRIVILEGE IN CONTEMPORARY CHINA

Jennifer Hubbert

Meng Jinghui's 2002 film, *Chicken Poets*, is a movie about Ouyang Yunfei, a thirty-something year old poet who has lost his voice in China's consumer society. Although Ouyang has published a book of poetry, it is not widely read, and the revelation of his occupation to security officers at the beginning of the film meets with derision and laughter. Finding himself suffering from a lack of remunerative employment and estrangement from his intellectual passion, Ouyang renounces his artistic mission and joins the latest business venture of a former college friend selling black chicken eggs, declaiming the worth of the product alongside laments over his inability to write "successful" poetry. Desperate to reclaim his intellectual voice, Ouyang enlists the aid of a magical compact disc that writes poetry for him, turning the artist into a money-generating celebrity whose face graces advertising billboards and television talk shows. However, such success arrives with a price. The Faustian bargain struck by Ouyang comes in the form of a "poetry" that is merely catchy televised, advertising ditties, accompanied by disco-dancing hipsters, reaping profits for large business conglomerates. In the end, technology and consumption ambush art, and Ouyang is left wondering about the place of poetry in the modern scheme of things. Mired in an existential dilemma on the nature of value, the intellectual is trumped by market mechanisms that determine individual worth.

Although Ouyang despairs the linguistic trivialization of his poetry, his dilemma is as much about the form as the content of this intellectual production. For him, the poetic narrative itself represents a particular moral formation and contestations over its value highlight some very fundamental tensions between intellectual subjectivity, moral authority, and state ideology: in contemporary China's rampant marketization project, what forms of knowledge are valued, what kinds of moral authority derives from those forms of knowledge, and what kind of subjects have access to them?

This chapter examines the contemporary narrative forms of retired intellectuals in Kunming, China who, like Ouyang, navigate the complicated relationship between knowledge, moral authority, and subjectivity as they confront market practices that devalue traditional forms of intellectual knowledge even as state ideology promotes the importance of intellectuals in China's modernization process (see Hubbert 2003). Specifically, I analyze how these intellectuals negotiated such changes through a process of narrative borrowing that deployed both Mao-era oral performances, called *suku* (speaking bitterness), and imperial-era techniques of remonstrance for voicing grievances and asserting moral authority in the post-Mao era. I draw upon Durkheim's (1974) notion of moral authority as a power source, referring to moral authority as the perceived legitimate right to represent the nation, portray its history, assess its present, and embody its modernity. Such narrative borrowing reveals how contemporary moral authority derives from the epistemological approaches of particular narrative forms and intellectual subjectivities and reflects a contingent relationship to material and political value.

These two different narrative techniques represent two distinct epistemological moments, are spoken through different subjects, present diverse paths to moral authority, and suggest different relations between the individual and the state. Dynastic era remonstrance narratives were the purview of scholar-officials who, after long years of concerted effort at mastering the classics of the Confucian canon and wading through an exhaustive imperial examination system, assumed formal positions in the government. Scholar-officials were in control of "ideological legitimacy and moral authority" (Tu 1996, 175) through their ability to interpret the Confucian moral code and define the correct order of the empire, inscribing and reinscribing structure and power in both government and universe (see also Zito 1997 and Spence 1990).

Scholar-officials relied on this moral code to evaluate governmental conduct. When such conduct failed to meet the morally rigorous standards of behavior, literati were ethically obliged to remonstrate—to protest and lodge public complaint (Bonnin and Chevrier 1991).[1] These scholar-officials were thus intended to be both participants in and critics of state structures of power. Some remonstrance performances appeared in written form, such as the poetic lament of Qu Yuan (ca. 340 BC—278 BC), "Li Sao," that chronicles the disillusionment and sorrow he faced during his exile from a corrupt government, while others involved highly ritualistic, public protests such as that of Ming Dynasty official Hai Rui who went to the palace court to reprove the emperor and suggested his impeachment and, anticipating trouble, brought his own coffin.[2]

Remonstrance narratives represented an epistemological perspective that equated power and authority with knowledge: "I know this is true (the failings of the state) because I have studied it (i.e. the Confucian code of conduct)." These narratives were performed by the privileged bodies of scholar-officials as critiques of the fallibility of the very governing body that practically speaking, enabled their existence. Thus the moral authority of the speaker was produced through a particular body of knowledge, and demonstrated and publicized through remonstrance applications of that knowledge, publicizing also a moral separation of scholar and state, even as the scholar was awarded by that state with elevated social and political positions and their attendant material rewards.

Suku practices, on the other hand, mastered during the Maoist era, were enacted not to protest governmental authority but to reinforce it.[3] These narratives were not spoken by the elite but by dispossessed peasants and workers who recounted harrowing tales of starvation, rape and torture, and exploitation, at the hands of local landlords and Republican officials—representatives of the "feudal" regime.[4] Frequently reducing members of the audience to tears, these narratives empowered peasants and workers through a language of suffering and sacrifice (Anagnost 1997).[5] Such performances had several important effects. First, they created class-consciousness among the peasants through speaking about and making public the common experience of exploitation and power (Anagnost 1994). Second, having voiced the experience of powerlessness, they were also represented as embodying the possibility for national growth. This played an important role in establishing a new social hierarchy, not only through constituting peasants and workers as a cohesive group, but also establishing their subject positions as moral authorities of the nation-state.

The epistemological angle of the *suku* narrative, in contrast with remonstrance narratives, reflected a path to authority that spoke of pain rather than privilege: "I know this is true (the authority of the Maoist state) because I have experienced it (the pain and suffering)." Yet, more than merely public venting with no tangible implications, these narratives had consequences beyond the ideological. For while they established peasants and workers as moral authorities for the nation-state, as a result of the land reform movement, they also often resulted, in the direct material improvement of the lives of the speakers. Interestingly, while these narratives highlighted individual and class-based oppression as the basis for knowledge and authority, they ultimately also reinforced the state and the communist party as the locus of power and control. The party not only stopped the oppression, but also provided the speaker a venue in which to have a voice and through which to obtain privileged citizenship, moral authority, and class-consciousness, but also gratitude and debt (Ci 1994, 82–83).

In the narratives presented in the following text, it will become apparent how the contemporary stories of these intellectuals drew upon both *suku* and remonstrance performances to produce a particularly post-Mao narrative claim to moral authority. These new narratives not only referenced the epistemological strategies of earlier narrative forms, but also laid claim to the subjectivities of both subaltern and elite speaking bodies.[6] This compels the problematization of the dichotomy between state and society, pushing one to consider the changing relationship between intellectual subjectivity, subalternity, and state discourse and the attendant implications for moral authority and value. Yet, as we consider these narrative borrowings from the past, we must also consider the possibilities for translating the value of moral authority into another form of value, that of material value, asking how the narrative content references the subjectivity of the market itself, as it too influences the locus of moral authority and value in contemporary China. Ultimately, referencing the subjectivities implicit in both narrative forms has proven inadequate at overcoming the disempowered structural positions in which the speakers found themselves in contemporary China.

Narrative Performances

Typically, studies of intellectuals in post-1949 China have primarily addressed the concerns of elite-level intellectuals.[7] In efforts to represent Chinese intellectual norms and ideas, many have turned to the writings and speeches of elite thinkers such as Fang Lizhi and Liu Binyan.[8] Eloquently spoken, these intellectuals have made heartfelt public appeals on the behalf of other intellectuals for such national transformations as wholesale Westernization and rejection of the party-state. However, public figures such as Fang and Liu, articulate as they are, occupy a special position in China's intellectual hierarchy and represent a unique relationship between intellectual and state. As internationally recognized "representatives" of China, their ruminations on the contemporary People's Republic of China are given great weight outside national boundaries, their treatment within those boundaries subject to intense scrutiny from an international media on the lookout for human-rights abuses and resistance to a perceived totalitarian state.[9] However, as the narratives below suggest, their opinions, concerns, and vision for the future of the nation were not necessarily shared by other intellectuals in China.

This chapter differs from many other studies of Chinese intellectuals in that it addresses the perceptions and conditions of "ordinary" intellectuals, not the renowned physicists and literary moguls. It takes as its object of study teachers, administrators, and researchers who played a role in the dissemination of intellectual expression at local levels and reflects a different relationship to state structures of power. Yet, even if these local intellectuals typically offered little to the national-level discourse directly, they saw their role in the nation-building project as no less important. Even if their intellectual mobilization efforts seemingly amounted to little of significant import, understanding them remains an important goal, for one of the objectives of anthropology is to understand local level practices and daily experiences, and the meaning borne through them. The analysis in this chapter thus offers a particular history of the grievance narratives of a local group of intellectuals and how these narrative forms produced and reproduced various ideals of moral authority within the context of larger state discourses on intellectual value. These narratives question the relationship between state power and legitimacy and demonstrate how struggles over the nation-state are perpetual struggles over individuals' efforts to offer themselves as the embodiment of particular value systems deemed necessary for the nation in its modernization struggles.

Professor Shen's Narrative

Professor Shen was a retired scientist approaching eighty who played two hours of tennis each morning. I got to know Shen when he asked me to tutor his granddaughter in English. Once a week, I went to Shen's house where he and his granddaughter and a half dozen or so of her teenaged friends were gathered. Shen typically selected a topic of conversation for the afternoon, something like religion in the United States, patriotism, or Western educational theory. The topics were predictably so complicated as to make English speaking with a group of fifteen year olds a near impossibility and the conversations quickly degenerated into animated Chinese language discussions of a diverse and always interesting range of subjects. After approximately fifteen minutes of this, several of Shen's friends, usually other retired faculty members or neighbors, would drop by and join our conversations. These discussions inevitably turned to the merits and drawbacks of contemporary Chinese economic reforms and comparisons between China and the United States, focusing particularly on the positions of intellectuals and educational practice. Shen held court over these gatherings, directing both the topics of conversation and their pedagogical effect. The direction of these "lessons" was definitely generational. These conversations were meant both to inform me as a Western, educated intellectual, but also to educate the high school students about the past, and about the moral and intellectual worth of those who had experienced that past.

Born in 1917, Shen went to college in central China for four years and then studied for an advanced degree in England for an additional four years. On returning to China in 1947, he took a job as a professor in Kunming. "Under the Guomindang," Shen informed, "conditions for intellectuals were pretty good, particularly in Yunnan where so many fled because of the Japanese occupation." When asked about his thoughts about liberation in 1949, he explained in a circumspect manner that it was "difficult to say" whether people welcomed Mao and the party.

Shen was married to a physician and had several children, one of whom was pursuing a graduate degree in the United States. He lived with his wife and several members of his extended family in a one-storey, dilapidated, campus dwelling with neither indoor kitchen nor private bathroom. This living situation was a constant source of chagrin to Shen. His intellectual service to the nation had met only with poor plumbing, a marginal pension, and a leaky roof. "Look at me," Shen insisted:

I have been a professor for over forty years and have such a low salary and decrepit living situation. I make one one-hundredth of what an American professor would make. I have had the devotion aspect but not the reward. Mao advocated struggle without unity and reward. That is why he failed...Mao destroyed us. Mao was like Qin Shi Huangdi, the emperor who chopped of the heads of so many intellectuals.[10] Mao feared us, he feared the intellectuals. Look at all that he destroyed. Mao was a despotic emperor who allowed nothing other than his own thought. We intellectuals loved the country and were highly patriotic, but devotion and reward must be united.

Although Shen hinted that he was not an early supporter of the communist regime, he frequently emphasized that for intellectuals like himself, devotion to the nation remained at the forefront of their practical endeavors. "What is important" he told me, "is to do something valuable for others, for the motherland." Yet often, Shen's objective of helping the motherland conflicted with the self-sacrificial policy of individual subjugation demanded by Mao. This was a policy that in the 1950s often mandated that intellectuals either move to places they did not desire, teach subjects in which they had no interest, or even give up academic endeavors altogether if the subjects were deemed superfluous or dangerous to Communist Party of China (CPC) ambitions and national guiding principles. Another retired intellectual, for example, an anthropologist who had studied at an American missionary-supported university in pre-1949 Beijing, was assigned to the politics department when anthropology departments throughout the nation were deemed tools of western imperialism and shut down.[11] After the death of Mao, he was relegated to the mailroom where he translated the addresses on incoming envelops from abroad into Chinese.

Shen balked at such sacrificial demands, arguing that helping the motherland occurred not through forsaking one's own interests, but through the pursuit of knowledge at the individual level and with individual reward for the accumulation of knowledge. While this knowledge was not purely for the sake of individual fulfillment but for the good of the nation, its attainment at the level of the *individual*, and of individual critical thought, was the requisite first step toward that individual's application of his or her knowledge to the national project.

In Shen's narratives, it was not just the individual pursuit of knowledge that enabled one to serve the nation-state, but the experience of a particular pedagogical process that enabled the production of the knowledge that in turn underscored the moral authority to which he laid claim. His grievance narratives were not only about individual suffering but also about what he perceived to be larger social problems. "Kids today depend on the teachers," he argued:

> They are not willing or able to think for themselves. When we were in school the teachers looked at our needs. Now it is all teacher focused... The education that I had was very different from today's. We were taught to be independent. We had famous teachers who were strict with us and pushed us to think for ourselves. We were pushed to focus on learning, on methods, not just on exams, not solely on the end result... Now students are too dependent. The purpose is just to pass. Knowledge is defined [for them]. The youth know the exact answers. There is no room for creativity... People today are just focused on living standards, they want money, high salaries... They want more than they can get and so get the money in corrupt ways.

Shen related the intellectual's duty to draw attention to problems with the state to the demands of a true nationalist who remains loyal to Confucian demands for remonstrance, disdaining blind obedience: "True Confucianism does not call for blind obedience. It says that if something is not right, you should not obey. People need to treat others well, not blindly follow orders or the collective."

Shen perceived the degeneration of educational standards to have led to a more general national crisis:

> The main problem is that we lack educated leaders. The next generation of leaders is not going to be any better. They are the kids of the big officials' families and they control all the money but they do not get educated.
>
> The problems in China are not necessarily those of population [numbers] but of education. The quality of the population is getting worse and

worse as time goes on. It's just not getting better because fewer and fewer are getting educated and the standards are getting worse...The outlook on the future—it is very difficult to see, it looks dangerous...Today they [youth] have nothing, just beliefs in money.

There is a latent crisis in China...What kind of crisis, it is difficult to say, but it feels like it will happen...I look at the future prospects of this country and feel we are in great danger.

Thus the initial crisis with which I began Shen's narrative, the decrepit apartment and inadequate salary, became a national crisis, the intellectual suffering directly related to future peril for the nation itself. For Shen, this crisis was directly linked to education, yet it was clearly not a case of the number of people getting educated in China, for in terms of sheer figures, the educated sector of the population has increased quite significantly in both the Mao and post-Mao eras (*Zhongguo Tongji Nianjian* 2002).[12] Rather, for Shen, the problematic factor was that of value, both the value assigned to particular forms of pedagogy and the concomitant value assigned to intellectuals who have worked to safeguard these pedagogical forms. For Shen, contemporary pedagogical methods, based on, in his perception, rote learning and prosaic subject matter, have led to a both national crisis and also a personal crisis. This "crisis" is one in which the independent, critical, western thought in which he was schooled has been met with suspicion and derision, resulting in a meager pension and dilapidated living conditions, decades after the death of Mao and the beginning of the reform era.

Professor Fang's Narrative

Professor Fang, a retired literature professor in his seventies, was a colleague of Professor Shen. Shortly after hearing about my presence at his university, Fang knocked on my door, in search of someone with whom to discuss his literary interests. Although Fang had suffered many of the same career dislocations and educational disappointments as Shen, he had not suffered a similar material displacement, relative to other intellectuals at least, and his newly built, upscale apartment reflected this. Fang and I would meet periodically at his campus apartment where he narrated his story to me in the living room of his seventh floor. As living space was at a premium, new apartment buildings were invariably multistoried; however, few were equipped with elevators. As a result, most occupants preferred second and third story flats. Particularly for older people, climbing six or seven flights of stairs was taxing, but the first story was considered undesirable for reasons of privacy and safety. Less mobile than Professor Shen, Fang spent much of his day shuffling around his campus apartment or settled in an easy chair rereading the literary classics of his young adulthood.

The focal point of Fang's home was an elaborate entertainment center on which rested a large photo of him in cap and gown at his commencement ceremony from a prestigious university in Beijing. Matriculated in the 1940s to study philosophy, Fang was drawn instead to the humanistic novels of the European realists. After graduation, he taught English language and literature in Beijing. However, in the 1950s, the state redirected him into the study of Russian, and he spent the next decade translating scientific documents and interpreting for Soviet advisors. In 1960, following the break in relations between the USSR and China, the party disbanded its cadre of Russian language experts located in the capital, sending Fang to the remote city of Kunming to teach because, as he put it, "There was not any use for all these Russian experts any longer and they had to find something to do with us."

Despite finding himself superfluous to the revolutionary demands of the party a decade into his career, Professor Fang revealed that he was an ardent supporter of the nascent Communist movement. Yet, it was apparent how important a role western education played in informing his idealistic understanding of Communism as he discussed his support drawing upon language of the humanistic ideas of his earlier pedagogical interests. "My friends and I were very influenced by humanistic ideals, by all the literature we had read. We thought that Mao's ideals were very humanistic.[13] There was a song the party sang, that we also sang, about going behind this remote mountain and finding a communist paradise where there would be no exploitation...I supported the Communist Party of China (CPC) because I equated it with democracy. The CPC said it was very democratic...We worshipped Mao."

In a separate conversation, Fang noted how such dreams of democracy collided with the realities of everyday life:

> There is a lot of nostalgia [for the early days of the revolution]. The nostalgia now is silly. These leaders were not democratic, they were not equal with people. Even as far back as the Yanan days, the leaders rode horses while the common people walked terribly long distances. Leaders had great privileges, it was just less conspicuous than it is today...Mao has his own swimming pool, his own train. He could fly anywhere at any time. How is this equal with others?...How is this democracy?

As quickly as Fang had proclaimed his earlier support of the party, he moved into a scathing critique, suggesting that Mao and the party cheated him through their false appeals to the precepts of humanitarian values that were espoused in his educational background and which formed the bases of his ideals of and claims to moral authority. Fang accorded moral authority to those whose commitment to humanitarian ideals remained intact. In his view, the party had sacrificed its authority precisely because it rejected the humanistic values that it once espoused. "Of course we would find that [Communism] attractive. We did not know what Communism was. We did not know of the massive deaths caused by Stalin. We were duped, cheated. Mao betrayed our ideals. Mao was a monstrous power, like Hitler and Napoleon. We were so innocent, so naive. We thought Communism was the humanitarianism we had read about in Tolstoy and Zola." Fang experienced this rejection of humanist ideology as personal suffering, a personal rejection of his authority, sacrificed by a duplicitous party organization.

Whereas Shen's narrative about educational value focused on pedagogical method, Fang's converged predominantly on discussions about content. Yet for both intellectuals, a key factor behind the downfall of early ideals was the deemphasis on the primacy of the individual, whether as an equal among others or as in terms of the individual's ability to foster independent, critical thought. In contrast, while Shen kept coming back to how his educational background led to the deplorable material state of his life, his decrepit apartment, his low salary, despite his devotion to the motherland, Fang highlighted the material benefits of contemporary Chinese policy,

> Today is the best era in modern Chinese history. Look at my apartment, it's so big. Life is so much better, there is so much more freedom to speak. Most have benefited, although some haven't. Look at the workers in the state factories, they have so much leisure. They can sit around and play cards. They can go do odd jobs to make money after work.

Fang was able to partake, relatively to many other intellectuals, of the goods and services made available in the newly capitalist system in China. Yet at the same time, he deplored how the content of his educational background, the humanism he had once trusted to revitalize the nation, had been perverted, the crisis one in which a humanism that promised an intellectual freedom failed to materialize, the personal suffering one of a rejection of ideology.

Nonetheless, despite the material benefits he had attained, Fang too saw an imminent crisis in China, laying blame on the lack of belief systems in China, offering his own faith in Christianity and humanism as an alternative.

> No one believes in Communism. It is a failure. Look at the Soviet Union, at Eastern Europe. Even if you got a group of CPC leaders together and if they were frank, they would admit that they do not believe. It is just a way of having power. People today only join for power reasons. People

need a belief system. People need a belief system. Christianity is the best one. Students today do have a "crisis of beliefs."[14] No one believes in Communism...Communism is the devil in disguise. You take the clothes off and it is only bad inside...Christianity is the best belief system. The CPC surreptitiously supports it because they see that the calmest villages, the most law-abiding places are those with citizens who are Christians.

Thus Fang's grievance narrative, like Shen's, begins with the self, with job transfers and ideological loss, and ends with a story of national crisis, linked directly to the nation's rejection of the premises of the two men's educational backgrounds.

The Politics of Narrative and Authority

As I begin to analyze the specific nature of Shen's and Fang's grievance narratives, it will become clear how these retired intellectuals selectively utilized the structure and content of *suku* and remonstrance narratives to lay claims to moral authority in the reform era. Interestingly, and seemingly paradoxically, Shen and Fang also drew on the various subjectivities of both *suku* and remonstrance speakers to reposition themselves, vis-à-vis governmental structures of power, as the legitimate representatives of the nation-state.

One of the paradoxes of these grievance stories, must surely be the mere existence of the narrative borrowing, the fact that contemporary intellectuals deployed aspects of a narrative form whose content in the past had been used to denigrate their claims to moral authority, utilizing an historical narrative form from which they were originally excluded and in which they were originally excoriated to illustrate their own contemporary value. Yet, when one considers the structures of contemporary and *suku* narratives, correspondences emerge. Typical *suku* structure went as follows: "Here is my life, I have suffered, I have been marginalized and oppressed. It is this marginalization and oppression that makes me the legitimate representative (moral authority) of the country, my historical experience." Such narratives, once begun, segued from personal suffering to national suffering, offering the experience of the speaking self and the production of particular forms of knowledge that accompanied that experience, as the answer to national suffering.[15] Shen's narratives, for example, frequently referenced the embodied suffering caused by his living situation and his low salary while Fang's often concerned the suffering inherent in his intellectual marginalization over the years.

Yet interestingly, this epistemological approach, that of "truth" being known through the embodiment of pain and suffering, typical of the *suku* narrative, through which they maintained their moral authority, was a direct result of social and educational backgrounds that resulted in their earlier exclusion from participation in the original *suku* sessions. Even as intellectual claims to moral authority, based on elite, humanist educational standards, clashed at the most fundamental level with Maoist ideals for a peasant and worker based socialist utopia, the manner in which "bitterness" and "suffering" became a recognizable category in Mao-era ideology, and such a key component in narrative strategy, renders similar narratives recognizable and categorizable today.

While employing the narrative structure of the *suku* performance, these intellectuals also stressed an epistemology that defined academic-based knowledge as the path to "truth" and understanding. References to "traditional" Confucian mores and practices dot these narratives, as does commentary about the superiority of their "Western"-oriented, humanist educational backgrounds.[16] In the manner of remonstrance practices, Fang and Shen referenced the knowledge obtained through adherence to these mores, practices, and philosophies, to critique state structures of power that rejected both the philosophies of their youth and the moral authority associated with them. Thus, it was the content of a remonstrance narrative form, intellectual experience, and knowledge, a content that was not only deemed superfluous and even antithetical to socialist revolution, but also rejected as a source of legitimacy in the original *suku* performances, that was injected into the structure of a *suku* narrative form, to construct a distinctly post-Mao narrative claim to moral authority. Linking the two narrative forms, these intellectuals explicitly noted how it was precisely this content, the epistemological energy of the remonstrance performance— the commitment to independent and critical thought, the love of and political commitment to humanism—that was the cause of the bitterness and suffering they had later endured. This was, their narratives suggested, precisely because it was used to disparage intellectuals as a group and persecute specific members, but it was then framed within the structure of the *suku* performance to accord it narrative power. For both men, this personal suffering was linked to the nation's suffering, the nation's loss, for they understood their particular intellectual training and skills to be the foundation of true progress. In their eyes, as the nation forsook the moral authority embedded in both the content and pedagogy of their educational backgrounds, and in the resultant suffering they experienced, it also forsook its chance for redemption.

Another important aspect of the content of these grievance narratives was their focus on marginalization. Yet, what is important here is not merely the trope of marginalization and how that validates moral authority, but also what it signifies about the subaltern subject. Following the death of Mao in 1976, the state officially rehabilitated many intellectuals who had been publicly humiliated and denounced in previous campaigns and reclassified them as workers (mental laborers) that enabled them to obtain improved housing and increased pay (Madsen 1990).[17] The contemporary official line on intellectuals is visually illustrated by the minting of a new version of the Chinese fifty yuan banknote. On it, standing regally beside a peasant and a worker, is a gray haired, bespectacled "thought worker" who has replaced the soldier in the previous trinity (Hubbert 2003, 273).[18] This links intellectuals to the nation through symbolic incorporation with monetary fungibles, important markers of contemporary success as demonstrated implicitly and explicitly throughout this collection (Hubbert 2003, 273).[19]

The post-Mao discourse on patriotism has also changed somewhat, having rejected the narrative of self-sacrifice that dominated the Maoist era, and offering instead a renewed emphasis on individual achievement as the source of national greatness, targeting intellectuals as crucial to the fulfillment of national modernity (Hoffman 2006). Mao's death, and the public recognition of the failure of his utopia, thus represented an opportunity for some of the previously disenfranchised, like intellectuals, to reclaim the moral authority of the national subject, to reassert themselves as enlightened conscience of the nation.

However, this era has also represented a paradox for intellectuals such as Shen and Fang. Although public discourse has rejected the Maoist experiment, the source of their displacement, these intellectuals did not feel that true emancipation or appreciation had materialized. As Shen remarked, "They've changed the soup but not the medicine" or as Fang contended "Now we have Socialism with Chinese characteristics. It's a code name for capitalism, but the worse of both worlds, capitalism and bureaucracy. It's worse than in England when the industrial revolution began. Child labor, slave labor, people working for low wages, bad conditions. No one believes the slogans anymore. It's just propaganda."

Theoretically, Shen's liberal, science-based, Western education and Fang's English language facilities, firmly embed them within the state's contemporary modernization project that is Western-oriented, science, and technologically driven, and within a social context that accords status to educated individuals.[20] However, it was precisely from the perspective of their educational backgrounds that these retired professors proffered a critique of contemporary practice and rejected it as lacking. For in fact, rather than revesting moral authority in the intellectual class, it has become the market, as a reified actor, with its discourse of financial return as individual achievement that dominates popular consciousness, evident in Wu's and Yang's chapters. Thus, the education and experience that Shen and Fang believed to have located them uniquely to participate was once again shunted aside in the interests of an alien national ideology, this one focused on capitalist models of material prosperity.

Clearly, the subjectivity of the Confucian scholar and the expectations for intellectual participation in the state apparatus, remain models for these retired, intellectuals, born and educated in the Republican era that despite its rejection of automatic intellectual advancement into state ranks of power, largely retained earlier notions of intellectual value and moral authority. Nonetheless, their continuous references to their own marginality through the Mao years and into the present, reflects strongly on the marginalization rendered so prominent and accorded so forcefully with moral authority among the original *suku* speakers. Yet, these intellectuals were not assuming the identity of the subaltern, but were, like the original *suku* performers, not about maintaining the status of the subaltern, but in using that status to gain moral authority and the forms of power and value concomitant with that authority. The original *suku* performances focused on the experiences of exploitation and powerlessness, but it was a powerless of the past that was to be transmuted, via the mechanism of an all-powerful party, into power in the future. *Suku* performances were not about demonstrating immediate power but about demonstrating the kind of status that subaltern subjectivity promised for the future. Although moral authority lay in the experiences of exploitation of the subaltern, voicing the marginalization was a prominent step in its erasure.

Neither Fang's nor Shen's narrative laid claim to desiring subalternity, but to the moral authority that subalternity suggests and the future power that it portended in party discourse. While scholars in the pre-Mao era claimed and were granted authority based on their educational experiences and the control over a particular body of academic knowledge, by the Maoist era claims to authority were laid and established with reference to the symbolic power of suffering and oppression. Although such intellectuals today speak from the relative positions of authority that come from being intellectuals in a post-Mao China, nearing the end of their lives, these intellectuals were acutely aware of the near impossibility of obtaining any other form of authority and power. These narratives positioned Fang and Shen to assume the authority of the subaltern rather than the position of the subaltern, essentially utilizing Maoist categories of power to subvert a post-Mao social apparatus that disavows their claims to legitimacy.

The hybrid subjectivities to which intellectuals laid claim in their contemporary grievance narratives compel an assessment of how these narratives structure the relationship between intellectuals such as Fang and Shen and the state. In the original *suku* performances, the party was the organizing force and the recipient of the power created and defended—even as the speaker benefited socially and materially and claimed moral authority through submitting to the ideologies of party supremacy. Remonstrance narratives also entailed a position in which the speaker's power was enabled by the state. Yet whereas in *suku* narratives, the speakers became proxy for the party, in remonstrance narratives the speaker acted as proxy for a more encompassing power, that of a Confucian moral order that mandated that the state's loyal subjects also became its critics. Nonetheless, both narratives ultimately reinforced the authority of the state, for remonstrance narratives, having pointed out the shortcomings of the government, were ultimately meant to reinforce its power through realignment with the correct order of the cosmos.

Fang's and Shen's performances explain the exploitation of the past as leading to a powerless also in the present that state recognition of intellectual value has been unable to overcome. Thus their own grievance narratives are performed within a new system of meaning, neither in uncontested defense of party political authority nor consistently in rejection of state power and indicate a complicated and frequently ambivalent relationship with the state. Even as Fang and Shen critiqued many forms of state power quite ruthlessly, they employed their narratives to assert their moral authority as in the best interests of the nation-state; it was the *effects* of state policy rather than the state itself that was rejected. They were critics, but not necessarily renouncers, of the state, revealing not a dichotomy of state and society, but a convergence of personal visions with state policy *intent* rather than consequence.[21]

Speaking of Value

Two forms of value dominated these stories. In these narratives, the most obvious form of value was the moral positioning that accompanied the knowledge and suffering these intellectuals had experienced. Yet, attending this form of value is another very real form of value, and here I speak of material value. In pre-Mao China, when these intellectuals received their educations, the two forms of value were immediately linked; the moral authority associated with these intellectuals' educations, knowledge, and experience translated directly into social status and monetary value. Although such links between education, material value, and moral authority were largely negated in Maoist China, *suku* narratives spoke to the intent of a Socialist policy that was again to equate material value and moral authority, albeit this time made present through suffering rather than academic learning. Although to a certain extent the links between moral authority and educational status have been resuscitated in the contemporary era, the market does not offer material recompense to the equation. Because of their ages and the forms of value associated with their educational backgrounds—the humanist individual versus the capitalist individual—Fang and Shen have remained unable to develop the moral authority associated with the forms of value that dominates their narratives.

Despite his sacrifices for the nation, Shen has not attained the material value that is indicated by intellectuals' picture on the post-Mao fifty yuan note. His leaky plumbing, his dilapidated housing, all reflected his inability to turn one form of value into another. Moreover, his kind of intellectualism no longer retained its earlier moral authority. Thus, in front of me, in front of his friends, and his granddaughter and her friends, he chose a form of narrative voice that privileged one notion of value over another. Drawing on his educational experience and the forms of knowledge that went along with that experience to pose himself, and others like him as moral authorities in contemporary China, as those with the legitimate right to represent the nation, portray its history, assess its present, and embody its modernity.

Fang on the other hand, relative to Shen, has benefited materially from the reforms, but emphasized his loss of that other form of value, the moral authority that was to accompany the forms of learning and modes of knowledge of his educational background. Their narratives became an assertion of value, of a moral authority to which they were no longer privy because they were too old and too firmly embedded in epistemological forms of belonging negated as the market becomes the ultimate arbiter of value in contemporary China.

Notes

1. For portrayals of intellectual remonstrance see the *sanwen* essays "Peng Shan" (Damage) by Zhou Zuoren and "Xiao de Lishi" (A Funny Story) by Zhu Ziqing. On remonstrance, see Nivison 1964 and Hucker 1964. The moral potency of remonstrance practices was demonstrated before a global audience during the demonstrations in China in 1989, as three student leaders knelt down before the entrance to the Great Hall and presented their petitions to the government.
2. On Qu Yuan, see Schwarcz 1996. The story of Hai Rui was made into a play in 1965 and is considered an important precursor to the Cultural Revolution (Fisher 1993; Wagner 1993).
3. The earliest *suku* narratives began in the 1930s to mobilize peasants against the landlords in areas where the Red Army was taking control. For English-language discussions and examples of *suku* narratives see Chan, Madsen, and Unger 1992; Belden 1970; Hinton 1967.
4. The term feudal was used in Maoist China to characterize the exploitative social relationships of the pre-Mao era.
5. Gender too became in important category of belonging in these narratives. See Rofel 1999.

6. Subaltern refers to individuals who either as individuals or as members of a group, exist outside hegemonic structures of power.

7. The following narratives are culled from discussions that took place over the course of a year. They reflect discussions on different days, weeks, and months, and they are presented to reflect a narrative story and structure rather than a strictly chronological succession of events, to highlight the defining features of the speaker's point of view. This chapter is part of a larger project examining narratives of national belonging and moral authority among four generations of Chinese intellectuals. This larger study involved multiple, extensive interviews with several dozen intellectuals who completed their educations in the pre-Mao era. Here I present only two of these narratives to represent the content of the data set from which they are drawn.

8. For example Link 1992; Chow 1991; Li and Schwarcz 1983–1984.

9. Xudong Zhang (1998) notes how elite Chinese intellectuals are divorced from the implications of everyday life for local intellectuals. Similarly, John Borneman (1992) notes how pre-1989 reportage on East Germany focused on dissident voices that while enjoying popularity in the capitalist West, met with widespread disapproval within the nation.

10. *Qinshi huangdi* was the Qin Dynasty emperor noted for his tyranny and mistreatment of Chinese scholars.

11. Politics departments in China at the time were devoted to the study of Marxism, Leninism, and Mao Zedong thought.

12. See especially Chapter 20, pp. 671–697.

13. Fang's observations on humanism and humanistic ideals typically referenced appeals to individualism, cosmopolitanism, and independent thought. However, they were always framed within references to applying such ideals in service to the country rather than of the self.

14. This phrase "crisis of belief" (*xinyang weiji*) was a common one at the time, referring (in this case) to members of the younger generations who did not grow up in fervently revolutionary times and did not have strong political beliefs.

15. Erika E. S. Evasdottir (2005) also notes how suffering plays a role in establishing claims to authority for what she calls the "oligarchs" of the academic, archaeology world.

16. It is important to note here how the meaning of the West and of a Western-oriented education changes over time. For these intellectuals, it signified a humanist education focused on the dignity of the individual. For contemporary youth, that same idea connotes an economic program focused on consumption (Hubbert 2003).

17. On the effects of the post-Mao reclassification of social categories, see Hubbert 2006.

18. Originally cited in Schwarcz 1992, 116.

19. This symbolic step marks a concession to the Confucian tradition that regarded the educated elite as the foundation of Chinese society and soldiers as the "lowest, most ill regarded rung of the social hierarchy" (Schwarcz 1992, 116).

20. One should also note the current importance, in terms of both cultural and economic capital, of English language skills and western educations.

21. Similarly, Judith Farquhar's and Qicheng Zhang's analysis of *yangshen* practices in Beijing reveals a convergence of personal views with state policies that is "neither surprising nor problematic in 'mainstream' Beijing" (Farquhar and Zhang 1995, 308).

References

Anagnost, A. 1997. *National past-times: Narrative, representation, and power in modern China*. Durham, NC: Duke University Press.
———. 1994. Who is speaking here? Discursive boundaries and representation in post-Mao China. In *Boundaries in China*, ed. J. Hay, 257–279. London: Reaktion Books.
Belden, J. 1970. *China shakes the world*. New York: Monthly Review Press.
Bonnin, M. and Y. Chevrier. 1991. The intellectual and the state: Social dynamics of intellectual autonomy during the post-Mao era. *China Quarterly* 127: 569–593.
Borneman, J. 1992. *Belonging in the two Berlins: Kin, state, nation*. Cambridge: Cambridge University Press.
Chan, A., R. Madsen, and J. Unger. 1992. *Chen village under Mao and Deng* (2nd ed.). Berkeley: University of California Press.
Chow, R. 1991. Pedagogy, trust, Chinese intellectuals in the 1990s—Fragments of a post-catastrophic discourse. *Dialectical Anthropology* 16: 191–207.
Ci, J. W. 1994. *Dialectic of the Chinese revolution: From utopianism to hedonism*. Stanford, CA: Stanford University Press.
Durkheim, E. 1974[1906]. *Sociology and philosophy*, D. F. Pocock, trans. New York: Free Press.
Evasdottir, E. E. S. 2005. *Obedient autonomy: Chinese intellectuals and the achievement of orderly life*. Honolulu: University of Hawaii Press.
Farquhar, J. and Q. C. Zhang. 1995. Biopolitical Beijing: Pleasure, sovereignty, and self-cultivation in China's capital. *Cultural Anthropology* 20: 308–327.
Fisher, T. 1993. The play's the thing: Wu Han and Hai Rui revisited. In *Using the past to serve the present: Historiography and politics in contemporary China*, ed. J. Unger, 9–45. Armonk: M. E. Sharpe.
Hinton, W. 1967. *Fanshen: A documentary of revolution in a Chinese village*. New York: Monthly Review Press.
Hoffman, L. 2006. Autonomous choices and patriotic professionalism: On governmentality in late-Socialist China. *Economy and Society* 35: 550–570.
Hubbert, J. 2006. (Re)Collecting Mao: Memory and fetish in contemporary China. *American Ethnologist* 33:145–161.
———. 2003. Signs of the modern: Intellectual authority, pain, and pleasure in reform China. In *Trans-Pacific relations: America, Europe and Asia in the twentieth century*, ed. R. Jensen, J. Davidann and Y. Sugita, 269–292. Westport, CT: Praeger.
Hucker, C. 1964. Confucianism and the Chinese censorial system. In *Confucianism and Chinese civilization*, ed. A. F. Wright, 50–76. Stanford: Stanford University Press.
Li, Z. H. and V. Schwarcz. 1983–1984. Six generations of modern Chinese intellectuals. *Chinese Studies in History* 17: 42–56.

Link, P. 1992. *Evening chats in Beijing: Probing China's predicament.* New York: W. W. Norton.

Madsen, R. 1990. The spiritual crisis of China's intellectuals. In *Chinese society on the eve of Tiananmen: The impact of reform,* ed. D. David and E. Vogel, 243–260. Cambridge: Council on East Asian Studies/Harvard University.

Nivison, D. S. 1964. Protest against conventions and conventions of protest. In *Confucianism and Chinese Civilization,* ed. A. F. Wright, 227–251. Stanford: Stanford University Press.

Rofel, L. 1999. *Other modernities: Gendered yearnings in China after Socialism.* Berkeley: University of California Press.

Schwarcz, V. 1996. The pane of sorrow: Public uses of personal grief in modern China. *Daedalus* 125: 119–148.

———. 1992. Memory and commemoration: The Chinese search for a livable past. In *Popular protest and political culture in modern China,* ed. J. Wasserstrom and E. Perry, 109–123. Boulder, CO: Westview Press.

Spence, J. 1990. *The search for modern China.* New York: Norton.

Tu, W. M. 1996. Destructive will and ideological Holocaust: Maoism as a source of social suffering in China. *Daedalus* 125: 149–179.

Wagner, R. 1993. "In guise of a congratulation:" Political symbolism in Zhou Xinfang's play *Hai Rui submits his memorial.* In *Using the past to serve the present: Historiography and politics in contemporary China,* ed. J. Unger, 46–103. Armonk: M. E. Sharpe.

Zhang, X. D. 1998. Intellectual politics in post-Tiananmen China: An introduction. *Social Text* 55 (16): 1–8.

Zhongguo Tongji Nianjian [China Statistical Yearbook]. 2002. Beijing: Zhonghua Renmin Gongheguo Guojia Tongjibu.

Zito, A. 1997. *Of body & brush: Grand sacrifice as text performance in eighteenth-century China.* Chicago: University of Chicago Press.

CHAPTER TWO
THE GENDERED EFFECTS OF MARKET REFORMS

Carrie Liu Currier

The reforms implemented since 1978 have done more than just change the Chinese economy, but also alter the relationship between state and society. Marketization can be considered as much an economic reform as a social reform when considering how the removal of the iron rice bowl, the privatization of housing, and the retrenchment of subsidies fundamentally changes the socialist contract. Unemployment, increasing costs of living, and inadequate health care are all emerging problems in the reform era, and they highlight the inability of the state to meet the basic needs of its citizens. Although the state is concerned about these trends, its modernization goals appear to outweigh the social costs associated with "development." The individualistic capitalist notion "to get rich is glorious" is replacing the socialist idea of personal sacrifice for the good of the collective, and inequality becomes a consequence of the transition from a socialist to a more market-driven economy.

The implementation and outcomes of the reforms clearly have been unequal and several groups have been left behind in this process. While Jennifer Hubbert examined intellectuals another such group is women, and although their experiences do vary, there are problems in how their roles collectively have been flexibilized and feminized under reform. Using a gender-sensitive lens to analyze how the state's reform strategy has affected urban women, we can see that women have been treated as both supplemental and secondary when it comes to their economic roles. Rather than "hold up half the sky" many women are being encouraged to return to the household, as one of several ways to reduce some of the employment pressures in the reform era, and as a result they are experiencing a resurgence of sex discrimination in the labor market. Women are simply not experiencing reform in the same ways men are, and these differences are central to understanding how the state has managed marketization. To illustrate the gender differentiated effects of reform and what these trends suggest about state-society relations, this chapter examines the changes to both the urban labor market and the household for women. I begin with an overview of women's employment, analyzing the revival of the male breadwinner model by the state. Although the socialist economy was not devoid of these same problems, the market economy's competitive and privatized nature has given employers greater discriminatory power in their hiring and firing practices. With the disappearance of full employment and the state no longer responsible for enforcing at least the idea of equality, women workers are seen as more expendable economically and socially when compared to men. The assumption is that women will be cared for by husbands or fathers; hence, they can return to their primary responsibilities in the home and leave the public sphere for men.

Treating women as secondary workers is not just a product of social norms that associate women with the household; it also has been institutionalized by state policies and campaigns. Therefore, this chapter also examines the state's use of "femininity" to assist in the push for women to return to the household. At different times the state has manipulated the images of what is gender appropriate, and it has in effect flexibilized women's labor, mobilizing them as a reserve labor force and withdrawing them from the public sphere when necessary. In the reform era, women have been encouraged to return to their household duties or to seek jobs that are feminine, based on gender stereotypes. The state has played an important role in this process, explicitly and implicitly, and is changing economic and social expectations for society.

This analysis of the relationship between women and the state shows us how the state has strategically pursued modernization and where its power has begun to weaken. Specifically the state's loosening of public sphere[1] control has led to an erosion of its power in the social realm, empowering societal members to become agents of change. Although the state has focused on economic modernization and development rather than social or political reform, the interconnectedness of these issues is apparent. Labor restructuring affects not only economic life, but also societal relations and the state must find ways to quell rising discontent. The question that remains is whether the state will be able to remain in control while overhauling economic structures and institutions, or whether the state's continued intervention will undermine economic reform and its citizens. The state admittedly cannot maintain its current pace of marketization without paying closer attention to the social costs. More specifically, these trends raise concerns about the future path of reform and the effect it has on women. To support these claims, I draw on evidence from a survey of

292 Beijing women on their employment opportunities/conditions, their home environment, and their attitudes toward reform to determine both how they have fared and how they perceive their futures. This in-depth case study shows that different cohorts of women are increasingly aware of the feminization and flexibilization of their labor, and it examines the types of pressures facing the state to adjust its modernization strategies.

Labor Restructuring and Redeploying Femininity

The urban labor market has undergone a significant overhaul in the last thirty years. In China's prereform economy, individuals did not have control over the allocation of their labor, as we saw in the case of Professor Shen and Fang in the previous chapter, but they were protected from the harms and inequalities present in capitalist systems. Although individuals could not readily change jobs, they also did not fear unemployment. The state had firm control over work and home life by demonetizing the economy and serving as the primary provider of jobs, housing, rations, and other benefits. In contrast, the post-1978 era fundamentally altered the Chinese economy by introducing a contract labor system to replace lifetime employment, downsizing several state-owned enterprises (SOEs) to promote economic efficiency, and removing price controls and rations. These incremental reforms have marked the beginning of the state's relaxed control over the economy and the move toward privatization. However, the effects of this transformation have not been gender-neutral and examining the reforms with a gender-sensitive lens shows that women have been instrumental to the state's successful management of reform up to this point.

In the early stages of reform, labor restructuring resulted in labor retrenchment. Among those targeted as redundant or expendable workers included both younger workers, who lacked seniority and were more likely to enter contract labor positions, and women. Under the contract labor system workers were not guaranteed lifetime employment, and more importantly firms were given greater freedom in their hiring practices (Meng 2000, 82). However, these changes applied mainly to individuals just entering the labor force, whereas workers employed before the contract labor system was introduced were essentially grandfathered in (Korzec 1992; Meng 2000). For women, these labor market changes created new challenges. Under the socialist economic model, which provided for full employment, women were employed at rates on par with men. According to Harrell, "women as well as men were expected to engage in wage labor during this time, so that there was no longer, in the ideology at least, a difference between the woman as the 'inside worker' and the man as the 'outside' worker" (2000, 71). Several public sphere opportunities existed for women, which were facilitated by the "gender-neutral, state-assignment employment system" (Tsui and Rich 1992, 18). However, when marketization gave employers the freedom to discriminate among workers on the basis of sex, women ended up on the losing side. One of the more notable effects was the reemergence of sex discrimination and gender stereotyping with respect to both hiring and firing. Although attention was paid to factors such as seniority, women were generally the last ones hired and the first ones fired when socialism gave way to marketization. In addition, in spite women experiencing many inequalities under socialism and never truly "held up half the sky," privatization meant employers' individual prejudices and preferences could dictate their personnel decisions. Hence, with the state no longer enforcing ideals of equality, traditional beliefs on the value and place of women as dependents resurfaced.

When SOEs had to identify redundant workers, women were readily considered more expendable because their livelihood would be less affected if laid-off. The rationale behind this argument can be tied to androcentric views of the economy that support the idea of the male breadwinner model. Traditionally men have been considered the main economic providers while women are seen as supplementary workers and their roles are associated primarily with the household. Thus, when the state sector is forced to make decisions on which workers are more expendable, men will generally be protected over women. Presumably, women will be provided for by either their husbands or fathers and can more readily be displaced, whereas men are considered primary breadwinners and their retrenchment would more negatively affect the financial well being of the entire household. This higher value attached to male labor was overinflated even before reform, where the allocation of benefits and subsidies through one's *danwei* (work unit) embedded gender inequalities. The allocation of housing and other benefits were typically assigned through the husband's *danwei*, further institutionalizing the idea that men are a household's primary workers. Therefore firing men would be more destabilizing to a household's livelihood. Consequently, we find evidence that when lay-offs occurred in the 1980s women were disproportionately pushed out of the state sector relative to men (Currier 2007a; 2007b).

During these first stages of reform, scholars have also noted a resurgence of sex discrimination as seen in: higher qualifications required of women applicants, a prevalence of "flower vase" hiring, forced retirement at rates five to ten years earlier than men, and the tracking of women into certain occupations deemed most suitable for them but lacking high pay or job mobility.[2] In addition, legal measures designed to prevent gender discrimination can end up having the opposite effect. Policies that protect women workers by enforcing maternity leave and reduced hours during pregnancy are sometimes used by employers to justify differential treatment or lower employment rates of women (Boserup 1989, 113). For instance, as employers must permit reduced work loads or work hours during pregnancy and grant maternity leave, women can be seen as more expensive to employ. When given a real choice regarding whom to employ, providing these additional benefits can negatively affect employer's decisions to hire female employees (see Kerr and Delahanty 1996; Korabik 1993; Wolf 1985; Woo 1994; Wu 1995). In addition, Article 25 of the *Protection of Rights and Interests of Women* law (1992) declares, "certain work categories or positions are unfit for women," granting employers the power to determine which jobs "suitable" for women (Woo 1994, 280). A combination of these factors arguably contributed to lower employment rates for women under reform and the use of policies like forced early retirement to push them out of the labor force. Even the All-China Women's Federation (ACWF), a state organ responsible for representing the interests of women, began raising awareness about some of these problems and the higher dismissal rates facing women in reform (White, Howell, and Shang 1996, 73).

Although patriarchal values are important for understanding why society views women as secondary workers, the state has been explicitly involved in institutionalizing these values and associating women primarily with the household. Rofel notes, "the state, far from receding in this process, actively involves itself in naturalizing femininity and masculinity" (1994, 219). In the past, the state targeted the female labor force with campaigns designed to return them to their household roles. In the 1950s, Evans argues that "to relieve the pressure of unemployment in the urban areas, women were encouraged to 'go back home'" and women's domestic role was "hailed as a contribution to 'working for the country'" (2002, 339). Later, during the Cultural Revolution, the state encouraged women to leave their home roles as "femininity was criticized as a petty bourgeois characteristic" (Perry 1998, 280). Thus, at different times the state has manipulated the images of what is gender appropriate and has in effect flexibilized women's labor, mobilizing them as a reserve labor force and withdrawing them from the public sphere when necessary.

Given the mounting pressures on employment, with many individuals searching for work in an increasingly competitive market, it comes as no surprise that the state has once again taken an active role in flexibilizing the female labor force. One way this has been accomplished is by creating an environment that encourages women to concentrate back on the household rather than on public sphere employment. Shifting women back into the home helps the state offset labor market pressures and naturalizes the association between women and the household. It is also the case that by creating a "happy home life," the state sees the opportunities and productivity of the entire work force will improve (Dalsimer and Nisonoff 1984, 35). Several scholars (Bian 2000; Hooper 1984; Kerr and Delahanty 1996; Summerfield 1994; Zheng 2003) have linked this reemergence of feminine roles for women with the increase in urban unemployment. Women were advised to "return home" to make way for male workers (Zheng 2003, 163), or to market their "physical attributes to get a job" (Kerr and Delahanty 1996, 38). According to Farris the rationale was, "if the workforce must be reduced because of growing unemployment, it seems more appropriate for women to be the ones to return home" (2000, 155). Overall, these labor strategies that target women as flexibilized workers are not new to the reform era, but they have reemerged with marketization pressures.

Howell argues that another reason women are treated as flexibilized or second-class laborers is they are seen as less threatening to stability when compared to male labor. She states that for the Communist Party of China "gender issues are perceived as politically less important, partly because the demand for women's rights and interests does not unsettle the political status quo too much...because women have not organized around broader political themes such as political reform, but in contrast, protests around labor issues such as strikes and go-slows and petitions about workers' conditions appear to threaten social stability and production" (2000, 371). Under the old system, when the state provided for housing, food, and a variety of other social welfare benefits through the SOEs, workers were dependent on the state and were not likely to act in a way that threatened that livelihood.[3] However with marketization, workers are less dependent on these extra benefits and are driven primarily by wages; free to move and sell their labor to the highest bidder. Therefore, the modern worker is less willing to accept low or worsening labor conditions and would be more likely to make demands on the state by striking, protesting, or demonstrating. Others have noted that labor unrest has clearly been on the rise in the reform era, particularly since Tiananmen in 1989. Perry notes that, "the Ministry of Public Security calculated for 1990–91 a total of 523 unapproved public rallies, marches, demonstrations and petitions involving ten or more people across the country..." and in 1992 that number increased to "more than 540 cases of illegal demonstrations and assemblies and more than 480 strikes involving hundreds of thousands of workers" (Perry 1995, 321). Howell notes that in 1997 the city of Xi'an reported as many as seventy-four protests in the first six months of the year, and that in China as a whole approximately 1,000 complaints on lay-offs alone were "lodged with local governments in 21 provinces" (2000, 365). Finally, Lee states that the Ministry of Public Security documented an increase in protests, which include those related to labor, "from 87,000 in 1993, to 32,000 in

1999," and "in 2003 the number of mass incidents reached 58,000 involving 3 million people, and increased to 87,000 incidents in 2005" (2007, 231). Thus, it is easy to see the growing number of labor protests correlate with the increasing number of SOE closures. These protests have become a regular occurrence in many areas as workers struggle with the dilemmas of increasing unemployment. Furthermore, Hurst and O'Brien (2002) argue that contentious pensioners from downsized SOEs formulate another significant challenge to the state, and the state has been forced to respond to these challenges to uphold the social contracts these workers were promised before reform. In contrast, women generally have not been seen as an organized and significant threat to the state, thus they will be viewed as more expendable compared to unsatisfied male workers.

Despite these efforts to retrench women from the public sphere and to place them into less secure private sector, women in the contemporary era have become empowered in new ways and are important actors that the state cannot continue to overlook. Although the state may have been able to treat women as a supplementary pool of laborers before, there are several trends raised by studying women's employment patterns that suggest greater agency and awareness among women about their changing roles in society. To better understand these issues, an in-depth case study of Beijing will demonstrate how different cohorts of women have experienced flexibilization by the state and what kind of roles they see for themselves with continued reform.

Gendered Reforms in Beijing

For women in Beijing, reform has had different consequences on their employment depending on their age and working status at the time of the different rounds of reform. To illustrate these differences, I draw on survey data that captures the experiences and attitudes of 292 women, in 3 different cohorts, between the ages of 20 and 60.[4] The survey was administered in 2002 in the Haidian district of Beijing only including women with urban *hukou* (residency), while excluding migrant or temporary workers. The Beijing sample referenced here was similar demographically to the greater Beijing population of 11 million, as determined by comparisons to individual and household data from the National Bureau of Statistics on Beijing. I obtained the sample of 292 women by using a combination of random, quota, snowball, and convenience sampling. The characteristics used to determine the quota sample included sex (female), age (20–60), and marital status (married, divorced, single, widowed), where categorization cells utilizing these divisions determined whether respondents were eligible for the study (Wuelker 1983, 163–164). I grouped the women into cohorts on the basis of their first entry into the labor force and the timing of labor market reforms in the state sector. As a result 3 distinct cohorts emerged and women were grouped according to age into: young (ages 20–32), middle (ages 33–45), and oldest (ages 46–60).

The survey was comprised of sixty-five questions, where I asked respondents to report on their employment status, household finances, household labor, and their attitudes toward reform. I also conducted open-ended interviews with the respondents to elicit more information on some of the survey questions. The attitudes of the women toward the past, present, and future of reform provides insight into the levels of satisfaction among different generations of women on the pace and path of reform as well as how they envision their roles in this process. By conducting a cohort analysis, I examine several factors that mark economic life differently for young, middle, and older cohorts of women. Some of the distinguishing characteristics across the three cohorts include the types of jobs they pursue, their reasons for seeking employment, and the emphasis placed on domestic responsibilities. The three cohorts also have very different economic experiences based on the timing of reforms. In this case, the cohorts can be used to examine the trends structuring both the labor market during the different stages of reform and how individuals adapted to these changes as workers. These snapshots of economic life for the three cohorts give us insight into the gendered nature of reform and how women were forced to reorganize their labor. More specifically, I use the cohorts to examine the factors influencing women's moves from SOEs into individually owned enterprises (IOEs), the state's role in this process, and the social consequences of these changes.

The primary factors differentiating the three cohorts include their date of entry into the labor force and the number of different economic reforms they have experienced. Women in the oldest cohort (age 46–60) are distinguished by their entry into the labor force during the socialist era, at a time when lifetime employment was still guaranteed. With an average entry date of 1972, these women have lower human capital investment and have witnessed the greatest variation in labor market conditions compared to the other two cohorts.[5] The middle cohort (age 33–45) is comprised of women who entered the labor market expecting lifetime employment, but immediately found themselves flexibilized from the contract labor system and SOE downsizing mentioned earlier. This cohort has varying levels of human capital investment and as a result, these women were expected to be more negatively affected by the reforms more than the others. Given their lack of seniority at the time of restructuring, these women did not have the same promises of employment stability that the oldest cohort had, making the transition seemingly most burdensome on this cohort. The youngest cohort (age 20–32) faced challenges similar to the middle cohort, in that employment was not guaranteed and the market was becoming increasingly competitive. However, they came of working age when reforms were already clearly under way, on average entering the labor market in 1996. They never had expectations of lifetime employment and have been encouraged to focus on the kind of skills that would be more marketable under reform. Thus their human capital investment is higher, and the kind of employment opportunities they have been presented are rather different. Their work sector concentration is also more varied than the other cohorts, as new opportunities in retail, real estate, and commerce have expanded for them.[6] As these three cohorts will show, the timing of entry into the labor market and the conditions under which they enter have contributed to different levels of success. Moreover, by examining how women have navigated reform we gain insight into the state's motives behind the labor patterns we see emerging and what challenges await the state with further reform.

The key area to examine is the effect of SOE downsizing and the development of the IOE sector. As the state began to loosen its control over the economy and allow the non-state sector development, there were many uncertainties regarding how the non-state sector would perform. It was a carefully managed change that was in line with the gradualist policies characterizing reform in general. According to Davis, one pattern that emerged when the IOE sector was created was that married couples divided their labor between IOEs and SOEs, with one typically staying employed in the SOE for benefits and subsidies, while the other entered the riskier IOE sector (1999, 27). Couples could therefore get the best of both worlds, having the perceived security of the state sector and the greater economic possibilities in the private sector (Tang and Parish 2000, 33). The security offered by the state was not the same type of security available before marketization, but the state sector did still provide access to housing, medical benefits, and subsidies that the IOEs were not necessarily offering. The risk associated with the IOEs was mostly that it was an untested area, so there were more fears about the long-term opportunities and growth potential in this sector. However, in time the IOEs would prove to be more valuable both monetarily as well as in terms of China's overall development.

The SOE-IOE split that couples experienced can be examined more critically for the gender biases in the allocation of spouses to the state and non-state sectors. Although many reform policies appeared gender neutral on the surface, affecting both men and women similarly, there are clear patterns that emerge in the Beijing sample that suggest these policies and labor shifts have disproportionately affected women and have varying results depending on the cohort. When using a gender-sensitive lens to examine labor redistribution in Beijing, some interesting trends material-ize. Among the three cohorts, it comes as no surprise that men and women of the oldest cohort have higher rates of concentration in SOEs than the other two cohorts. Older workers were generally protected from the flexi-bilization the contract labor system created, because they were grandfa-thered in. However, as the cohorts get younger there are fewer individuals concentrated in the state sector and higher rates of employment growth in the non-state sector. Rates of female employment in SOEs reduces by one-third as the cohorts get younger, and male employment also decreases though at a much slower rate (Currier 2007a, 72). These are trends related to the development of the IOE sector and the downsizing of the SOE sector, affecting labor market opportunities for workers who were just entering the market as these changes began. However, in terms of gendered trends several studies (Bian, Logan, and Shu 2000; Fredrich Nauman Stiftung Foundation 1994; Maurer-Fazio, Rawski, and Zhang 1999; Riley 1996; Rosenthal 1998; Summerfield 1994) have shown that women were more frequently labeled as redundant workers, and the middle-aged cohort of women suffered disproportionately from lay-offs in the late 1980s and early 1990s. The women in the Beijing sample demonstrate that this shifting of labor out of SOEs and into IOEs was not gender-neutral, but the outcome is not as bleak as the aforementioned studies would suggest. In fact, men remained heavily concentrated in the state sector, whereas women actually benefited from the shift by experiencing more rapid gains in the non-state sector, particularly those in the middle cohort.

The middle cohort is unique in that those women were shifted out of the state sector into the private sector early in their careers. They suffered from being both new entrants into the labor force at the time of restruc-turing, thus were more likely to fall under the more flexible contract labor system, and from being seen as supplementary to male labor. In addition, the rationale for shifting them out of the more secure state sector was sup-ported by both state campaigns and societal norms reinforcing the idea that women were not breadwinners. With the IOE and private sector con-sidered less secure, it became a new outlet for these women to move into as they were forced out of the state sector with early retirement or lack of contract renewal. Within the sample, we therefore see the SOE-IOE split among couples that Davis (1999) documents, but there is a clear pattern in the middle cohort of women that when an SOE-IOE split occurs, the husband remains in the SOE and the wife moves into an IOE. In contrast, the oldest cohort maintained high levels of SOE concentration for both spouses, since they were less likely to be forced to change their labor from the state sector. The youngest cohort did not experience the same couples effect, since they entered the labor market at a time when the non-state sector had already begun to bloom. This non-state sector no longer had the same degree of uncertainty attached to it that the middle cohort benefited from, and it quickly became the more desirable option for workers entering the labor market.

The data from the sample support these claims as we find that women in the middle cohort have high rates of non-state sector concentration relative to both men of their age cohort as well as women across the other two cohorts. These patterns suggest the situation was unique to women in the middle cohort and did not affect both sexes similarly. One of the biggest benefits to shifting into the non-state sector was the greater financial value attached to this labor, a factor also reflected in the cohort data. Women in the middle cohort reported the highest rates of entrepreneurship than any cohort of either gender and the highest median earnings. For many of the women, higher earnings contributed to a greater sense of financial power within the home as well. One woman reported that she felt more control over household spending than she had before because she knew the money she spent was "her own" and the product of *her* hard work (Personal communication June 21, 2002). These findings are also supported by the ACWF, where their own survey reported that nearly 20 percent of China's entrepreneurs are women, 80 percent of these women are between the ages of 30 and 50, and more than 95 percent of the enterprises led by women are making profits.[7] Both studies show that women in the middle cohort have been able to make a significant claim in the public sphere despite SOE retrenchment and market reform. Moreover, it calls attention to the growing economic power that these women are accumulating relative to their peers of both sexes. Although these women are clearly taking an active role in the economy and have been successful in terms of entrepreneurship, the political implications of these changes have not been as widely examined.

The gains experienced by the middle cohort, have not continued as the cohorts get younger, a problem that brings attention back to the role of the state in managing reform. The middle cohort of women did well for themselves, but this is despite being pushed out of the state sector at an early age. Thus, the gains must be considered unexpected rather than an intentional effort by the state to help economically, and indirectly socially, empower middle cohort women. Meanwhile, the youngest cohort has experienced a different trend in terms of employment patterns. Younger women are finding their employment less rewarding both monetarily and in terms of the personal value they attach to it. Women in this group report higher instances of wanting to change jobs in an effort to put their talents to better use or to gain greater responsibility (Currier 2007b). The resurgence of gender discrimination that these women reported in their jobs is a by-product of the unexpected gains we saw in middle cohort women. As individuals see the benefits of the non-state sector, experienced by women in the middle cohort, they begin to shift their labor interests and actively seek out these opportunities. The more lucrative non-state sector thus creates the necessary push and pull factors to draw individuals out of or away from the state sector and into the non-state sector. Middle cohort women were among the first to test the possibilities of the non-state sector, and their success served as an example to others that it was a better option than SOE employment. However, with greater competition for these new opportunities, the state must find ways to meet the increasing demands of the labor force and ensure those individuals who have the greater potential to challenge the state are not encouraged to do so. Under these conditions, the state easily resorts back to gendered policies that treat women as supplemental. Therefore the kind of jobs the youngest cohort of women secures end up being in low-wage "jobs" in basic services or retail, but do not represent "careers" in the sense of long-term stability and investment into their occupation (Currier 2007b, 89–90). Moreover, the competitive labor market they enter is over-saturated with male workers, who are still viewed as primary breadwinners and more deserving or valued workers by both state and society.

Overall, the cohorts demonstrate that the state's management of inequality continues to rely on the flexibilization of women's labor, which is designed to offset the decline in security and opportunities for men. Women in the oldest cohort were protected in the state sector from significant retrenchment based on the state's willingness to uphold the socialist promise of lifetime employment for those already working at the time restructuring began. The middle cohort was pushed out of the state sector by the implementation of the contract labor system in the mid-1980s, as well as efforts by the state to encourage women to retreat to the household, leaving more jobs for men. However, several women in this cohort experienced success and younger generations have adapted accordingly with their labor more heavily concentrated in the non-state sector. The youngest cohort, although better equipped with higher human capital investment does not have the same degree of success that the middle cohort had. The problem is that once again state campaigns to return women to the home were promoted, and the value of women as workers was lessened. This differential treatment of women as workers can be tied to their lower perceived political value by the state. When the question of political importance is raised, it becomes clear that the flexibilization of women workers is another strategy to offset mounting unrest arising with the increasing unemployment of men. Men are treated as primary workers, as first-class citizens, and as a greater overall threat to the power of the state. In comparison, women are seen as upholding a lesser role in their ability to challenge the state and are more easily retrenched. Thus, the middle cohort has reaped the greatest benefits from the timing of the reforms and their early entry into an untested sector of the economy, while the other cohorts have found marketization less amenable to protecting their interests as workers, particularly as reform has continued to unfold. The question that remains is whether the greater economic and social power we see emerging in women can serve as a catalyst to change the gendered practices that are endorsed explicitly and implicitly by the state.

Challenges to the State

The gendered nature of reform is a potential stumbling block for Chinese state development, as it struggles to loosen its grip over the economy while still restricting political and social reform. Throughout the reform era, the state has been able to implement economic policies with relative ease, given the cohesiveness and centralized nature of decision-making. The top-down structure of political power in China has given the state a great deal of authority and influence over all aspects of public life. Moreover, through a series of tight controls on community organization and media outlets, and the use of "campaigns," the state has effectively moderated the lives of individuals in the private sphere. These characteristics of the Chinese system support the argument that China has best been characterized as an example of strong state corporatism. State corporatism allows states to remain relatively insulated from interest-group pressures, to adopt perspectives that emphasize "consensus overseen by the moral authority of the leadership, reflected in a moralistic father-knows best paternalism," and to hierarchically create and order organizations without outside competition (Unger and Chan 1996, 98–100). With the state managing business, labor, and social groups through formal restrictions on the types of organizations that can be formed, it has been able to solidify its power through institutional control. However in China, corporatism is being used "not as a mechanism for yet further strengthening the state's grip over the economy and over society, but rather the reverse, a mechanism through which the state's grip could be loosened" (Unger and Chan 1996, 105). Unger and Chan (1996) claim that under reform the state is engaging in a managed devolution of power, whereby groups are increasingly able to secure a public space for their interests. I argue that women represent one of these groups that are gaining strength, but remain underestimated by the state.

One problem is that the connections between politics and economics have been widely addressed in the literature primarily regarding *male* labor in China, in the sense that growing unemployment has raised speculation that a labor crisis may lead to a political one if left unchecked. However, rarely there is a connection made between economic roles and expanding political influence for *women*. The difference can be explained by the fact that researchers have not emphasized or acknowledged a rising urban middle class led by rising female entrepreneurship. Instead, the literature has more often focused on female retrenchment under marketization. Retrenchment has been problematic and has negatively affected many women, but as I have shown here, there is significant variation across cohorts that deserve further consideration. With a detailed microlevel cohort analysis one sees that reform has benefited some women, specifically those in the middle cohort, and that economic gains have not bypassed women entirely under reform. This study expands on the existing literature by drawing attention to these cohort differences and examining the degree of (dis)satisfaction women have with reform.

By pitting men's and women's labor interests against each other, the state has helped shift the focus of male labor dissatisfaction toward female labor rather than labor retrenchment in general. Asking women to return home or to take on traditional roles to make room for more men in the public sphere draws attention to the idea that women are in jobs that "belong" to male breadwinners. Although the state has underestimated the importance of women as an organized interest group, the expanding economic power of certain cohorts of women poses an unmistakable challenge to the state. The Beijing sample has shown that women in the middle cohort have gained considerable economic power under reform. This cohort is unlikely to adhere to further calls to return home when they have already carved out a niche for themselves in the new economy. They also reported seeing future reforms as bringing new challenges to women, with the sample perceiving further restructuring to be 20 percent less favorable to women than before. The difference that we see between past and future assessments shows that women are aware of the negative economic conditions that await them as marketization continues. The relevance of examining women's attitudes toward reform is to gain a sense of the "specific motivations and constrains under which people act" (Peter 2003, 13). More than just examining how people feel about their work environment or their standards of living, attitudes can reveal the likelihood individuals will take an active role to change their situation.

Where the state should be concerned is that women in the middle cohort have more at stake in the transition than just wealth, especially if the state continues to forward policies that ask women to return to the home, allowing the economy to better absorb dislocated male workers. When asked about the likelihood of returning home to assume more traditional duties, a woman asked in somewhat disbelief, "What would I do? I've always worked." (Personal communication June 23, 2002). In addition, the limitations on family size with the One Child Policy (1979) have reduced some of the care-giving demands formerly placed on women. Grandparents frequently assist with the raising of their grandchildren, and while the double burden still exists for women, it is not necessarily as time consuming as it was before population policies were introduced.

Although claiming the state is facing a new social movement may be an overstatement at this point, it is clear that women in the middle cohort have the resources in place to organize their interests effectively. These women have more at stake with further retrenchment than the other two groups, as far as the economic setback it would entail. Therefore, it is in the state's interest to avoid policies that pressure these women to return home. Since these women are already active in economics and in social organizations such as the ACWF, a more prominent political agenda would only be a short step away.

For the youngest cohort, who already perceives present conditions to be less than favorable, further retrenchment or deterioration in working and living conditions could inspire a greater sense of agency. In a 1995 study on public opinion in Beijing, Dowd, Carlson, and Shen found "the fact that younger people are more likely to select individual freedom as their most important value would suggest that their will be greater pressure in the future for a more open society and perhaps even democratization" (2000, 202). This cohort of women, facing a tougher labor market with heavy competition with men in their cohort as well as laid-off men from older cohorts, has already reported high rates of dissatisfaction on all aspects of urban life, from employment opportunities, to housing conditions, to the overall lack of adequate infrastructure and services in the city. When considering the youngest cohort is the most educated, the least satisfied with a variety of social and economic issues, and that they perceive future reforms to bring even greater difficulties, it is easy to see how their dissatisfaction could lead to more organized activism. A separate study conducted by Chan found that students have "low efficacy and low trust in the system," and they are for "reform, democracy, and legality" (2000, 226–227). As the youngest cohort continues to have their rising expectations met with disappointment and decreasing economic opportunities under marketization, and more organizational tools at their disposal, they represent yet another future challenge to the state.

Finally, the organization potential of the oldest cohort should be considered. Marber has argued that the transition from an egalitarian society to one of the most unequal societies has several destabilizing effects for China, which can lead to political dislocation (2003, 78). The oldest cohort is the only one of the three groups who has truly known the full range of this transition from socialism to the present version of capitalism. As the research by Hurst and O'Brien (2002) shows, older people have been more engaged in demonstrations over pension payments and severance packages than other groups, because they have both the time and the most to lose if their concerns are ignored. More specifically older individuals become more active once their livelihood is directly threatened, such as with the loss of retirement benefits and increases to the cost of living. These are just some of the problems that appear to be worsening for the older generations, and the state still has not established an effective safety net or adequate pension program for retirees. However, at this point the oldest cohort of Beijing women reported being rather apathetic about organizing their interests and challenging the status quo, but with the social and economic changes occurring around them the possibilities for greater activism, that can thereby threaten the state, cannot be ruled out.

The focus of this chapter has been on examining the changing relationship between women and the state during the reform era, and the gendered effects of marketization. Moreover, it is important to understand how different cohorts of women have been flexibilized and feminized by the state during different periods of reform, in an effort to satisfy the more potentially volatile male labor force. Using the Beijing sample, I have shown that economic reform is creating more inequality, less economic stability, and increasing dissatisfaction among women as the state allows marketization to run its course, but that there is variation among women that deserve further analysis. I argue that if the state continues to intervene by adopting gender-biased policies that favor the male breadwinner model over female employment, it will face challenges from an affluent middle cohort of women, who will not readily accept further retrenchment, and a discouraged young cohort of women, who has had high expectations accompanied by great disappointments under reform. These cohorts are increasingly finding a space to express their dissatisfaction as the state moves from a strong-state to more of a societal-corporatist system, which is allowing for the managed devolution of power and is paving the way for social change. Thus the tests facing the state as it enters the next stage of reform are how it can accommodate the concerns of these different cohorts and continue to intervene and maintain a sense of social and economic stability by treating women as second-class workers. The problem is that the further retrenchment of female labor does not adequately solve the growing problems of male unemployment and labor unrest and does not appear to be a viable option across all cohorts. Greater state involvement and control also present a challenge to the neoliberal reforms firmly rooted in the present economic system and have the potential to undermine economic growth. Therefore, the Beijing case-study provides insight into how reform has unfolded at the microlevel, and the growing pressures women will place on the state as marketization continues.

Notes

1. Public sphere is used to refer to the formal economy or paid workforce. In this sense the "public sphere" includes the state-controlled sector as well as the privatized sector, since both are part of the formal economy.
2. Flower vase is a term used for women hired to look pretty, but where their actual job qualifications are not a priority. See Currier 2007a; Hershatter 2007; Kerr and Delahanty 1996; Khan and Riskin 2001; Wang and Hu 1999.
3. Tang and Parish (2000) examine the work of Stephen Crowley (1994) on the Soviet Union and argue that workers were made dependent on the state; therefore, they were docile and unwilling to challenge the state for fear of losing that safety net. Therefore, "workers can be expected to be more docile when they work for firms that provide housing and other in-kind benefits..." (Tang and Parish 2000, 129–130).
4. The Beijing data used in this article are from surveys and interviews I designed and administered in 2001–2002 with the assistance of a Fulbright Research Grant.
5. Of the factors contributing to lower human capital investment, one important point of consideration is the disruption to education created by the Cultural Revolution in the 1960s, a factor many women in this cohort noted as reasons for why they did not pursue their education.
6. These are just three of the high scoring categories among women in the youngest cohort. The categories are from the standard occupational classifications used in the National Bureau of Statistics Labor yearbooks (*Guojia Tongzhiji* 1996).
7. Statistics reported in *People's Daily Online*, "20 Percent Chinese entrepreneurs women."

References

Bian, Y. 2000. *Work and inequality in urban China*. Albany: State University of New York Press.

Bian, Y., J. R. Logan, and Z. Shu. 2000. Wage and job inequalities in the working lives of men and women in Tianjin. In *Re-drawing boundaries: Work, households, and gender in China*, ed. B. Entwisle and G. Henderson, 111–133. Berkeley: University of California Press.

Boserup, E. 1989. *Woman's role in economic development*. London: Earthscan.

Chan, C. 2000. The political pragmatism of Chinese university students at the dawn of the twenty-first century. In *China and democracy: Reconsidering the prospects for a democratic China*, ed. S. Zhao, 207–232. New York: Routledge.

Currier, C. L. 2007a. Bringing the household back in: Restructuring women's labor in Beijing. *American Journal of Chinese Studies* 14: 61–81.

———. 2007b. Redefining "labor" in Beijing: Women's attitudes on work and reform. *Asian Journal of Women's Studies* 13: 71–108.

Dalsimer, M. and L. Nisonoff. 1984. The new economic readjustment policies: Implications for Chinese urban working women. *Review of Radical Political Economics* 16: 17–43.

Davis, D. S. 1999. Self employment in Shanghai: A research note. *China Quarterly* 157: 22–44.

Dowd, D. V., A. Carlson, and M. Shen. 2000. The prospects for democratization in China: Evidence from the 1995 Beijing area study. In *China and democracy: Reconsidering the prospects for a democratic China*, ed. S. Zhao, 189–206. New York: Routledge.

Evans, H. 2002. Past, perfect or imperfect: Changing images of the ideal wife. In *Chinese femininities/Chinese masculinities: A reader*, ed. S. Brownell and J. Wasserstrom, 335–360. Berkeley: University of California Press.

Farris, C. 2000. Contradictory implications of socialism and capitalism under "East Asian modernity" in China and Taiwan. In *Democracy and the status of women in East Asia*, ed. R. Lee and C. Clark, 143–168. Boulder, CO: Lynne Rienner Publishers.

Fredrich Nauman Stiftung Foundation. 1994. The impact of economic reforms on the situation of women in China. In *Occasional Papers-Policy Analysis No. 7* (December). Beijing: Fredrich Nauman Stiftung Foundation.

Guojia Tongzhiji. 1996. *Zhongguo Laodong Tongzhi Nianjian* (Chinese Labor Statistical Yearbook). Beijing: Zhongguo Tongzhi Chubanshe, State Statistical Bureau.

Harrell, S. 2000. The changing the meanings of work in China. In *Re-drawing boundaries: Work, households, and gender in China*, ed. B. Entwisle and G. Henderson, 67–76. Berkeley: University of California Press.

Hershatter, G. 2007. *Women in China's long twentieth century*. Berkeley: University of California Press.

Hooper, B. 1984. China's modernization are young women going to lose out? *Modern China* 10: 317–344.

Howell, J. 2000. Organising around women and labor in China: Uneasy shadows, uncomfortable alliances. *Communist and Post-Communist Studies* 33: 355–377.

Hurst, W. and K. J. O'Brien. 2002. China's contentious pensioners. *China Quarterly* 171: 345–360.

Kerr, J. and J. Delahanty. 1996. *Gender and jobs in China's new economy*. Ottawa, ON: The North-South Institute.

Khan, A. R. and C. Riskin. 2001. *Inequality and poverty in China in the age of globalization*. New York: Oxford University Press.

Korabik, K. 1993. Managerial women in the People's Republic of China. *International Studies of Management and Organization* 23: 47–65.

Korzec, M. 1992. *Labor and the failure of reform in China*. London: Macmillan.

Lee, C. K. 2007. Is labor a political force in China? In *Grassroots political reform in contemporary China*, ed. E. Perry and M. Goldman, 228–252. Cambridge, MA: Harvard University Press.

Marber, P. 2003. *Money changes everything: How global prosperity is reshaping our needs, values, and lifestyles*. New York: Prentice Hall.

Maurer-Fazio, M., T. G. Rawski, and W. Zhang. 1999. Inequality in the rewards for holding up half the sky: Gender wage gaps in China's urban labor market, 1988–1994. *China Journal* 41: 55–88.

Meng, X. 2000. *Labor market reform in China*. New York: Cambridge University Press.

Perry, E. 1995. Labor's battle for political space: The role of worker associations in contemporary China. In *Urban spaces in contemporary China*, ed. D. Davis, R. Kraus, B. Naughton, and E. Perry, 302–325. New York: Cambridge University Press.

———. 1998. Holding up half the sky: Women in China. *Current History* (September): 279–284.

Peter, F. 2003. Gender and the foundations of social choice: The role of situated agency. *Feminist Economics* 9: 13–32.

Riley, N. 1996. Holding half the economy. *China Business Review* 23: 22–25.

Rofel, L. 1994. Liberation nostalgia and a yearning for modernity. In *Engendering China: women, culture and the state*, ed. C. Gilmartin, G. Hershatter, L. Rofel, and T. White, 226–249. Cambridge, MA: Harvard University Press.

Rosenthal, E. 1998. China's middle class savors its new wealth. *New York Times* June 19: A1, A8.

Summerfield, G. 1994. Effects of the changing employment situation on urban Chinese women. *Review of Social Economy* 52: 40–59.

Tang, W. and W. L. Parish. 2000. *Chinese urban life under reform: The changing social contract*. Cambridge: Cambridge University Press.

Tsui, M. and L. Rich. 1992. The only child and educational opportunity for girls in urban China. *Gender and Society* 16: 74–92.

Unger, J. and A. Chan. 1996. Corporatism in China: A developmental state in an East Asian context. In *China after Socialism,* ed. B. McCormick and J. Unger, 95–129. New York: M. E. Sharpe.

Wang, S. and A. Hu. 1999. *The political economy of uneven development: The case of China*. Armonk, NY: M.E. Sharpe.

White, G., J. Howell, and X. Shang. 1996. Urban women and the Women's Federation. In *In search of civil society: Market reform and social change in contemporary China*, eds. G. White, J. Howell, and X. Shang, 69–97. Oxford: Clarendon Press.

Wolf, M. 1985. *Revolution postponed: Women in contemporary China*. Palo Alto, CA: Stanford University Press.

Woo, M. Y. K. 1994. Chinese women workers: The delicate balance between protection and equality. In *Engendering China: Women, culture and the state*, ed. C. Gilmartin, G. Hershatter, L. Rofel, and T. White, 279–295. Cambridge, MA: Harvard University Press.

Wu, N. 1995. Employment and Chinese women. *Beijing Review* 38: 8–13.

Wuelker, G. 1983. Questionnaires in Asia. In *Social research in developing countries*, ed. M. Bulmer, and D. P. Warwick, 161–172. New York: John Wiley and Sons.

Zheng, W. 2003. Gender, employment and women's resistance. In *Chinese society: Change, conflict and resistance,* (2nd ed.), ed. E. J. Perry, and M. Selden, 158–182. New York: Routledge.

Chapter Three

Developing Minority Nationalities in Contemporary Urban China

Reza Hasmath

It is not unusual for gender and ethnic studies to borrow from each other. In the previous chapter, we saw that economic reforms from the late 1970s onward have altered the relationship between state and society for women. Using Beijing as an example, Currier demonstrates urban women workers are increasingly marginalized by the state, encouraged to return to more "traditional" household roles. The growing tension between the state and ethnic minority groups is another segment of the population deserving attention. Interestingly, when it comes to ethnic minorities in China the discussion is often directed toward the country's under-developed, bordering Western provinces, where nearly three-quarters of the 106 million ethnic minority population reside (NBS/EAC 2003). Little is written in either English or Chinese literature about the nation's growing ethnic minority[1] population in the relatively developed urban centers such as Beijing. At core, ethnic minority management in China is operated by a cocktail of central government decrees, public policy protections, and local attempts to promote ethnic minority culture such as festivals, food, sport, or dance in the mainstream. In Beijing for example, local officials have stressed a loud confidence that the municipality promotes and respects the religious affairs, education, culture, and sport of ethnic minority groups. In fact, interviews conducted in late 2006 with officials from the Beijing Municipal Commission of Ethnic Affairs point to the Muslim population—comprised of approximately 300,000 persons spanning 10 ethnic groups, including the Hui, Uyghur, Uzbek, and Kazak—who practice their religion in the city's 80-odd mosques, as a successful case study in managing ethnic difference. Officials argued this illustrates that social policies were successful in promoting ethnic tolerance. Moreover, this also illustrates that discussing the management of ethnic difference in the relatively developed urban spaces of China is not necessary given this rosy reality.

Yet, despite long-standing efforts to integrate ethnic minorities at both the national and urban level, there has been a deep history of strained ethnic relations and tensions, rather than a Confucian-inspired, socialist vision of harmony in ethnic interactions (Mackerras 1994; Mittenthal 2002). For example, the separatist activities of the 1990s in Tibet and Xinjiang trickled down to the streets of Beijing, where severe crackdowns on Tibetan and Uyghur activities occurred. During the period of Deng Xiaoping's state funeral (February 1997), bus bombings in Beijing signaled Uyghur contempt for the Chinese state (Mackerras 2001; Rudelson and Jankowiak 2004). Similarly, during the march for Tibetan sovereignty, the Beijing government forbade any meetings among Tibetan community associations. To this day, there still resides a stigma among key local government circles that such ethnic community associations are there for malice—suspected of encouraging drug trade or inciting "rebellious activities." Although the integration of ethnic minorities into the urban milieu is a matter of great importance for Beijing's development, suffice to say, it is conducted in a background of often tense ethnic relations.

Coiled in this background, there is seemingly a growing paradox in ethnic minority development in the capital city. When examining local ethnic minorities' education attainments, they either outperform or are on par with the dominant Han population. However, when analyzing the ethnic minority demographics of those working in high-wage, education-intensive (HWEI) employment sectors, the Han population is most prevalent. What accounts for this discrepancy? What does this mean tangibly, in respect to the management of ethnic difference in Beijing? And, what steps can we take to improve this situation?

This chapter draws on recent findings, investigating the integration and social development of ethnic minorities in Beijing. It proceeds in four sections. First, it details exactly what is meant by ethnic difference in the Chinese context as the logic of ethnic difference is fairly distinct. This is followed by outlining the background conditions to Beijing's strategies for managing ethnic difference. The third section elaborates on the paradox of ethnic minority development, drawing on rare, publicly available statistical information, and interview and ethnographic data. The chapter concludes by offering future steps to be taken, by both state and civil society actors, to improve the urban management of ethnic minorities.

Ethnic Difference: The Chinese Perspective

In the People's Republic of China, the concept of ethnicity is fairly straightforward, definitive, and by some accounts rigid (Mackerras 1994).

The term "ethnic minorities" refers to people officially identified as minority nationalities (*shaoshu minzu*), stemming from the categorization of ethnic minorities by the Communist Party of China (CPC) since 1949. When the CPC came into power, they commissioned studies to categorize ethnic groups within the boundaries of the People's Republic, whom in 1953 numbered more than 400 registered groups. Teams were sent into regions heavily populated with ethnic minorities to conduct research and field work, investigating minorities' social history, economic life, language, and religion. After detailed study, they found that there was a lot of overlapping and a significant number of groups that claimed to be separate, actually belonged to existing groups (albeit with different names). As a result, thirty-eight ethnic minority groups were officially recognized in 1954; and by 1964, another fifteen were identified, with the Lhoba ethnic group added in 1965. The Jino, were added in 1979, solidifying the official fifty-five ethnic minority groups of China.

In determining what constituted an ethnic minority group, a criterion in the Stalinist tradition was used to identify nationalities distinct from the majority Han. The official criterion was fourfold: (1) distinct Language—although there are virtually hundreds, perhaps thousands, of dialects spoken across China, a minority language is not simply a dialect. It is a language with distinct grammatical and phonological differences, such as Tibetan. Twenty-one ethnic minority groups have unique writing systems; (2) a recognized indigenous homeland, a common territory, within the boundaries of China; (3) distinctive customs, ranging from dress, religion, foods; and (4) a strong sense of identity—although at times, loosely interpreted.

Although the categorization of fifty-five ethnic minority groups was a step forward from Sun Yat-sen Nationalist Party's denial of the existence of different ethnic groups in China; and from the derogatory names commonly used to refer to ethnic minority groups (officially abolished in 1951), criticism was rampant as it reduced the number of recognized ethnic groups by eightfold. In fact, the *wei shibie minzu*, literally the "undistinguished ethnic groups," presently total more than 730,000 people (Mackerras 1994). Examples of these groups include the Gejia, Khmu, Kucong, Mang, Deng, Sherpas, Bajia, Yi, and Youtai (Jewish). The number of undistinguished ethnic groups could even rise, as most commentators do not include groups that have been classified into existing groups, such as the Mosuo who were effectively assimilated into Naxi or the Chuanging into Han. Certain official ethnic groups are even near extinction or borderline assimilated into Han, which begs whether a recategorization or abolition of official ethnic minority groups is needed in the near future. For example, typical of many interview responses when asked,

"What does it mean to be an ethnic minority?" Joanna, an ethnic Xibo, replies, "We don't eat dogs or horses. Otherwise we are the same as Han." Elaborating further, her explanation was her grandparents will wear traditional clothing during festivals, otherwise, their cultural and social lives are virtually the same as other Han. Few Xibos she knows can speak the traditional dialect fluently, a trend that will most likely continue as the numbers of elders diminish. Joanna, like many young ethnic minorities interviewed in Beijing, can barely speak their ethnic language or dialect and does not practice it everyday. Although officially she is considered a member of an ethnic minority, her way of life are indistinguishable from a Han. In fact, many Chinese scholars interviewed believed that a "multi-ethnic" Beijing will not last long, because, in the words of the current Minister in charge of the State Ethnic Affairs Commission, an ethnic Korean, Li Dezhu (1998, 109) "like a grinding shed, the city will grind off ethnic [minority] features."

Interestingly, the purpose of officially classifying ethnic minority groups in China lies in the logic that official ethnic minorities are guaranteed systematic and procedural "special rights" and preferential treatments under China's constitution, and reaffirmed in various national (e.g., 1999 National Minorities Policy) and local (e.g., Beijing Minority Rights Protection Policies) policies. The "one-child" policy typifies such a preferential treatment. Since 1982, and reinforced by the Population and Family Planning Law in 2002, China's population policy seeks to control the size of the population, calling for late marriages and fewer births. In effect, it strongly encourages couples to have only one child. Special exemptions in the population policy have however been afforded to ethnic minorities, whereby couples from ethnic minorities are usually exempt or have a higher quota for children. In short, due to like-oriented "special rights" and preferential treatments afforded to ethnic minorities in China, the status of an ethnic citizen cannot be altered at discretion.[2] What we will see in the following sections is that this idea of preferential treatment and "special rights" promoted by the state have played a tremendous role in increasing the educational attainment levels of ethnic minorities in Beijing—even to the point where it has surpassed the Han population.

The Background Conditions

Unknowing to many, even some locals, Beijing's demographics encompass all fifty-five ethnic minority groups, who total nearly 600,000 legal residents. As one of China's largest urban communities, Beijing is dominated by a Han population whereby many are descendants of Mongolians and Manchus, but identify themselves as Han. For example, although

43 percent of the ethnic minority population are officially Manchu, this number can be significantly higher as many with Manchurian ancestry choose to identify themselves as Han to protect themselves from the stigma of being seen as "outside colonizers" (as Manchus were initially portrayed by Sun Yat-sen) or "imperialists" (as portrayed by the CPC). Interviews in the outskirt districts of Beijing, where a sizeable ethnic Manchurian population exists, suggest there was a growing trend of those who are mixed Han/Manchu or have strong Manchurian ancestry attempting to reidentify themselves as Manchu in present-day. Many interviewed were upfront, claiming they sought to reidentify themselves as Manchu not only because of ethnic pride and due to a more favorable environment where the negative stigma of being Manchu is weak, but also due to the preferential treatments ethnic minorities tend to receive. Yet, the reidentification process is quite difficult, especially in adulthood. Most are often not successful due to strict state policy and for some, a lack of formal records to prove ethnicity.

Other groups such as Tibetans and Uyghurs in Beijing harbor resentment against the majority Han due to the CPC's treatment of their large populations in the Western provinces. In contrast, certain groups such as the Zhuang and ethnic Koreans are well adapted into Beijing's urban milieu. The ethnic Korean population in particular can be seen as one of the most successful minority groups in terms of economic capital and social integration. Their history in migrating to the city was often due to famine and war in the Korean peninsula from the 1860s onward. Most famously the Japanese, who occupied Manchuria in the 1930s, organized a series of collective migration from southern Korea to parts of Northeastern China, which eventually lead to thousands of ethnic Koreans settling in Beijing (Kim 2003). After the Sino-Japanese war and civil war between the Communists and Nationalists during 1945–1949, Koreans in China who allied with the Communists were granted formal citizenship and were encouraged to maintain their ethnic language, education, and culture. As Jin, an ethnic Korean who experienced the rise of the Communists remembers, "Koreans became enthusiastic supporters of China and were proud to be Chinese citizens." However, during the Cultural Revolution (1966–1976), Koreans encountered setbacks as an ethnic minority group when the Communists sough to abolish bureaucracy and feudalistic elements of society. After realizing the vulnerability of being a minority group and the danger of nationalism, many ethnic Koreans in Beijing seemingly adopted a strategy of full accommodation to the authority of the state. They even obeyed the population control policy so enthusiastically that most ethnic Korean families interviewed have opted to have just one child. As a result, Yu (2000) points out that their birth rates and population growth statistics are much lower than Han and all other ethnic minorities.

With widespread economic reforms in the 1980s and 1990s, South Korean firms began entering Beijing markets. Ethnic Koreans, who mostly retained their native language, were positioned to greatly benefit from the introduction of such firms who had preferences in hiring cheaper, domestic employees who were able to communicate in the Korean language and relate to its cultural values and practices. As a result, Koreans in Beijing today are more highly represented in corporate and small-medium enterprise occupations than other ethnic minority groups. Commentators such as Kim and Yu further believe that the entrepreneurial class is likely to grow among ethnic Koreans because they are adopting capitalist values and high earning economic activities more rapidly than other ethnic groups. An observation that can be confirmed in the Wangjing neighborhood of the business-oriented Chaoyang District and Wudaokou area in Haidian District, where ethnic Korean businesses such as electronic repair shops, information technology, and restaurants are increasing in numbers to cater to South Korean firms and their employees; as well as, an increasing expatriate community.

One noticeable attribute in the neighborhood characteristics of Beijing is that it lacks defined and distinct ethnic enclaves. Although there were small Tibetan enclaves near the Central University of Nationalities in Haidian District, pockets of Manchurian enclaves in the city's outer districts, and very small Muslim-ethnic enclaves scattered throughout the city, today, due to Beijing's unparalleled, rapid development and lack of physical space, virtually all ethnic enclaves have been absorbed to make room for high-rise residential and corporate buildings. Although there are several original Tibetan temples and Islamic mosques that still remain in tact, they often do not reflect the ethnic demographics of the local area. This makes the Niujie area more remarkable as one of the last important historical and present-day ethnic enclaves in Beijing.

The Niujie area in Xuanwu District is centered by one of the oldest mosques in Beijing and China. Built in 966 during the Liao Dynasty and enlarged by the Qing Emperors, Niujie or Cow Street Mosque is the spiritual center for 10,000 Muslims, mostly Hui, living in the area. As the Mosque's Imam confirms, more than 200 Muslims attend the Mosque each day. Niujie is beyond an average ethnic enclave. The Beijing Municipal Government has invested millions in rebuilding a residential area mainly inhabited by Muslims. It has successfully revitalize Ox Street into a Muslim-style commercial street, home to numerous Muslim restaurants, a Hui Primary School, Islamic-Chinese styled buildings (from apartment blocks to the post office), and a street community center, which in effect, serves the needs of the Hui community. In typical CPC fashion, there are signs present that remind the locals about the recent historical achievements of the community and the role the municipal government has played in improving water, electricity, and gas supplies to the area. As a ninety-two-year old male Hui, who has lived in the Niujie area since birth, puts it: "We are all happy about the renovation projects and we are grateful for the government's religious policy."

In general, the younger generations in the area share a different sentiment. Most young Huis interviewed in the Niujie area did not attend the Mosque, save in "important festivals" where they often felt obliged by their parents and grandparents to attend. In fact, an observation both in the Niujie Mosque and various Mosques throughout the city confirmed that a majority of those who attended the Mosque regularly was an older demographic, usually in their fifties and beyond. Many older and middle-aged Muslims expressed concern that their children do not practice or adopt the Islamic culture. They assert their children are Beijingers, educated within a Han-dominated community. They do not eat traditional foods, except to occasionally go to "ethnic" restaurants (which are increasing in popularity among Han Beijingers) that are, for the most part, not even staffed or owned by ethnic minorities. But even moving away from the obvious (ceremonial) cultural rituals, their children do not speak the minority language fluently, they are, in the eyes of many Muslim interviewees, products of education and employment systems that promote a Han-dominated culture.

Although an ethnic minority population has been entrenched in Beijing arguably since the existence of the capital city, the most significant recent additions to the ethnic population are the result of waves of internal migration by university students from minority regions. Students often migrate to complete their studies in one of the numerous tertiary-level institutions in the city and are often granted legal residency status as they take up employment thereafter. As we will see, the education of ethnic minorities in Beijing is taken very seriously.

The Paradox of Urban Ethnic Minority Development

Education

In China, formal education is seen as the equalizer for ethnic minorities when it comes to ensuring their future economic and social security. As such, Beijing have taken strong efforts to improve educational opportunities for ethnic minorities, often working in combination with higher-level government agencies to institute preferential treatment and equal opportunity programs.

In many regards, the CPC views itself as the "enlightened element" and sees its mandate as raising the standards of common people (Heberer 1989, 11). One measure the CPC takes in pursuing this mandate is to increase the formal education and skills of ethnic minorities through the establishment of national minority universities and institutes. The first of these, the Central University of Nationalities (formerly called the Central Institute of Nationalities) was established in Beijing in 1951, and it was originally designed to train cadres from all minority nationalities who should be familiar with local languages and customs; thus, serving as liaisons between local ethnic minorities and the state. The formation of national minority institutes was an opportunity for minorities to be educated in CPC ideology and provided a platform to integrate minorities into the Han mainstream.

In this vein, other tertiary institutions and vocational secondary schools in Beijing often give preferential treatment to applicants of ethnic minorities. This usually equates to lowering minimum requirements for entrance exam marks to gain acceptance into a tertiary institution. A prestigious university in Beijing may lower its threshold slightly, which normally requires a score of 850 out of 900 for entrance; while other universities may require only 600. At the Central University of Nationalities, a minimum score in the mid-400s is accepted, ranking it one of the lowest entrance requirements among all Beijing universities. Some universities may set ratios between ethnic minorities and Han applicants for their incoming class. The Central University for Nationalities allocates spots to ensure all ethnic minority groups are represented each year, to the extent that on several occasions scores are further lowered to ensure that the least represented ethnic groups are represented. Ethnic minorities who come from poorer income geographical clusters may also be granted even lower qualified entry marks to enter higher education. Further, minority students enrolled in ethnic minority-oriented specialties are provided with generous scholarships and on numerous occasions, pay no tuition and are granted a monthly stipend of around 100 yuan (US$12). There are even bridging programs—with tuition paid in full by the CPC—designed to select high-achieving ethnic minority secondary school students to attend the Central University of Nationalities to prepare them to enter Beijing's top universities, such as Peking or Tsinghua.

At the primary and secondary school levels, Beijing also has a multitude of ethnic and cultural schools. For instance, numerous Muslim (mostly Hui) primary and secondary schools are spread across the city and often have close relationships with a Mosque. The children are educated in a standard curriculum that every school in China must abide by, but their curriculum is supplemented with a Muslim education. The Principal of a Hui primary school in the Chongwen District expands, "The children are not taught about differences at all. They learn to respect each other and ethnic differences. Here, they are taught by both Muslims and non-Muslims alike." Those attending ethnic primary schools have the option of attending an ethnic middle/high school later on or a regular Beijing school.

When examining the education attainment of ethnic minorities in Beijing, they reflect the tremendous efforts to improve the education standards of their minority populations. In fact, the city's ethnic minorities clearly outperform the rest of the nation as table 3.1 demonstrates. Owing to the high number of ethnic primary and secondary schools in the city, as well as an emphasis in social policy to constantly improve education for ethnic minorities, secondary school education attainment in Beijing outperforms the national ethnic minority average by 23.1 percent. More impressively, Beijing takes advantage of the high number of universities within its boundaries—totaling 77 universities in 2004—whom, for the most part, practice an effective preferential treatment system for ethnic minority entry. This has contributed to Beijing enjoying an 18.8 percent higher average in university education attainment than the national level. One can simply dismiss these education figures on ethnic minorities as a clear case of a relatively developed urban environment, stacked with greater financial and teaching resources outperforming the not-so-developed areas, where a significant number of ethnic minorities reside throughout the nation. Yet, table 3.1 also illustrates a very interesting trend that provides further insight into the success of Beijing's education outputs for ethnic minorities. What is observed is that even the ethnic minority population in Beijing outperforms or is on par with the local Han population in educational attainment. In the key university education attainment statistics, ethnic minorities outperform Hans by nearly 5 percent. What this tells us is that the management of education for ethnic minorities in Beijing, as measured by educational attainment, has been successful.

Table 3.1 Education attainment by ethnic population in Beijing

	Non-Schooling %	Primary school education %	Secondary school education (1) %	Tertiary level education (2) %
Ethnic minorities* (National average)	13.1	45.0	36.5	2.7
Ethnic minorities	**2.8**	**15.8**	**59.6**	**21.5**
Hans	4.4	17.6	60.5	17.5

Source: Author's calculations based on 2000 Census.

Notes:
(1) Includes Junior and Senior Secondary Schools, and Secondary Technical School Education.
(2) Includes Junior College, University, and Post-Graduate Education.

Employment

High education outcomes for ethnic groups, dominant or minorities, bodes well for employment possibilities. To ensure that ethnic minority groups in particular are not denied access to employment reflecting their educational outcomes, the CPC has enacted several laws and policies in principle. For example, China's Labor Law stipulates that workers must not be discriminated in employment due to their ethnic identity, race, sex, or religious belief. The CPC also has a very active affirmative action program in the public sector that recruits ethnic minority cadres. In terms of figures, the success of the CPC's affirmative action program is resounding: China currently has 2.915 million cadres from different ethic minorities, accounting for 7.4 percent of the nation's total; this is up 2.6 percent from 2000 (*People's Daily* February 24, 2007). The State Ethnic Affairs Commission proudly points out, "as leaders at all levels, these cadres are acting as the backbone in the political, economic and social development of minority areas" (quoted in *People's Daily* June 28, 2000).

However, the enforcement and monitoring mechanism to protect discrimination in the workplace lacks. Although in theory one can officially complaint to public authorities on employment discrimination, this occurrence is rare and few. In fact, the costs, financially and time-wise, for the average worker in Beijing makes this an unattractive option. In short, although there are laws that seek to protect ethnic minorities against employment discrimination, the enforcement and monitoring mechanisms are lacking in Beijing; and this is reflected in the ethnic demographics of HWEI employment.

When examining the ethnic demographics of those working in HWEI employment, an interesting paradox seemingly arises. One will expect given similar educational attainment levels among the ethnic minority and Han population this will be reflected in the ethnic demographics of HWEI employment in Beijing. Rather, when looking at table 3.2 we see Hans dominate. Bearing in mind, the average gross income is 34,191 yuan (US$4,400) per annum; Hans dominate each employment sector above this. Put another way, only 20 percent of the ethnic minority population works above the average gross income in Beijing. The remaining 80 percent of the ethnic minority working population can be found in labor-intensive employment sectors (e.g., farming, forestry, and animal; construction; manufacturing; and, hotel, restaurant and retail trade).

Explaining the Paradox

One possible explanation behind this paradox may be that the HWEI employment is dominated by an older, working generation. Thus, the

Table 3.2   Occupation and avg. gross income per annum by ethnic population in Beijing

Occupation sector	Ethnic minorities %	Han %	Average gross income (RMB)
Banking, security, and insurance	1.58	2.42	92,764
Scientific research and technical services	2.81	9.61	57,870
Electricity, gas, and water (production)	0.90	1.25	49,776
Public management and social organization	5.44	6.07	47,277
Health, social securities, and social welfare	2.63	3.40	42,925
Education, culture, sports, and entertainment	6.60	10.14	40,032
Geologic prospecting and management of water conservancy	0.18	1.58	34,950
Hotel, restaurant, and retail trade	18.13	12.22	32,109
Other professions	1.05	9.43	31,699
Real estate	1.86	4.37	29,811
Transport, storage, and post	4.84	7.36	27,655
Manufacturing	21.4	21.27	24,958
Mining	0.81	0.45	23,774
Construction	7.77	7.83	23,300
Services to households and other services	10.97	1.99	18,159
Farming, forestry, and animal	13.03	0.61	16,125
Average wage			**34,191**

Source: Author's calculations based on 2000 Census.

younger, highly educated, ethnic minority generation has yet to reap the benefits of top positions in HWEI employment. Owing to the legacy of the Cultural Revolution and relatively new nature of economic reforms (and subsequent boom), the city's HWEI employment are dominated by those under the age of 40. As such, the idea that it is just a matter of waiting to see educated ethnic minorities breaking through the ranks of HWEI employment does not hold to a great extent in the capital city. There is something more to this that goes beyond statistical analyses.

Interviews revealed a very troubling situation for educated ethnic minorities working in Beijing. There is a general stereotype among Hans in HWEI placements that ethnic minorities will have a more difficult time adapting to the working environment and are thus, less likely to be employed. Among 78 local ethnic minorities interviewed, 64 percent responded they perceived they were unable to advance in a past or current working placement, as their bosses saw them as ethnic minorities.

Forty-eight percent responded they have had or are having a difficult time finding jobs in HWEI employment as they perceive they were negatively stereotyped by their potential employers. Although the majority of ethnic minority respondents have lived their entire lives in Beijing, the main stereotypes perceived were language difficulties and vast differences in (family and working) culture.

The case of Khang, a young, PhD educated, female of Tibetan ethnicity illustrates the depths of this situation. Khang graduated from one of Beijing's (and Asia's) top universities, Peking University, and immediately sought job prospects. When applying to HWEI placements, Khang faced a lot of challenges convincing her prospective bosses that she was capable. As it is a common requirement when applying for a job placement, her ethnic nationality was written on the resume and career folder (a mandatory file that contains one's educational background, including transcripts and teacher appraisals; and working history, including former work placements, appraisals, and recommendations). Beyond that, her facial features revealed that she was not Han. Her prospective bosses often asked about the Tibetan culture and what it is like living there. According to Khang, this was done in a very patronizing manner. Khang lived her entire life in Beijing, and the knowledge that she knew about Tibetan culture was passed down from her parents. Out of twelve HWEI job interviews, Khang received one offer, which she accepted. In her present job, she finds that her coworkers always treat her differently as she is an ethnic minority. They always ask about her "hometown" and the Tibetan way of life. She reveals her office workers cannot see her as simply Chinese. "There is still prejudice [by her coworkers] although not malicious," but nevertheless they cast her as an outsider in the office. She believes she is not able to climb the corporate ladder due to the fact she is perceived not to fully understand the Han-dominated working culture.

Khang's case is not unique. Throughout many interviews these were common documented cases. Among 33 interviewed with post-graduate qualifications, 82 percent shared related experience as Khang. Among another 17 interviewed with other tertiary qualifications, 71 percent had like experiences. Although educated ethnic minorities should on paper have better prospects finding a HWEI placement, evidence suggests otherwise for many. In Beijing, this may be the result of Hans believing there are fundamental differences between ethnic minorities and themselves—from language/dialect spoken to cultural rituals. Although most of the ethnic minorities interviewed grew up in Beijing, can speak Mandarin Chinese fluently, with no noticeable accent, and are assimilated into the Han culture, many in HWEI placements still believe, in effect, that their ethnicity could possibly be a disadvantage in the workplace.

Improving Ethnic Minority Development

Ethnic minorities are the most educated groups in Beijing. When it comes to HWEI employment, in general, minorities are seemingly paying an "ethnic penalty." Although there are sufficient public policies in Beijing designed to legally discourage employment discrimination, many ethnic minorities continue to face hidden discrimination that is, denied promotions, stereotyped or excluded from influential inner circles. Steps to improve the development of ethnic minorities will require the attention of three main actors: the state, community, and the individual.

Chinese education, especially at the tertiary level, is highly subsidized. Thus it is in the interests of the state to ensure that ethnic minorities realize their potential in the labor market and economic losses that come with the under-utilization of their human capital are minimized. Both the central and local Beijing governments should promote a more active approach to improving ethnic representation in the public and private sectors. There is, in effect, an affirmative action policy in education for ethnic minorities, thus the logic can be extended to the public and private workplace. However, when querying ethnic minorities and stakeholders about this possibility, it is met with strong opposition. In fact, an overwhelming 96 percent of all ethnic respondents interviewed answered an overwhelming "no" to this proposition. In many respects, the notion of affirmative action in Mandarin denotes a negative connotation. Two words are often used to describe it: *zhao gu*—"to take care of" or *you hui*—"discount" or "special." By implementing an affirmative action in the workplace, it is seen as actively signaling to Hans that ethnic minorities are different, inferior, and are in need of state assistance to get ahead. This in turn, further perpetuates negative stereotypes and increases prejudice toward ethnic minorities—the very idea that fuel the paradox of ethnic minority development in Beijing. What is accepted by those interviewed, is that the state should attempt to promote, in a very covert manner, more ethnic minority leaders in the workforce, especially in the upper echelons of management in HWEI public and private workplaces in Beijing. Consensus in the manner in which this should be conducted, however, has not been fully realized.

The state can also initiate programs to improve the perception of ethnic minorities in the city. It is apparent that ethnic minority realities are not fully understood by the local Han population. There has been, to a large extent, a mentality among many Hans that their "culture is better," stretching over thousands of years, and even more acutely in the capital city. There is a lot of misunderstandings and stereotypes when it comes to the livelihoods of ethnic minorities, especially in the urban context. The state can play a major role in reducing the stereotypical imagery of ethnic minorities as being "backward," "barbaric," and having an urban culture that is dramatically different than Hans. It may be beneficial that local education authorities promote cultural education in mandatory elementary and secondary school curriculum—teaching about the history and traditions of ethnic minorities in a nonpatronizing and noncommodifying manner. Combating deep-seated stereotypes is a difficult proposition for any state-oriented social policy. However, this does not mean that the state cannot implement strategies to assist in changing the commodified perception of ethnic minorities among many urban Hans.

Local ethnic community associations can also be a valuable resource in improving the situation for ethnic minorities in employment. Ethnic associations act as a social forum or an information point to promote ethnic minority issues (e.g., Muslim Association or Tibetan Information Center). Ethnic associations can play a greater role in providing support for urban ethnic minorities by acting as a networking mechanism to encourage greater access to HWEI work placements. Support from the state can go a long way in assisting in this venture. As mentioned, there is still a stigma of distrust in Beijing among many local government officials toward such community associations—many continue to believe they are there for malice. One would hope this line of thinking will slowly change over the course of time. Suffice to say, ethnic associations can be an impetus for providing a greater network for employment prospects in HWEI sectors.

It is at the individual level where most opportunity lies for reducing the paradoxical effects of ethnodevelopment in Beijing. Young ethnic minorities, who are soon-to-be university-graduates, have the greatest chance of breaking through the barriers of HWEI positions. They are the most optimistic group interviewed, eager to "climb the employment ladder." For the most part, ethnicity does not factor into their calculus of whether they are able to attain a HWEI position in the future. And, like many before them they have experienced a dual life. They are socialized within the dominant culture, and although they may not fully practice their ethnic traditions, they have garnered some understanding of their own ethnic culture. Whether they will suffer from an "ethnic penalty" experienced by many in this current working generation—who will be their employers and bosses in the future—is yet to be determined; and thus, there is still an opportunity for positive change in the near-future.

It is the present-day CPC's stated goal to build a *Xiaokang* society, that is, to build a "well-off," "equitable," and "harmonious" society. In many respects, this goal has been successfully achieved when examining educational attainments among ethnic minorities in Beijing. However, another key ingredient in achieving a *Xiaokang* society envisioned is to have equity in the employment market, in both ethnic terms and gender terms as demonstrated in the previous chapters. It is troublesome that the major reason for this ethnic paradox is due to the public and private sectors' institutional working cultures and prevalent minority stereotyping. With a projected increase in the ethnic minority population in China's urban areas, it is vital not only on the basis of social equity, but also in terms of economic imperatives, to effectively capitalize on untapped ethnic minority human capital. The effective management of urban ethnic minority development demands this.

Notes

1. This figure represents the legal population as defined domestically and will be the basis of analysis throughout the chapter. According to Beijing's Public Security Bureau, there are an estimated 2.5 to 3.5 million *min gong* (migrant workers) living illegally in Beijing, that is, they do not have *hukou* (permanent residence) or temporary residence status in the capital districts. Among this group, an estimated 15–20 percent are ethnic minorities.
2. Save in the situation where a child is born by parents of different ethnic backgrounds. Here the ethnic status will be determined by the parents before the child reaches 18 years of age. However, when the child reaches 18, s/he can choose which parent's ethnic status s/he chooses to adopt. By the age of 20 no alteration can be made. In practice, the large majority adopts the ethnicity of their father.

References

Heberer, T. 1989. *China and its national minorities: Autonomy or assimilation?* New York: M.E. Sharpe.

Kim, S. J. 2003. The economic status and role of ethnic Koreans in China. In *The Korean diaspora in the world economy,* ed. C. F. Bergsten and I. B. Choi, 101–127. Washington, DC: Institute for International Economics.

Li, D. 1998. City: An important arena to display ethnic cultures and ethnic development. In *Urban Culture and Urban Ecology in China,* ed. H. Yang, 107–113. Beijing: China Urban Anthropology Association.

Mackerras, C. 1994. *China's minorities: Integration and modernization in the twentieth century.* Hong Kong: Oxford University Press.

———. 2001. *Xinjiang* at the turn of the century: The causes of separatism. *Central Asian Survey* 20: 289–303.

———. 1994. *China's minorities: Integration and modernization in the twentieth century.* Hong Kong: Oxford University Press.

Mittenthal, L. 2002. Inter-ethnic strife prompts review of migration policies. *China News Digest.* Available at http://www.hartford-hwp.com/archives/55/343.html (accessed June 18, 2008).

National Bureau of Statistics and Ethnic Affairs Commission (NBS/EAC) 2003. Tabulation on Nationalities of 2000 Population Census of China, Vols. 1 and 2. *Beijing*: Ethnic Publishing House.

People's Daily. 2000. Number of ethnic minority cadres soaring up. June 28. Available at http://english.people.com.cn/english/200006/28/ eng20000628_44161.html (accessed June 18, 2008).

————. 2007. China has nearly three million cadres from ethnic minorities. February 24. Available at http://english.people.com.cn/200702/24/eng20070224 _352120.html (accessed June 18, 2008).

Rudelson, J. and W. Jankowiak. 2004. Acculturation and resistance: Xinjiang identities in flux. In *Xinjiang: China's Muslim Borderland*, ed. F. S. Starr, 299–319. New York: M. E. Sharpe.

Yu, P. H. 2000. A study on the crisis in Korean-Chinese population in China. *Studies of Koreans Abroad* 10: 135–159.

Chapter Four

Abstracting the City: Urbanization and the "Opening-Up" Process in China

Ian Morley

Urbanization has historically shown itself to be both an effect and also a cause of societal changes initially instigated by the onset of industrialization. So closely allied is urban growth with industrialization, and so significant are they in terms of how a society perceives itself, that they collectively in effect act as an age marker, that is they are culturally defining processes that mark a society's advancement from the traditional to the modern. In such a light therefore urbanization is integral to the acuity a society has of itself and its influence can be reinforced through moral imperatives and political strategies so as to, for instance, deal with age old problems connected to impoverished rural locales. In this chapter, a detailed examination of the urban perspective of China's modern development is given, in doing so offering a means to appraise not only China's shifting state-society relationship since circa 1980 as part of what is commonly known as China's "opening up," but moreover to appreciate how the evolving economic and political approach in China since the economic reforms initiated by Deng Xiaoping have manifest themselves into a changing urban landscape. By investigating the Chinese economic determinism to progress, the work shall elucidate the significance of the modern global city concept to Chinese society, a notion that has led in recent decades to an aggressively modern institutionalizing of the market economy, a reorganization of goods and services through local, regional, national, and international markets, a restructuring of everyday life through consumption, and new urban scales and proportions. Focusing on issues such as the clearing and redeveloping of city districts and the construction of skyscrapers, this treatise will demonstrate how urbanization in capitalist China has explicitly been encouraged by the elites to radiate the benefits of modernity and actualized by government plans of replacing rural environments, that is places associated with poverty and little food, with urban ones defined by city officials by their city axes lined with high-rises. Observing how elites in modern China speak of shared values yet present bases for local critiques, attention is given to the values, abstractions—which make the once unimaginable now socially useful, and practices to reveal how the urban not only symbolizes the promises of the modern world but can also in literal terms be exploited to build a modern society. The chapter thus explicates the redefining of the post-1980s city in the "abstract" by the elites in China, at the same time noting how the new definition of the city equates with a fresh array of associations between various stakeholders within the city, that is in particular the Chinese citizen and the Chinese state, as the nation moves from its agrarian foundation.

Background

For almost thirty years, China has been experiencing major transition as a consequence of the adoption of an economic paradigm commonly referred to in the West as "opening-up," that is a modernizing process founded on national economic restructuring from a Soviet styled command economy to a market economy with Chinese characteristics (Broudehoux 2004, 8–10), and the reorganizing of goods and services through local regional, national, and international markets. In accord with this economic alteration, and the introduction of land and housing reforms, the momentum for urban growth has expanded, and the morphology and appearance of China's urban places has changed. Large numbers of towns and cities have, for instance, grown in terms of their complexity, demographic size, and spatial extent, with the 295 settlements listed in the *Chinese Statistical Yearbook for Cities* (1985; 2005) having a built-up area of 8,842 square kilometers in 1984 having expanded to almost 24,000 square kilometers by 2004. Hitherto rural environments previously distant from the urban fringe have thus been swallowed by the expanding sprawl of urban communities. The vertical nature of Chinese cities has likewise been transformed. Old low-rise buildings have been replaced by edifices of a greater vertical scale as a result of the need for office buildings, the necessity to increase housing stock so as to ease the problem of housing shortages, (Wu 2002, 155) and the rising cost of urban land. Yet of note as well is the actuality that Chinese settlements have undergone alterations broader than just their appearance as more than 180 urban settlements in China now perceive themselves as being "internationalized." Consequently, the meaning of contemporary China's cities contrasts with previous times.

During the past few decades much scholarly attention has been placed on China and its evolving economic, political, and urban contexts. Given the nature of this work, there is little need to provide detailed comment on circumstances and events widely written about previously. Nevertheless, a few basic comments are pertinent. By way of illustration, China's "opening-up" has allowed the national economy to enlarge by 10 percent or more per annum since the late-1970s. The expansion of China's economy, now one of the largest in the world, has helped increase the country's levels of national income and peoples' disposable income, which despite being comparatively low by world standards is rapidly rising. Indeed the expansion of China's economy in the past few decades has meant that the average Chinese citizen is wealthier than they have ever been in their country's history with, for example, per capita income in Beijing now exceeding US$6,000 each year (China News April 3, 2007) and in Shanghai more than US$7,000 per annum (*People's Daily* February 8, 2007). Yet, as profitable as the use of economic determinism to national progress has been, it has also led to the onset of numerous urban-based predicaments (Atkinson 2007).

Although many of the problems evident in contemporary Chinese urban places shall be raised and subsequently explained some need to be commented on immediately. As a case in point, one of the most easily recognizable present-day predicaments occurring in China's cities has been the municipal approved destruction of a large number of historic urban districts. Consequently, many homes have been destroyed and architectural artifacts of note, including the renowned *siheyuan* houses (traditional four-sided residences planned around an open space at their center) and *hutong* (narrow alley) quarters of Beijing, and *li-long* (low-rise historic residential settlement) blocks of Shanghai have been torn down because they are old (*People's Daily Online* 2007) and do not match the modern urban image Chinese elites are manufacturing. Of note too, frequently in the place of razed structures are erected standardized concrete-built edifices of unoriginal and repetitive design. Hence China's urban transformation may be said, among other things, to be occurring at the detriment of a built environment of local and national culture and identity (Chang 1990, 73). Not only has cultural heritage thus come under serious threat, but the matter of replacing the old city with a "new city" based on modern design and spatial arrangements in accord with contemporary urban planning principles has led to a divergence in urban spatial patterns. The appearance of new abstract urban design values and an urban vision where new ideals are exercised through the implementation of monumental scales of high-tech industrial zones at the urban fringe (Gaubatz 1995, 45), skyscraper office buildings at the urban core, and high-rise apartment blocks or luxury villas for the wealthy.

Cities, the Opening-Up Process, and Its Impacts

When examining the modern urban history of China, it is imperative to appreciate the intertwining matters of economic development, political ideology, demography, and culture, and the influence they have had on urbanization. Moreover, it is also imperative to grasp China's profundity of empiricism, and the experience of grave social problems throughout the nation's history, for example, famines, natural disasters, poor housing, and rural poverty—matters labeled as the struggles of the peasantry (Boyd 1962, 21). Accordingly to underestimate the legacy of social matters on the Chinese psyche would be reckless, for even up to the 1960s famines were a genuine threat to the nation's stability. Hence Yeh and Xu's remark that governmental attitudes and policies regulating urban growth in the densely populated eastern provinces during the last century were pragmatic enterprises in population control given the experiences, predicaments, and lessons of China's past (1989, 4). Moreover this management situation was further shaped by the moral perceptions of the elites, who between the late-1940s and 1970s associated urbanization with free economic enterprise, immorality, social pollution, and the avant-garde (Au and Henderson 2004), that is, decadent Western values. Yet, despite the elites holding an iron collar around urban growth it would be erroneous to label Chinese authorities as being intrinsically antiurban. Indeed it would be more accurate to note how the elites adopted acuity to urbanization that respected both the advantages and disadvantages of urban growth given their nation's circumstances and history, and evidence for such a statement may be derived from Mao Zedong's broad political and cultural dialectical view of "walking on two legs" (Sit 1995, 13). Nonetheless in December 1978 a turning point was reached when the 11th National Congress of the Communist Party of China (CPC) under the leadership of Deng Xiaoping adopted a decree to instigate economic development so as to achieve "Four Modernizations" (agriculture, industry, science and technology, and national defense). Since this time urbanization has been integral to rejuvenating China's economy, (Kwok 1992, 72) and its accumulation of capital. Under such a framework cities have, in effect, been given formal sanction to guide the national modernization process (Cook 2006, 63).

In the open policy era, that is the time following on from the CPC's 1978 economic advancement decree, the ensuing policy of employing city growth to promote national advancement should be recognized as being a stratagem utilized to both propel China forward, and concurrently resolve age-old social problems. In this milieu, the coupling of economic growth with urban growth may be recognized as being a moral imperative, and under such a context large cities and their development have acquired a number of complex meanings. To highlight this point China's largest cities, such as Beijing, Shanghai, Guangzhou, and Tianjin, are now "expected to serve as growth centers for the countryside through externalities and spill-over effects" (Batisse, Brun, and Renard 2006, 49) and in Guangdong Province this was encouraged further by the creation of "Industrial Satellite Towns" (Woo 1998, 363). As such cities at the top of the urban hierarchy are motors for regional progress, and they are the sites to actualize the replacement of archaic environments and problems through the construction of new surroundings of vastly different imagery and meaning. In other words, large cities are the nucleus of the procedure to literally raze "old China" and its associated problems, and means by which this is achieved is through urban renewal, suburban expansion, and state policy to encourage township industry. To more adequately clarify the effect of this process, economic development on China's urban places a number of briefly raised points shall now be elucidated:

- Rising number of cities. Due to administrative changes and urban growth, China now has more than 650 cities, a monumental increase from the 13 cities in China in 1978.
- Increasing urban populations. Since 1978 cities, particularly the largest ones have substantially increased their population sizes due to natural increase, in-migration (Batisse, Brun, and Renard 2006, 47), and enlarged administrative borders. Places like Beijing and Shanghai have respectively grown from approximately 9 million and 10.75 million people in the late-1970s to approximately 15.25 million and 16.1 million people by 2005, respectively. More than 50 cities in China now have 1 million or more people, and in total more than 540 million Chinese people live in urban places, a figure more than 300 percent higher than the national urban population in 1978.
- Growing intra-urban heterogeneity. As Chinese cities have attracted migrants, generally young adults (Day 1994, 30), and as cities are more attractive to migrants than towns (Yeh and Xu 1989, 3), Chinese city populations now contain large numbers of nonlocal citizens. Consequently, the ethnic composition of communities has shifted. This is particularly evident in cities like Beijing, a place traditionally dominated by one ethnic group, the Han. At the same time, the vast influx of migrants has led to enormous pressure for housing and by 2004, 489 million square meters of built land was being added annually onto existing towns and cities.

- The reconfiguration of urban space. As Lu (2006, 160) has noted the reordering of urban space reflects the restructuring of social relations but in China this process has also been influenced by factors such as the rescaling of the state (Shen 2005, 39), comprehensive municipal plans, detailed plans for specific site development (Gaubatz 2005, 100), and the opening-up of the housing market. The economic hegemony of land in China should not be overlooked for it increasingly determines who will profit (in the social sense) from the rebuilding of cities.
- The reorganization of land uses. Since 1978, Chinese cities have adopted a broader number of functions than what they once had. Whereas once urban districts were typified by a complex street-based juncture of workplaces, shops, markets, schools, social institutions, and parks, the modern city instead defines itself on spatial-functional specialization via the establishment of single land use districts (Atkinson 2007), a manifestation claims Gaubatz (1995, 60) of the increased diversity in the social and economic spheres. The move to single land uses has also been heightened by modern urban planning trends that draw attention to land use zoning within citywide schemes, (Gaubatz 1995, 60) and the state's intervention in matters relating to the production of urban space and capital accumulation (Ma and Wu 2005, 4).
- Changing status. Authors like Atkinson (2007) and Cook (2006) have noted that economic developments have fueled a desire to develop "internationalized" metropolises (Cook 2006, 63). To fulfill such an objective, China has engaged its cities with the world economy and given the need to maintain its participation in global networks modern offices, high-tech facilities and cultural institutions have been built, and prestigious sporting and trade events held. At the same time such a policy had the benefit of augmenting national prestige (*mianzi*) and so the reputation of China's cities. On this very matter Esherick (2000, 1–16) noted how the overall aim was to invite notice so as to be seen as "somebody in the world."
- Exceptional urban growth in Special Economic Zones (SEZs), trade and development zones as a result of the magnetizing of financial investment and management capital (Shen 1999). Urban growth of more than 1000 percent between 1980 and 2005 is not unheard of in SEZs in Guangdong Province.
- Rising GDP of cities. As settlements have expanded their manufacturing and service-orientated economic bases, their GDPs have also grown rapidly. From 1978 to 2000, urban places in Guangdong Province have seen their per capita GDP rise by approximately

1000 percent. In the case of Shenzhen, its GDP has risen annually by 33 percent since 1980 (North American Representative Office of Shenzhen Web site).

- Vertical construction and the remodeling of cityscapes. Wu (2002, 163) has pointed out that the unparalleled rise of urban redevelopment in China, in part due to enthusiastic local governments' acquiring revenue from land development and the need to participate in the global economy, has led to the refashioning of Chinese cityscapes with high-rise construction, a built form that is fundamental, states Gaubatz (2005, 98–99) to making cities be internationalized.

- High-rise suburban living. Owing to its benefits of land saving and development efficiency high-rise housing has developed rapidly since the 1980s (Lu, Rowe, and Zhang 2001, 242). Yet as advantageous as it is to build high local authorities are aware of the detriments of tall buildings, and their contrast with the existing cityscape. Consequently many cities, including Beijing, in the 1980s put strict controls on building at the urban core so as to protect the traditional cityscape, but likewise made looser restrictions for building high at the urban fringe. Hence, in many cities low-rise cores and high-rise peripheries (Ibid.) have materialized.

Out with the Old, and Globalizing the New

Earlier in this chapter, it was noted how Chinese urban development is closely allied to economic and political contexts, and that a number of transformations regarding urban scale, complexity, and heterogeneity have become apparent after the 1978 modernization diktat. In this section, consideration is given to the endeavor of bestowing an abstract vision of social transformation, advancement, and modernity through the remodeling of Chinese cities. A few generic observations are thus relevant to begin with.

Cities, irrespective of their pasts, locations, and natures are complex entities. They are subject to a plethora of influences that can affect their nature, size, and urban form. They are also sites of political and economic expression, these being markers of a nation's cultural position at a given point in time (Sit 1995, 29). As already touched upon, economic advancement and urban transition in China has been propelled by globalization. Yet despite Chinese governments at the national and local level utilizing worldwide economic forces to propel the nation forward, Broudehoux (2004) has revealed that the impact of exogenous economic factors has led not only to new insights about cities, economic expansion, and modernity, but also new forms of inequality and spatial segregation too. One such predicament stems from the state-approved process of razing and rebuilding neighborhoods, the outcome of which has permitted the displacement of many poorer members of urban society yet concurrently permitted the elites "to isolate themselves behind the barrier of real estate pricing. Through their economic control of space, entrepreneurs and property investors have the power to determine who will dominate, use, live in and profit" (Broudehoux 2004, 6). Significantly too, this process of transforming urban land and establishing a new housing market has led to the commoditizing of urban space, a reflection of the broad commodity culture that has emerged in open-era China. Furthermore, given the milieu to internationalize Chinese cities, an extensive process to further expand cultural activity through civic consumption has begun. Thus, with the construction of high-class residential enclaves for the emerging middle classes, many using pseudo-European design through "adopting the colors, column order, artificial molding and roofs of Western classic architecture" (Lu, Rowe, and Zhang 2001, 276) has also surfaced the redevelopment of urban cores with building types such as art galleries, museums, shopping malls, hotels, and restaurants.

The cultural development of cities has, in some instances, been considered essential by the local elites to elevate the perceived unsophisticated nature of urban places. Guangzhou, the capital city of Guangdong Province, for example, in light of its reputation for money-making, industry, and a lack of urbanity has been "uplifted" by the policies of public authorities since the 1990s. Not only have massive offices and housing complexes been built, for example, the 1283 feet-high CITIC Plaza, 597 feet-tall Metro Plaza, and 466 feet-high Sky Central Plaza Apartments, but also a number of major public edifices that include the Guangzhou Opera House, Guangzhou Library, Children's Palace, and Guangdong Museum have been erected, so as to boost the city's cultural ambiance and status. In this way, Guangzhou's government may be perceived as endeavoring to fill a perceived contemporary void based on the need for first-class civil facilities so that the city can proudly define itself as a modern, internationally renowned settlement. Yet, to reiterate for a moment, the way in which culture has been imposed on urban society through the proposing and construction of cultural institutions goes hand-in-hand with how the modern Chinese city has been conceived as an object strongly connected to consumerism (Schein 2001, 225). In such a milieu, the amount of culture evident in cities thereby visibly indicates its and its citizens' sense of modernity and their affluence, and therefore the local standard of living too. Accordingly, the more culture the city has to be consumed by its citizens, the wealthier the city can reveal itself to be, and the more it can reveal itself to be nonparochial in both form and nature. Moreover, as wealth has long been an ideal in Chinese culture (N. N. Chen 2001, 166) the cultural significance of providing new amenities that are collectively countable and characterized by their scale and modern design styles as observable gauges of prosperity, should not be underestimated.

International Icons and Reflections

It is difficult to think about China and its cities without certain age-old images immediately coming to mind, such as the Forbidden City in Beijing, the terracotta warriors in Xi'an, or the historic architecture of the Bund in Shanghai. However, many of China's icons are also contemporary in nature, like the new Beijing National Stadium, and the impressive skyline of Shanghai's urban core. To discuss Shanghai, albeit briefly, its buildings have long been the international symbol of the city, which as mentioned earlier have for most of the last century been based on the appearance of the Bund, although during the 1980s and 1990s the city, along with other places, for example, Beijing and Guangzhou, has engaged in altering its images to a new economically defined vision based on skyscrapers and cultural facilities. To a great degree, the modern-day image of Chinese cities has been very carefully managed as Broudehoux (2004, 150–160) has eloquently documented. Taking Beijing as a case in point the selling of this city was borne out of the "One World, One Dream" scheme, a lofty agenda with the 2008 Olympics at its core that has promoted the city as the capital of a modern nation, a city of the world, and a place to share the global community and its culture (*China Daily* June 27, 2005). For Shanghai, its image has been based on the radical transformation of one of its boroughs and creating the Lujiazui Financial District, a glittering new Central Business District (CBD) whose built environment presents a vision of corporate and cultural might comparable to Asia's original world city, Hong Kong—Asia's key node in the networked global economy and internationalization of capital production (Yusuf and Wu 2001).

In creating modern, large-sized cities in China, certain tools have been employed to display the nation's path to economic determinism and progress. During the 1980s, SEZs and the rank of "Open Coastal Cities" were created, and by the 1990s, for instance, a device employed to accentuate the advancing economic substance of Chinese cities was Economic and Technological Development Zones (DZ), often located in central areas within which high-rise office buildings can be erected, in so doing giving the superficial impression that Chinese settlements are "becoming" Hong Kong in terms of their economy and appearance (Yang 2006, 136). One such place that has taken on the characteristics of Hong Kong, at least in the visual sense, is Shenzhen, a place described by the mid-1980s as being among the most dynamic and modern-looking cities in all of China (X. Chen 1987, 57).

Located in Guangdong Province at the border with Hong Kong, Shenzhen before the granting of SEZ status in 1979 consisted of numerous agricultural and fishing communities. From having a population of approximately 30,000 people at that time Shenzhen has exploded into a cosmopolitan boomtown with an official population of more than 8 million residents by 2005. Being the world's fastest growing city in the past 25 or so years, and now covering more than 2,000 square kilometers in area, Shenzhen is an ideal place to witness the unfolding of modern Chinese urbanism and to observe the meaning of the modern, international city in China.

Described by Shen (1999) as being China's gateway to the modern world, the rapid growth of Shenzhen is an outcome of massive business investment, a rapidly expanding industrial platform, and huge sways of in-migration due to the city's appealing image based on its prosperity, SEZ status, and high-quality living environment. From having just one construction company in 1979, the demographic explosion of Shenzhen was apparent from as early as the mid-1980s when the number of workers engaged in the construction of factories, offices, public edifices, and houses exceeded 100,000. (*Shenzhen Statistical Yearbook* 1985) In environmental terms Shenzhen, the self-proclaimed "City of Sunshine and Modernity" (Shenzhen Municipal Government Web site), the community with the highest quality of life in China (*China Daily* September 21, 2006) currently offers little resemblance to what it was less than thirty years ago. The city of today has a vertical nature that towers above the village forms that Shenzhen once was, and its citywide plan now containing large axial lines consisting of broad boulevards lined by buildings in excess of fifty floor levels. Acting somewhat as a idealized environment for China's transformation and national development, Shenzhen explicitly speaks the values in abstract and pragmatic terms of China's modernization, and although the elites in the city, like elsewhere in the country, make reference in their policies and actions to shared modern values these ideals are repeatedly the bases on which local critiques are founded, as shall now be explained.

Actors, Standards, and Critiques

When attempting to grasp notions regarding the values of modernity and urbanity in China a number of points need addressing. Therefore within this section attention is given to the contemporary urban meanings that have emerged in China as it has undergone social and economic transition. In explaining these matters, consideration is put upon anthropological matters such as the theory of value in so as to demonstrate the fundamental meanings of city development within the context of China's process of social advancement.

In broad terms, when any society engages in social and economic development new spatial forms are produced. These new spatial expressions have in the milieu of this work been shown to include the emergence development zones, skyscrapers, and cultural facilities. This is not to say though that other spatial expressions have not been formed, because gated communities, grand hotels, luxurious restaurants, and large-sized shopping malls are also common sights within Chinese cities. Although Wu and Ma (2005, 268) have suggested that these urban elements may be examined individually they contend that it is best to view them collectively when attempting to understand the changing meaning of Chinese settlements. In view of this observation, a broad outlook is now adopted and considering the role of the elites a number of points may be raised:

- The value of the modern metropolis has become especially meaningful to Chinese leaders as it differentiates the contemporary city, and so open-era society, from environments and the social problems of prior ages.
- The impression of modernity is architecturally expressible, and it is articulated by the presence of certain design styles and scales.
- The value of the modern urban settlement is expressed through specific tokens by which it may be ranked. These include the size of its population, its number of cultural institutions, the vertical scale of the cityscape, the height of the tallest skyscraper, the number of tall buildings (i.e., more than 100 meters in height), and the magnitude of the road and transport infrastructure, for instance. As Graeber (2001, 75–76) has outlined this is of a great weight in constructing civility as the application of abstract notions such as presence and ranking are the means through which values, for example, of social progress, can be realized. Along these lines certain building types, architectural forms, vertical scales and others bring conceptual values into being and make them culturally perceptible to both local and national society. This is very important to the agenda of the elites who wish to put forth shared values about social and economic betterment.
- Certain building types, road infrastructures, architectural forms, and the like are not only means by which conceptual values and ranks are brought into being but are ends in themselves. Elaborating the work of anthropologist Terence Turner, Graeber (2001, 76) asserts that tokens of rank are both tools through which values are mediated and are the manifestation of values in themselves. With reference to the

urban environment therefore this premise allows the city to become a symbol and a setting of values, a setting where modern life and social progress can be qualitatively defined. In reality though it is also the platform on which critiques are founded as economic advancement has not brought a growth in wellbeing for all citizens.

Considering the issue of abstracting the modern Chinese city and its values, certain items just mentioned need further elaborating. The first point of significance with regards to the ranking of Chinese cities is the fact that their standing is indexed through the production of visual concepts easily observable to the onlooking eye. This should not be undervalued for anyone in China can thus easily grasp certain connotations from the design and plan of the contemporary environment and be aware of contrasts between it and the old. To adopt a Lefebvreian perspective for a moment,[1] the implications of this visual reading of the urban setting is enormously influential for the elites. Firstly, it rather obviously confers edifying values through the language of sight irrespective of people's age, class, wealth, or life experiences. Second, as noted earlier, it grants a sense of time, a sense of now, and a sense of differentiation between the antiquated and the present-age. In addition, the evolution of the urban situ makes people conscious of society's growth, for as long as anyone can see urban buildings of a height and design different from Chinese architectural traditions they can grasp to some degree the progressiveness of society. Also, in such a context, the modernity and advancement of other societies, what was the once imaginary to the average Chinese citizen, becomes real, and so what was once otherworldly now becomes socially beneficial given the sense of national empiricism. As philosopher Henri Lefebvre has contended (1991, 179) the outpouring of energy into making the once imaginary real is a defining aspect of the concept of a "living body" (an evolving society) and its association with itself, the surroundings in which it is set and the world at large. Likewise insists Lefebvre (Ibid.), the expenditure of energy into transforming a society can be deemed productive as "long as some transition, no matter how small, is thereby effected in the world," which in the evolving Chinese urban context means energy can be judged useful when the skyline alters and, for instance, it replicates the wealth and supposed rise in life quality.

As much as urban transformation can help put forth modern cultural values similarly double meanings of urban and social development can occur. In other words, as much as the elites intend to speak of shared values owing to, for instance, the lack of arbitration in the economic hegemony of land, the unequal distribution of national wealth, and augmenting social and economic division criticisms of national progress arise. With regards to the aforesaid issue of razing old districts, while it ultimately creates new standards of housing far superior to that beforehand, it similarly must be appreciated for establishing social and spatial division, as resultant gated communities on cleared land establish feelings of separation for those who have been displaced from where they once resided due to not being able to afford modern housing at the market price. Consequently, those relocated may be said to experience the costs of modernism/social progress, for their displacement and movement to unfamiliar communities diminishes their access to centrally located urban resources but additionally because of their lack of wealth and inability to compete in the land/housing market, feelings of difference, a lack of well-being, and inattentiveness to contemporary political thinking become produced. In this light, the new scales and proportions created by clearing land provoke the manufacture of alternative identities as an expression of contemporary urban citizenship. In this manner, the actions of demolishing and rebuilding even though designed to speak common values of betterment and progress in due course fabricate varying interpretations as to what benefits are being created by the new direction society is heading toward. As such, the actions of razing and reconstructing have different meanings to different urban actors. As a final point, the noticeable growth of settlements and their spatial and architectural transitions, allows not only for the above-mentioned observation of cities and society to be made but it moreover allows for hierarchical observation as Lefebvre (1991) labels it from which rivalry surfaces between cities, their governments, and elite social groups. Within this background those of influence encourage the erection of more large-sized offices, high-rise housing estates, modern architectural forms for public buildings, and more comprehensive road systems and transport infrastructures to be laid down so as to demonstrate the high ranking of their community within the region and nation. In such a situation lengthy roadways reminiscent of Parisian boulevards, roadways junctions of three or more spatial levels, new and lengthy city bridges (Gaubatz 2005, 99), and skyscrapers of ever-increasing height become lauded by city officials as defining the contemporary nature of the settlement even if in more pragmatic terms they are also imperative to promoting regional development (Fingerhuth and Joos 2002, 99). Hence, in cities like Kunming in Yunnan Province the laying out of roadways up to 30 kilometers in length have been utilized to explicitly demonstrate regional capital status and be an alternative to unplanned peripheral sprawl, in so doing establishing provincial economic development axes (Ibid.) to coordinate advancement between the city and its hinterland.

The materially realized nature of Chinese society, a consequence of the application of economic determinism to social progress, have led to a number of visual and urban morphological alterations during the past thirty or so years, of which some have been described. These changes, such as the increased vertical scale of cities, may be said to be what Graeber (2001, 75) terms "medias of value," that is, the means to bring abstract notions and modern values into being. Although many of the urban transformations, and their meaning, have been discussed before some matters nonetheless require further explanation. By way of example, while the modern Chinese urban environment might appear to contrast what it once was a degree of symmetry between the contemporary and the past are evident in many settlements. This is due to many new environments, particularly residential areas, retaining old village gates and replicating existing urban features, for example, old gardens in Suzhou, Jiangsu Province, or having their planning lines guided by the foundations of the former locale. Put simply, new settings are sometimes constructed directly on the foundations of the old communities but as modern edifices have more floor levels than traditional buildings as a result ill-lit and damp environments are created. Significantly too, the new surroundings are characterized by design homogeneity and an overall lack of aesthetic charm, in so doing they present a standardized face that offers no indication of local heritage, traditional culture, or geographical individuality, and instead it offers a dreary impression of modern urbanization.

In contrast to the production of gloomy environments, the evolution of Chinese urban society has led to radical new expressions. Whereas it has just been mentioned that planning lines in many instances have been guided by building patterns existing before the razing of sites many brownfield redevelopment plans have utilized the opportunity to build new living arrangements. These can include housing units many times larger than typical living arrangement in the mid-1970s (Perkins 2006, 4), great attention being given to the exterior design to provoke notions of exclusivity within the household consumption market, the consolidating the high-rise housing tradition that has emerged in recent decades, and constructing car parking areas, for example, underneath garden terraces. Moreover through building high, embracing Western design and building techniques, and erecting large units of accommodation, China has been able to meet the enormous demands of the commoditized housing market yet this has come about, as already touched upon, at the cost of displacing those in older housing, and magnifying existing housing inequality (Huang 2005, 194). However, as significant as these transformations and problems are one other new urban phenomenon that has arisen relates to micromorphologies within new housing communities. Not only has urban space become fragmented because of the rise of gated neighborhoods, many often with non-Chinese names such as "Plaza" although in Songjiang near Shanghai communities are based on European and American models, such as the English community named Thames Town, but even inside such communities distinct social-spatial structures have arose as the wealthy yearn to express their wealth and status as part of a constructed syntax of living in grand villas or high from the ground. In such a scene where the cost of housing is based on the which floor a family resides on, and the cost rises with floor levels, thus the higher the floor level a person resides the wealthier the resident appears to be. In other words the floor level, or estate name, where someone lives is an expression of individual status. Consequently, an amelioration of tensions results as those with wealth assertively act to acquire upper floor levels and villas in posh enclaves so as to present a particular face to urban society. In many respects therefore space and its production in China among the elites have become materialistic, and as Lefebvre rationally argues (1991, 172) in such a context it, and so people, will naturally be perceived with implications of difference.

Conclusion

An overview has been offered with regards to the changing face of cities in China, the evolving social and economic contexts since 1978 and their impact on the abstract meaning of urban communities. As has been demonstrated, the Chinese quest for societal advancement has focused upon moving from one economic sphere to another, and following on from 1978 a plethora of local, national, and global factors, many of which have been raised in this work, have been influential in transforming the cityscape and its meaning. Of much significance, for instance, has been the local and central political legitimacy given to globalization as a means to solve age-old problems: "The restructuring of the Chinese city is a local process that exploits and constitutes 'global' processes" (Wu and Ma 2005, 276). The development of China's cities in the open-era, as reflected in their evolving structure and meaning thus must be appreciated for providing a map that charts of the nation's economic emergence in the late-twentieth century, and a means to gauge to economic, social, and architectural imaginations.

As has been commented on the transformation of the Chinese city has stemmed from a variety of complex, interrelated factors, and in a work like this one it is impossible to highlight and explain each matter in detail. But, importantly, given the context of this chapter the shifting nature of Chinese society and the altering of social and spatial relationships have been shown to not be inert. With regards to the elites' abstraction of the city, the wider changes in society accordingly must be appreciated for leading to a new understanding of the city due to the potential of society created by economic transitions. In this manner, this work complements the work by authors such as Gaubatz (2005) who have outlined how the post-1978 move to globalized large city economies, along with shifting local-central government relations and a marketization of housing in terms of its provision and consumption, has led to an idealization of the Chinese city.

In explaining the contemporary urban situation in China sociospatial reconfigurations have been emphasized. In morphological terms specialization of land uses, the development of comprehensive transport systems and road infrastructures, and a growing verticality of the cityscape, have been noted to be fundamental to the process of modernization and ultimately achieving global city status. The reshaping of the Chinese urban world thus reveals an unfurling vision of social and economic betterment, one in which new spatial structures help brings abstract values into being. The move therefore to spatial specialization, a high-rise environment, and a growing visual resemblance to Hong Kong, should be viewed as part of the strategy to modernize China but, as demonstrated, due to the influence of the past at the same time it also provides the means to better manage the scarcity of national resources.

Note

1. The perspective put forward by Lefebvre centers on interpreting the urban environment through a theoretical lens so as to grasp the production and meaning of the urban place. Contending thus that urban space, for example, is a social construct, an outcome of particular principles and ideals in society, Lefebvre notes that social values will affect how space and the environment is perceived and built. In such a context, Lefebvre argues that space reflects the hegemony of particular social classes, who use urban space and the environment as a means to perpetuate the reproduction of society, a means to have control over it, and to ultimately exert authority. For a generic understanding of Lefebvre's theoretical approach to the urban situ please refer to Eleonore Kofman and Elizabeth Lebas, *Writing on Cities: Henri Lefebvre* (Oxford: Blackwell, 1996).

References

Atkinson, S. 2007. *A revised framework for the design of Chinese cities.* Presented at The Third International Conference on Urban Development and Land Policy in China, Hangzhou, PR China, October 12.

Au, C-C. and V. Henderson. 2004. *How migration restrictions limit agglomeration and productivity in China.* New York: World Bank.

Batisse, C., J-F. Brun, and M. F. Renard. 2006. Globalization and the growth of Chinese cities. In *Globalization and the Chinese city,* ed. F. Wu, 47–59. Routledge: London.

Boyd, A. 1962. *Chinese architecture and town planning, 1500 BC to 1911 AD.* Chicago: University of Chicago Press.

Broudehoux, A-M. 2004. *The making of post-Mao Beijing.* New York: Routledge.

Chang, C-Y. 1990. *Towards a culturally identifiable architecture.* PhD diss. Virginia Polytechnic Institute and State University.

Chen, N. N. 2001. Health, wealth and the good life. In *China urban: Ethnographies of contemporary Culture,* ed. N. N. Chen, C. Clark, S. Gottschang, and L. Jeffrey, 165–183. London: Duke University Press.

Chen, X. 1987. Magic and myth of migration: A case study of a Special Economic Zone in China. *Asia-Pacific Population Journal* 2: 57–76.

China Daily. 2006. Southern comfort: Shenzhen best to live. September 21.

———. 2005. Beijing 2008 Games: One world, one dream. June 27.

China News. 2007. GDP per capita in Beijing to reach US $6,210. April 3.

Chinese Statistical Yearbook for Cities. 1985. Beijing: China Statistics Press.

———. 2005. Beijing: China Statistics Press.

Cook, I. 2006. Beijing as an "internationalized metropolis." In *Globalization and the Chinese city,* ed. F. Wu, 63–84. London: Routledge.

Day, L. 1994. *Migrants and urbanization in China.* Armonk: M. E. Sharpe.

Esherick, J. 2000. Modernity and nation in the Chinese city. In *Remaking the Chinese city: Modernity and national identity, 1900–1950,* ed. J. Esherick, 1–16. Honolulu: University of Hawai'i Press.

Fingerhuth, C., and E. Joos. 2002. *The Kunming project: Urban development in China.* Basel: Birkhaüser.

Gaubatz, P. 1995. Urban transformation in post-Mao China: Impacts of the reform era on China's Urban Form. In *Urban spaces in contemporary China: The potential for autonomy and community in post-Mao China,* ed. D. Davis, R. Kraus, B. Naughton, and E. Perry, 28–60. Cambridge: Cambridge University Press.

———. 2005. Globalization and the development of new central business districts in Beijing, Shanghai and Guangzhou. In *Restructuring the Chinese city: Changing society, economy and space,* ed. L. J. C. Ma and F. Wu, 98–121. London: Routledge.

Graeber, D. 2001. *Towards an anthropological theory of value.* New York: Palgrave.

Huang, Y. 2005. From work-unit compounds to gated communities: Housing inequality and residential segregation in transitional Beijing. In *Restructuring the Chinese city: Changing society, economy and space,* ed. L. J. C. Ma and F. Wu, 192–221. London: Routledge.

Kwok, Y-W. 1992. Urbanization under economic reform. In *Urbanizing China,* ed. G. Guldin, 65–85. New York: Greenwood Press.

Lefebvre, H. 1991. *The production of space.* Oxford: Blackwell.

Lu, D. 2006. *Remaking Chinese urban form: Modernity, scarcity and space, 1949–2005.* London: Routledge.

Lu, J., P. G. Rowe, and K. Zhang. 2001. *Modern urban housing in China, 1840–2000.* London: Prestel.

Ma, L. and F. Wu. 2005. Restructuring the Chinese city: Diverse processes and reconstituted spaces. In *Restructuring the Chinese city: Changing society, economy and space,* ed. L. J. C. Ma and F. Wu, 1–20. London: Routledge.

North American Representative Office of Shenzhen Web site, About Shenzhen. Available at: http://www.shenzhenoffice.org/about_shenzhen.htm (accessed March 2008).

People's Daily. 2007. GDP per capita in Shanghai over US $7,000. February 8.

People's Daily Online. 2007. Calls for halt to demolition of hutong. Available at: http://english.people.com.cn/200705/15/eng20070515_374679.html (accessed December 2007).

Perkins, D. 2006. *The challenge's of China's growth.* Washington DC: American Enterprise Institute Press.

Schein, L. 2001. Urbanity, cosmopolitanism, consumption. In *China urban: Ethnographies of contemporary culture,* ed. N. N. Chen, C. Clark, S. Gottschang, and L. Jeffrey, 225–241. London: Duke University Press.

Shen, J. 1999. Urbanization in southern China: The rise of Shenzhen city. In *Problems of megacities: Social inequalities, environmental risks and urban governance,* ed. A. G. Aguilar and I. Escamilla, 635–648. Mexico City: Universidad Nacional Autonoma de Mexico.

———. 2005. Space, scale and the state: Reorganizing urban space in China. In *Restructuring the Chinese city: Changing society, economy and space,* ed. L. J. C. Ma and F. Wu, 39–58. London: Routledge.

Shenzhen Municipal Government Web site. http://english.sz.gov.cn/ (Accessed March 2008).

Shenzhen Statistical Yearbook. 1985. Beijing: China Statistics Press.

Sit, V. 1995. *Beijing: The nature and planning of a Chinese capital city.* New York: Wiley.

Woo, E. 1998. Urban Development. In *Guangdong: A survey of a province undergoing rapid change,* ed. Y. M. Yeung and D. Chu, 355–384. Hong Kong: Chinese University Press.

Wu, F. 2002. Real estate development and the transformation of urban space in China's transitional economy, with special reference to Shanghai. In *The new Chinese City,* ed. J. Logan, 154–166. Oxford: Blackwell.

Wu, F. and L. Ma. 2005. The Chinese city in transition: Towards theorizing China's urban restructuring. In *Restructuring the Chinese city: Changing society, economy and space,* ed. L. J. C. Ma and F. Wu, 260–279. London: Routledge.

Yang, C. 2006. Cross-boundary integration of the Pearl River Delta and Hong Kong: An emerging global city-region in China. In *Globalization and the Chinese city,* ed. F. Wu, 125–146. London: Routledge.

Yeh, A. G.-O. and X-Q Xu. 1989. City system development in China, 1953–86. Working Paper No. 41. Hong Kong: Centre of Urban Studies and Urban Planning, University of Hong Kong.

Yusuf, S. and W. Wu. 2001. *Shanghai rising in a globalizing world.* Policy Research Working Paper No. 2617. New York: World Bank.

CHAPTER FIVE

THE DUAL SYSTEM OF LAND USE POLICY AND ITS RELATED PROBLEMS IN CONTEMPORARY CHINA

Xiaogang Deng*, Lening Zhang, and Andrea Leverentz

Land ownership is a crucial issue. Nearly all social struggles in history are "essentially for the ownership and use of land" (Weber 1988, 343). Throughout China's history, land and its distribution have been central to any understanding of the country's complex relationship between power, politics, and economics (Brenner 2004). Various land tenure policies provide an insight to the historical changes and to gauge rapidly changing social and economic landscape in contemporary China. China's dual land tenure system has become a critical source of debate in China's rising housing costs and widespread official corruption in land transactions. The dual system of land use reflects the transitional nature of Chinese economic structure that attempts to maintain centralized administrative control over land use and at the same time allows land allocation to those who can pay the highest price for commercial lease. The dual system creates an unparalleled opportunity for widespread corruption and various social problems.

This chapter examines China's dual land tenure system in the context of China's transitional economy. The focus of this chapter is to assess the impact of official corruption and abuse of power in land acquisition on widespread social unrests in China. It reviews basic characteristics of China's dual land use policy and analyzes related problems such as official corruption and inequality. The dual system of land use creates an institutionalized opportunity structure for government officials to abuse power for personal gains at the expense of the rural and urban underclass. It has become a major method by which people engage in illegal economic activities for financial gain.

Land Tenure System in China

The Ideological Basis of Public Ownership of Land

China is a socialist country where public ownership of land is enshrined in its constitution. Its economic system is based on public ownership, including land as a means of production. Several important factors affect China's preoccupation with public land ownership. First, Marx's view of state ownership of the means of production still considerably affects Chinese communists' perception of public ownership of land. According to Marx, inequality and private ownership of productive property, including land, was the source of all social evils (Clarke 1982). The private ownership of property divides the society into two opposing sides: capitalists who own productive property (or means of production) and laborers who have only their own labor. Land is a component of the means of production, and land ownership may reflect the hierarchical social relationship between the two opposing classes. Increasing rent-seeking and higher profit may motivate capitalists to exploit laborers and contribute to the dehumanizing of workers and ever worsening living conditions. Marx argued that the only solution was to destroy private ownership of productive property and establish a communist state that would have public ownership of property (Ibid).

Second, throughout Chinese history, land dispute has been a major source of social unrest (Brenner 2004). When the conflicts between landlords and a large segment of farmers in the society became intolerable, peasants riots occurred and new rulers replaced old ones. In more than two thousands years of Chinese history, "a prosperous, free-holding peasantry had been both the norm and ideal" (Wright 1951, 256). When rulers managed land disputes well, there was a firm basis for peace and prosperity. If not, land disputes may become a fermenting ground for social unrest and dissolution of dynasties.

Finally, the Communist Party of China has a close association with farmers and their land. The Chinese revolution in 1949 was essentially a peasant revolution. Before 1949, land was highly concentrated in the hands of landlords, government officials, and businessmen. Farmers leased a piece of land to provide a certain amount of rent in return (Wright 1951). Farmers were extremely dissatisfied with the existing land tenure system and were the major source of military manpower in Mao's army. It was the Chinese peasantry that helped install the communist regime in power. For many orthodox communists, the mere label of land owners or landlords in a socialist China would not be conceivable because it would deprive the party's legitimacy and violate the basic principle of state ownership of public land. Many top-ranking party leaders were from the rural regions and had direct personal experiences with inequality in land ownership before the revolution. These factors became China's ideological justification for prohibiting private land transactions and thus shaped China's land tenure system (Kremzner 1998).

Land Tenure under the Centralized Economy 1949–1978

China's land tenure system is based on the socialist ideology that emphasizes equality and social justice and intends to terminate the exploitative nature of landlord-tenant/farmer relationships and make full use of land values for the benefits of all people (Zhang 2007). From 1949 to 1978, the Chinese economy was under strict state control and state-owned firms. According to its 1975 Constitution, "the state sector was the dominant force in the national economy" (Article 6 of the Constitution of the People's Republic of China 1975). The state had to ensure its dominant position. All natural resources including land were owned by the state. Although the Communist Party used somewhat different property regimes for rural and urban areas, its socialist doctrine has remained influential throughout the People's Republic of China's (PRC) history.

After 1949, when communists took over the power in China, the Communist Party launched a nationwide land reform that confiscated all private lands from landlords in rural areas and redistributed it to farmers who could then have necessary resources to grow their products. In 1954, China started its rural collectivization and gradually all farmers' land became communal property or collectively owned. For such collectively owned land, farmers had the right to grow agricultural products but did not have land ownership. Under the planned economy, the state had the right to turn to rural land for urban development and this practice has continued. If the state wanted to use farmers' land, farmers usually received a compensation package that may include an urban residential permit, housing costs, and compensation for the loss of crops (Ding 2003). Although the settlement price was low, the urban residential permit was high in demand because it could enhance farmers' living standards, improve occupational choices, and provide access to medical treatment and education.

In urban areas, the state owned all land. Many urban residents had their own houses but they did not own land after 1949. Their land titles and land certificates were not legally binding (Ding 2007). Many property owners were considered enemies in the class struggle and were persecuted with their properties confiscated during the Cultural Revolution. The concept of property rights did not really exist since the 1975 Constitution declared that all properties were owned by "the whole people." The administrative allocation system was the only method used to appropriate land.

Administrative land appropriation meant that all state enterprises, state governments, military, and nonprofit organizations could use the land without charge; it was not necessary to pay rent for land use as land was not considered to have any commercial value (Chan 2003). Collectives or cooperatives had to pay a nominal fee and had no time limit for land use (Lei 2005). Land users could use land without time restraint, and land ownership was not transferable. Administrative allocation was consistent with China's centralized economy at that time.

Dual Land Tenure System after 1978

Since China started its economic reform, its economy has become more diverse and private and foreign firms, town-village enterprises, and hybrid ownerships have played increasingly important roles in the national economy while inefficient state-owned enterprises (SOE) have seen a decline in their share of the national gross product (Walder 2003). China started to adopt a hybrid economic system in which many firms moved toward the market economy while SOE still operated under the centralized economy. Similarly two land tenure systems emerged: the traditional administrative allocation system and the market-oriented land transactions.

China revised its constitution to adapt to the rapid economic changes and allow market-oriented transferring of land use rights. In 1988, a constitutional amendment was passed to confirm public ownership of land but allow land use rights. It recognizes the existence of private or other types of enterprises, but it makes sure that the state economy is in the leading role. "The socialist economy under the ownership of the whole people is the leading force in the national economy..." and the state has to "ensure the consolidation and growth of state-owned economy" (1988 Chinese Constitution Amendment Two Article 10). It stipulates that "no organization or individual may appropriate, buy, sell or otherwise engage in the transfer of land by unlawful means. The right to the use of land may be transferred according to law" (1988 Chinese Constitution Amendment One Article 10).

It was the first time that the state recognized the right to use land that indicates a significant transition from the preoccupation with orthodox communism to the acknowledgment of land as a commodity with commercial value. The establishment of a system with well-defined property rights is a critical step in the transition from a centrally planned economy to a market-oriented economy and involves a series of institutional changes in economy, law, and society (Brandt, Rozelle, and Turner 2004). China has adopted a gradual approach to the transition.

If we conceptualize the extent of land marketization in a continuum from a totally free market on the one hand and to complete state administrative control or allocation on the other, China's land tenure system during the reform era has undergone two major periods. The first period took place between 1988 and 2000 that is termed a submarket configuration period (Lei 2005). Submarket configuration refers to the old administrative allocation system that still has substantial influence over land transactions while the market mechanism is not fully effective yet. The main characteristics of this period include the transformation from free use of land to use with payment, the setting of time restraints on land use,[1] and allowing the transferability of land use right. However, administrative allocation had a much larger share of land transactions than market-oriented land transactions. Even in those market-oriented land transactions, there were significant interventions by government officials and the potential for market mechanism could not be fully operational. Land transactions through the market were not open and fair (Ibid). Land pricing was largely determined by government officials who did not have skills in the real estate business and did not have to care about the land market as long as they could benefit from it personally. Although land is owned by all people in legal terms, officials directly control state property and do not necessarily share the same interests with ordinary citizens. There is a separation between ownership and actual control of public property. In China's booming housing market, land has become the most desirable commodity and real estate developers can quickly turn into instant millionaires if they obtain a piece of desirable land at a lower price. High-level officials cannot personally benefit if they abide by the state regulations on land use. But they have the power to determine land price and may gain substantially by accepting bribes from developers or let their own relatives benefit from land transactions. For instance, Wang Wulong, former mayor of Nanking and the vice chairman of the People's Congress of Jiangsu Province used his official position to help his brother obtain several primary plots in downtown Nanking at exceptionally low prices. His brother then could make huge profits by reselling land to the developers who built high end condominiums. Wang was charged for receiving several million yuan of bribery in 2006.

The second period emerged between 2001 and 2007, and it represents the coexistence of both submarket and market configuration (Ibid). As discussed earlier, during the submarket configuration period, the dominant mode of land transactions was administrative control of land appropriation and land pricing. Starting from 2001, market-oriented land transactions have gradually become more popular. Although several land related laws and regulations were passed, these laws and regulations did not clearly specify how to operationalize market-oriented land transactions and thus created numerous loopholes for local governments and corrupted officials to sell land illegally. In 2001, the State Council issued Document No. 15 entitled *Regulations on Strengthening the Management of State Owned Land* (Ibid). It requires all commercial use of land and other types of land supplies to undergo a bidding process. In 1999, only 2 percent of land ownership transactions went through the market-oriented mechanism. The rate increased to 15 percent by 2002 and 35 percent by 2005 (Editorial Office of China Land and Resources Almanac 2006). It is not only a significant improvement but also indicates that there is still a substantial portion of land under the administrative allocation that may deserve closer scrutiny due to widespread land corruption.

China's Administrative Law of Land (1998) specifies that four market-oriented transactions can be used: (a) land use right transaction through agreement, (b) listing, (c) open bidding, and (d) auction. On a continuum from strict state control to the free market, land use right transaction through agreement is a submarket method and bidding and auction are standard market transaction methods. Land transactions through agreement means that new land users have to pay the original landholders for using land, but land transfers are neither open nor fair because only two parties are involved and other parties who may want to buy are excluded from transactions (Lei 2005). In 2003 and 2004, approximately 70 percent of all market-oriented transactions still used the agreement method (Editorial Office of China Land and Resources Almanac 2005). Even when open bidding or auction methods are used, many of these transactions are already decided behind the scenes and open market is only for show. For instance, Shanghai is China's economic engine and has experienced the most booming housing market in China. Yin Guoyuan, the former vice bureau chief of Shanghai Municipal Housing and Land Bureau was in charge of all land transactions during 1995 to 2005. From 2000 to 2003, Shanghai had more than 2,000 hectares of land for commercial lease (a 70 year lease period) each year and 80 percent of the land sales were through the agreement method that could provide opportunities for rent seeking behavior. He illegally approved land transactions and has accumulated more than 150 million yuan (US$22 million) of unaccountable personal wealth, including many buildings and houses and a large amount of cash (Hu 2007).

Problems of the Land Tenure System

The original purpose of dual land tenure system was to adjust China's socialist market economy. To a certain extent it has contributed to China's rapid urbanization process (Palomar 2004). The urbanization rates were 18 percent in 1978, 36 percent in 2000, and 40 percent in 2004 (Ding 2007).

It has also contributed to China's economic success of the past three decades. However, the system also has serious flaws and has led to widespread social problems ranging from extensive land law violations, official corruption, a rapid increase in economic inequality, and social unrests.

Widespread Land Law Violations

The dual land tenure system allows the coexistence of administrative allocation and market-oriented land transactions. The system gives government officials substantial power to monopolize land supply and benefit financially through land sales that have become a major source of revenue. Huge price differentials in land procurement processes between administrative allocation of land and high costs of land for commercial use has created institutionalized incentives for rent seeking behavior and wide spread land law violations. The 2007 official report by the Ministry of Natural Resources and Land (2007) indicates several common violations: (1) discrepancy between claimed purposes of land use (such as industrial use or medical/educational use) and actual use (commercial use) to gain illegal benefits, (2) obtaining land through administrative allocation methods at lower costs in the name of public interest but illegally constructing buildings or houses for commercial use, (3) illegal taking of farm land and constructing residential buildings for sale without any approval, (4) using illegal long-term leases to rent land and building commercial structures without formal approval, (5) falsified land approval documents, and (6) bribery in any illegal land transactions.[2]

[handwritten marginal note: Common violations of dual land tenure]

We used available data from *China Land and Resources Almanac* from 1999 to 2004 to extrapolate the national patterns of land law violations.[3] As figure 5.1 shows, from1999 to 2004 there was a total of 784, 247 land law violations. In 1999, there were 157,958 cases of land law violations that involved approximately 26,925 hectares of land. By 2000, it reached 1,717,082 violations that included 29,069 hectares of land. Although the total number of violations was reduced in each of the following years, a significant increase was observed in the total hectares of land involved in 2003 (56,711 hectares) and 2004 (70,130 hectares). There was a 160 percent increase in the total hectares of land involved from 1999 to 2004, suggesting that illegal land taking increased at an alarming rate. Figure 5.1 also includes social unrests during the same period. There is a close relationship between increased hectares of land and more social unrests during the same period.

Since public ownership of land allows the state to monopolize land resources, officials and institutional users such as firms and nonprofit organizations are likely to have more opportunities to take large areas of land illegally. Figure 5.2 shows the percentages of involved areas

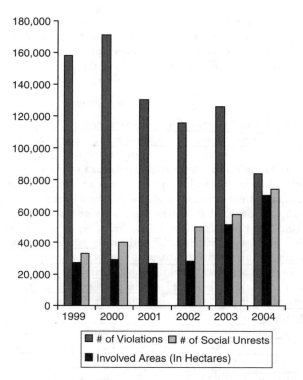

Figure 5.1 Number of land law violations and involved areas (in hectares) and number of social unrests, 1999–2004

Source: China Land and Resources Almanacs 1999–2004.

by three types of offenders: officials; firms and nonprofit organizations; and individuals from 1999 to 2004. As the figure shows, the total area of land law violations by government officials was 30 percent (70,940 hectares). Enterprises and nonprofit organizations constituted approximately 50 percent (116,759 hectares) of violations, and they account for 81 percent of the total land involved. There were 611,822 individuals involved in land law violations that account for 19 percent of the total land involved (44,336 hectares). These data indicate that institutional offenders are the major land law violators in terms of their impacts measured by land areas.

Official power or hierarchy in China has important implications. In the centralized economy, official power allowed the authorities to enjoy various privileges such as cars, high quality food, or medical care that were not

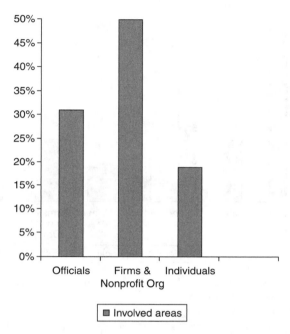

Figure 5.2 Percentages of involved areas by institutional and individual offenders
Source: China Land and Resources Almanac 1999–2004.

readily available for ordinary people. Corruption was therefore less likely involve monetary transactions because there was practically no market and only high-level officials could enjoy certain special privileges (Lu 2000b). In a market economy people can buy various modern comforts through the market as long as people make enough money. Thus, corruption in a transitional economy is likely to be transactional. Since China has both centralized and market economy in operation at the same time, officials at a higher level have more control over resources such as land. The higher the officials, the more power they have and the higher corruption incentive. Figure 5.3 examines the relationship between officials' ranking and the average involved areas of land law violations. It includes seven ranking categories: provincial, city and municipal district, county, town, village, firms/nonprofit organizations, and individual levels. A common pattern is one that moves along the administrative hierarchical ladder, so that those in higher administrative positions are more likely to be involved in land law violations with large hectares of land. For instance, provincial level officials have higher administrative position and the average involved area

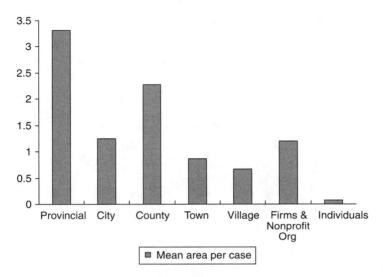

Figure 5.3 Average area of land law violations by officials at different levels of government, 1999–2004 (in hectares)

Source: China Land and Resources Almanac 1999–2004.

Note: The numbers here indicate the average area of land law violation per case by different levels of government officials from 1999 to 2004.

of land is approximately 3.31 hectares. At city (or municipal district) and county levels, the average area are 1.25 hectares and 2.28 hectares respectively while at the town and village level, the numbers are 0.86 hectares and 0.67 hectares respectively.

Land and Inequality

Excessive profit in real estate and corruption has contributed significantly to the unequal redistribution of wealth and inequality in China. Land is the single largest state asset in China. It was estimated that in 2002 the total state owned land was worth 25,000 billion yuan (US$3,572 billion) was accounting for approximately 76 percent of all state assets or 2.44 times of national gross product in the same year (Zhao 2005). Power elites or government officials as nominal holders of state asset are fully aware of the financial potential of their power and can easily become wealthy by manipulating critical resources under their control. Business elites would also seek to maximize their returns. As a result, the two groups have formed strategic partnerships to take advantage of loopholes in the land tenure system to benefit themselves at the expense of the poor and state interests. Real estate has consistently been rated as the number one excessive profit business in China (J. H. Chen 2006) and the majority of top billionaires are in real estate in China. In 2002, more than 40 percent of the top 100 wealthiest persons in China were in real estate, 47 percent in 2003, and 45 percent in 2004. Among top ten billionaires, six were involved in real estate in 2006 (Ibid).

According to Boston Consulting Group's estimates (2007), the total number of Chinese with at least US$1million financial assets, excluding real estate assets, increased from 124,000 in 2001 to 310,000 in 2006. It was ranked number five in the world after the United States, Japan, Britain, and Germany. On average the annual increase of millionaires in China is approximately 23 percent during the same period. In 2006 the top 50 richest real estate billionaires had 200 billion yuan averaging 4 billion yuan per person. The profit margin in real estate is extraordinarily high. For instance, it is estimated that the total profit in Beijing estate market alone in 2004 was approximately 24.98 billion yuan averaging 68 million yuan per day. It is estimated that approximately one-third of all official bribery cases are related to land according to the Communist Party's internal investigation (Zhao 2005). For some officials who are in charge of land, it is incredibly easy to make money. Hu Xing, the vice Chief of Transportation Bureau of Yunan Province broke the corruption record in China for receiving a bribe of 14.45 yuan million in a single land transaction (*Southern Daily* July 9, 2007). He was charged for receiving briberies of more than 40 million yuan. According to the Communist Party's internal investigation report, land law violations are closely related to nearly all official corruption cases (Shao 2007).

On the other hand, according to a 2004 World Bank's estimate, China has 134 million people or 10 percent of the population living in poverty. Their average monthly income is US$30 per (Ravillion and Chen 2004).[4] Although the majority of poor people live in rural areas, urban poverty has also become a serious issue. In urban areas the poverty rate was roughly 3 percent in 1986, increasing to 7.7 percent in 1996 and 11.8 percent in 2001 (W. Chen 2002; Wang, Tai, and Wang 2006). China was once the most egalitarian societies in the world but it is now one of the most unequal societies in the world. The income inequality index, or Gini coefficient, was 0.2 in 1984, 0.38 in 1992, and 0.40 in 1998 (H. Li 2004; Lu and Wiemer 2007).

As China develops economically, its urbanization process also develops at an extraordinarily fast rate. The urbanization rate of 18 percent in 1978 increased to 36 percent in 2000, and 40 percent in 2004 (Ding 2007). Nevertheless, rapid urbanization is achieved at high human costs. The communist state controls all critical resources and can easily project its will on disadvantaged farmers who, unlike urban residents, are not on the governmental payrolls and do not have any other resources except their physical labor. Zhou (2004) found that the state acquired approximately 100 million *mus* (Chinese unit of land measurement) or 6.6 million hectares from farmers from 1979 to 2002 and that the total financial costs of land acquisition were at least 10 trillion yuan. The acquired land contributed significantly to China's booming real estate market, but farmers on average received only one-twentieth of the land value in compensation. The state's land acquisition has contributed to persistent poverty in rural China where the average income of rural residents is one-third of urban residents. Approximately 100 million farmers are working in urban areas. This is juxtaposed against 2.5 million farmers losing their land in each year (Phan 2005). At the same time, the fortunate few in the real estate business have become extraordinarily wealthy. Many scholars (Zhang 2007; Zhou 2004) argue that China's rapid economic development is built on farmers' sweat and blood, and urban elites are created at the expense of rural poor. It is ironic that the Communist Party does not want to be perceived as landlords, due to China's recent history of revolutions, but in reality, the state is currently the largest landlord.

Farmers in China are frequently considered as second-class citizens in comparison to their urban counterparts due to lower living standards, life chances, and quality of life. Even when injured at the workplace, they are entitled to a lower compensation than urban residents in the eyes of the law. This bias is also reflected in farmers' compensation when the state reclaims their land. According to Chinese land law, the total compensation includes three components: (a) the farm land compensation payment is six to ten times its average agricultural production value in the three years before the state's acquisition; (b) the resettlement payment is approximately four to six times but no more than fifteen times of the average production value of the land in the past three years; and (c) the compensation for agricultural losses is approximately four to six times the annual production value (Chan 2003). The land laws and regulations allow local governments to decide the specific price to pay and thus provide the opportunity for abuse of power given the extraordinarily high profits in real estate. Moreover, even though the compensation is very low by any standards, these compensations are likely to trickle down to individual farmers and what they actually receive is much lower than what the land law states. Insufficient compensation often becomes one of the major sources of social unrests. Farmers frequently feel they are not fully compensated and journey to Beijing or the provincial capital to file their complaints with higher level officials (Larson 1998; Pils 2005).

Although farmers have worked on the land for many years, they do not have the rights to own land. They really can not benefit from land sale. Twenty to thirty percent of land sale revenues go to local government and enterprises. Farmers can only get 5–10 percent compensation fees but frequently have problems getting the fees because many government officials also take a little bit from farmers' compensation fees. So the current Chinese land sale system creates a social category of people that Chinese scholars call *san wu*, that is, people without land to farm, without job to work, and without minimal social security. There are approximately 40 million farmers who fall in this category (Zhou 2004).

Another critical issue in land acquisition is that farmers or local collectives in the village cannot share the profits from land transactions. According to the Chinese Constitution and the land law, farmers and rural collectives only have land use rights and do not have the right to transfer ownership. A group of farmers may live near a major urban area but they cannot sell their houses because their land is not assigned for urban development. Only the state has the right to assign land for urban use. The same piece of land can increase in value ten or twenty times more after going through the government's reassignment process; and farmers are not allowed to share in any of the subsequent profits. It is quite common for businessmen to profit highly after purchasing their land through local governments and then reselling it immediately. Since the administrative allocation method is practically free, many developers work together with corrupt officials to obtain land without or at low cost Then they can change the purpose of land use to build commercial housing in order to turn a quick profit.

Social Unrest

Unfair compensation and violent land acquisitions have generated increased social unrests. Land is a critical asset for farmers. Displaced farmers face significant risks in relocation, including finding jobs in a demanding labor market where typical college students can only make 2,500 to 3,000 yuan per month. Even if they find jobs in urban areas, those jobs are usually seasonal or temporary without any job security. Researchers (Li, Li, and Xie 2004; Wang 2007) found that 60 percent of displaced farmers faced significant difficulties, and their actual income is reduced by nearly 50 percent due to the added costs of living in the city, and some become beggars or homeless. Displaced farmers' living expenses in the city are far greater than their compensation because farmers usually have their own houses in rural areas. Displaced farmers deserve fair compensation that can assure them of having a quality of life that is comparable to what has been lost, but China's exceptionally low compensation standards makes it very difficult for farmers to maintain a basic living standard (Keidel 2006). Farmers usually do not have legal means to protect themselves, even if they take local governments to court, the Chinese judges are not impartial as they are appointed by local officials (Pils 2005).

When displaced farmers or urban residents cannot obtain reasonable compensation, they often refuse to compromise. However, real estate developers have vested interests in the construction projects to turn profits as soon as possible and any delay will mean reduced profits. They may ask for local governments to intervene for them since both sides often share common interests (Ibid). Thus land conflicts often become very violent and sometimes thousands of police are deployed. According to the Chinese statistics on public security, social unrests include mass incidents such as sit-ins, riots, strikes, and demonstrations (Keidel 2006). Official data show that there has been an upward trend of more social unrests as shown in figure 5.1. There were 32,500 social unrests in 1999, 40,000 in 2000, 50,400 in 2002, 58,000 in 2003, and 74,000 in 2004 (Ibid). Social unrests are closely correlated with the illegal acquisition of land.

A well publicized case in Longquan city of Zhejiang Province may reflect how farmers feel about the officials and developers who grab their land (Guo 2007). The farmers' land was located in the suburbs of Longquan city and the market price for land in a similar location was approximately 1 million yuan per *mu* but the local government only paid farmers 40,000 yuan per *mu*. The farmers claimed that their land was "one of the best cultivated land" in China, and they could get10, 000 yuan per *mu* per year by growing vegetables. "Land is our wealth for our future sons and grandchildren but the state only gave us a couple of thousands yuan. If we spend up all the money, we have nowhere to go but become beggars on the street" (Guo 2007). The nature of land taking in this case was administrative allocation; the state took away farm land in the name of "public interests." However, the farmers did not believe what the government's justification. The farmers showed a reporter several pieces of land that were taken away in the name of industrial development but instead became commercial residences. The farmers maintained that they signed the contracts with the state that guaranteed them thirty years of lease from 1995 and could not accept why their land suddenly became state owned. In addition, the state acquired their land several years earlier and paid the village a resettlement compensation, but the farmers received nothing as the village leaders appropriated the money. The farmers' accusation was that the village leaders secretly collaborated with corrupt officials to sign the land purchase agreement without their approval. The conflict escalated in 2004 with the local government deploying several hundred police and government workers and attempted to use bulldozers to eradicate crop field. With farmers demonstrating against the government's action and many threatening physical violence, the local government blocked all media access and prohibited any reporters from entering the village (Guo 2007).

Influential Factors of the Problem

The Political System

China has a large and complicated bureaucratic system. Administratively, China has thirty provinces, 320 cities and districts, 2,000 counties, 91,000 towns, and 680,000 administrative villages (Walder 2003). Thus, there are some 93,000 local governments above the village level. Each locality has two sets of officials: local administrative officials who are in charge of the daily management of local affairs and party officials who supervise and ensure that the Communist Party's policies and directives are correctly executed. Party officials also monitor job performance of local government officials and make important decisions. Although the People's Congress nominally exists at various jurisdictions, unlike their American counterparts, they have limited control over the operation of the executive branch and have little influence over personnel issues except for the annual meeting of People's Congress. Such massive governmental branches and officials and the lack of people's supervision and monitoring on governmental power leave prime opportunities for corruption in land handling and use.

Apart from the monopoly of political power, the state-guided and state-planned economy is another major pillar of the Communist system. As China has gradually transformed from the planned economy to the market-oriented economy, the central government has gradually decentralized its excessive control over the economy and grants provincial and local governments more power to make important decisions. Fiscally, the central government previously collected all revenues from provincial or local governments and then developed a spending plan for local governments in each province (Jin, Qian, and Weingast 2005). After the economic reform, the central government altered its fiscal policy to allow local governments to pursue their own economic development but still retain a certain percentage of local revenues. Local governments are permitted to keep all extra-budgetary revenues that usually include administrative surcharges, fees, some earnings from SOEs, and other miscellaneous revenues, including land sales (Ping 2006). Local governments do not share their extra-budgetary revenues with the central government and can spend these revenues however they want and do not have any accountability for these revenues. Thus, land sales has become a critical source of revenues for local governments.

Rent Seeking Behavior

Fiscal decentralization has reduced the central government's budgetary commitment to local governments. This means local authorities must find additional funding resources to keep their government functioning. Local officials in across the country must find ways to establish more competitive enterprises and market their products outside their jurisdiction (Walder 2003). As a result, different types of enterprises have emerged and economic ownerships have become more diverse. Before 1979, there were only two major types of firms: SOE and collective owned enterprises. After 1979 different types of ownerships have developed rapidly in different jurisdictions, town-village enterprises (TVE), joint venture, foreign enterprises, private enterprises, and many "red hat" collective firms that are actually private firms but register as collective firms to enjoy the tax and loan benefits of collective enterprises. These firms usually pay 30 percent of their profits to local governments (Nee 1992).

Local government officials are deeply involved in managing these business operations and become cadre-entrepreneurs whose interests are closely tied to "property rights that codify local government's role as shareholder and/or tax authority. These cadre-entrepreneurs—frequently include local party secretaries—have incentives similar to those of private businessmen, but they rely on their position in the state bureaucracy to preserve their 'quasi-ownership rights'" (Solnick 1996, 232). Oi calls this type of government local corporatism because local officials "act as the equivalent of a board of directors and sometimes more directly as the chief executive officers" (1995, 1132). The closeness between business and government elites indicate a shared common business interest, while the interests of the citizens are likely to be secondary or ignored. Local corporatism has the political characteristics of Mao's socialist state but also contains resemblance of a capitalist developmental state (Oi 1995). This dual characteristic also contributes to corruption in land handling and use. Officials utilize their position in the government to benefit financially but also seek to job promotion for the potential of greater financial gains.

Lu (2000a) argued that the current economic literature depicts the local governments in a positive light of advancing market-oriented reform but ignores the state's illicit and market-distorting activities that may hinder the development of market-oriented economy. The proliferation of hybrid ownerships, convergence of interests of enterprises, and officials as shareholders has blurred the boundaries between state, collective, and private companies. Companies that benefit from such close political connections through easy access to land approval, building permits, contracts and advanced knowledge of regulatory changes may distort market mechanisms and create hurdles for fair competition (Lu 2000a). The socialist state, in Lu's term, may become predatory or "boot socialism."

Generally urban areas have limited land for further development while rural areas tend to have a much larger pool of available land. In China's hierarchical structure, acquisition of farm land requires at least the approval of the county officials. China does not have a clearly defined property regime, and its land laws and regulations are ambiguous and leave more room for personal interpretations. Ambiguous property rights, loopholes in the law, and decentralization have greatly enhanced the range of discretion power at local level. Increased discretion allows local officials to develop informal land rules or de facto property rights to reduce investor anxiety for lack of formal legal protection (Zhang 2007).

De facto property rights allow local officials to manipulate rare resources to grant land use informally and foster patron-client relationship to seek rent (Ibid). They can make formal legitimate land applications intolerably difficult and demand unreasonably high land prices. At the same time they also grant kinship groups or "in-group" clients, who show appropriate respect for paying rent, land approval at low or no costs to consolidate client basis for higher subsequent returns. Both local officials and their in-group or kinship clients can benefit from these transactions. They may voluntarily continue their cooperation and self-enforce informal rules because such rules do not need formal contracts and do not require formal expansive monitoring or sanction from independent parties (Svendsen 2003).

Land corruption may reflect the basic economic principle, maximization of returns, and minimization of costs, and offenders make calculated decisions and select the course of action that best fits their self-interest (Cheung 1996). This is especially true when government officials monopolize public services and have exclusive access to land (Kreuger 1974). In Kreuger's view, the cause of corruption or rent seeking activity is due to governmental interference in the economy. Public ownership of land allows government officials to have exclusive control over land and creates an imbalance between land supply and demand. The imbalance may contribute to the emergence of a black market in which public service is provided at a price (Ibid).

Government officials throughout the country use their sole monopoly of land resources to make deals and seek rent from developers before official approval of land transactions. Land transaction is a complicated process and requires a litany of approvals and signatures. In every stage of land transaction from the initial planning, reclaiming the use of land, setting prices for land and compensation fees, deciding resettlement fees, to land taxation, officials themselves have benefited greatly from transactions. In a transitional economy, administrative power can be easily transformed into capital. In China government officials, especially those in charge of land resources, benefit greatly, particularly in financial terms from land transactions.

Discussion and Conclusion

We use China's land tenure system as a window to examine China's complex economic, political, and social relationships and review historical changes in its land tenure policy during its transition to a market-oriented economy. In the past four decades, we have observed significant but gradual changes in China's land tenure policy. It has shifted from the highly centralized authoritarian control of land to the gradual relaxation that kept administrative allocation in the dominant position while tolerating the emergence of market-oriented transactions of land during the submarket configuration period. It is during this period that the dual land tenure system started to operate. It allows land to have two drastically different values: procurement of land for public interests without payment or at extremely low costs and land for sale to the highest bidders. China's rapid urbanization and the rising expectations for better housing in the most populous country in the world have turned land into one of the most expansive commodities in contemporary China. The design of the dual tenure system makes land the single most valuable state asset in the hands of government officials. Decentralization may reduce the vertical power of the centralized hierarchy but create more horizontal power and discretion for local officials (Lu 2000b). The Communist Party's political monopolization of power ensures its exclusive control of power and eliminates any external accountability. In the meantime, government officials have little political risk as long as they can satisfy their immediate bosses and the party personnel departments at various levels of government for personal promotion (Olofsgård and Zahran 2007).

As China's economic reform continues, it has entered the coexistence period of submarket and market configuration in which market-oriented transaction methods have become more popular due to increased clarification of land laws and regulations. There has been a major improvement since all commercial use of land has to go through the market mechanism. However, only 35 percent of land ownership transactions in 2004 actually used the market-oriented land transaction system (Editorial Office of China Land and Resources Almanac 2005). Land related corruptions continues to rise. Our data show that while the total number of land law violations decreased over time, the impacts of land law violations have continued to rise due to the increased hectares of illegal land grabbing. An unprecedented number of land seizures are taking place throughout

China. High profitability of land price differentials, concentration of power in managing state owned land, legal and regulatory loopholes, little or no accountability, and low detection rates of corruption have reinforced the misuse of power by local officials (Shao 2007).

The converging interests of developers and opportunistic government officials has contributed to the emergence of elite power groups that may block or restrain market competition in order to ensure that their power will continue to translate into more personal profits. Both real estate developers and corrupt officials have become rich at an unparalleled speed at the expanse of farmers and the urban poor (Boston Consulting Group 2007). They take advantages of the flaws in the land tenure system and provide insufficient compensation to farmers for their land, thereby displacing millions farmers. Many are then forced to seek employment in urban areas with poor working and living conditions. Subsequently, scholars argue that Chinese farmers have sacrificed too much for China's urbanization and economic success and deserve to become legitimate owners of their own land (Zhang 2007; Zhao 2005; Zhou 2004).

The Chinese land tenure system has asymmetrical bias against individuals and unequivocally favors the state and institutional interests (Larson 1998; Zhang 2007). Extremely low land compensation has driven millions of displaced farmers into absolute poverty. Unfair compensation and exclusion of farmers from sharing profits in land transaction have guaranteed that developers and government officials have the exclusive rights for obscene profits. If displaced farmers or the urban poor refuse to move, violent means are frequently utilized to protect vested interests of developers and officials. Officials can take land away in the name of public interests and change the purpose of land to satisfy developers and their own personal gains. Given all these facts, one has to wonder whether China is really a socialist state that is meant to protect the interests of all working people and whether the government should do much more to protect workers' property rights rather than protect the interests of elites.

The land tenure system is an important issue and directly touches the lives of millions of people. It has drawn attention of many scholars who strongly advocate changes in China's land tenure system to give peasants more rights to solve China's persistent rural poverty and reduce incentives for corruption (Shao 2007; Zhang 2007; Zhou 2004). However, it is doubtful whether the central government can throw away the Marxist doctrine and allow farmers to have control over their own destiny. This is an important area of research that the existing literature has yet to address adequately (Ding 2003; Zhang 2007). Further research is needed to tackle the causes of land law violations and corruption. In addition, future research ought to assess organizational factors in land transactions and explore the linkages between organizational and individual corruption. Researchers should also examine patterns of land related corruption more closely and assess the decision process of the offenders in order to gain an insight into the institutional arrangements that allows for such corruption.

Notes

*The first author of this chapter would like to express his appreciation for Professor Cai Jiming of Qinghua University, Beijing, China. He was inspired by Professor Cai's talk on China's farm land compensation issue at China at a Crossroads: Searching for a Balanced Approach to Development at Harvard Law School in Cambridge, Massachusetts on November 5–6, 2005.

1. If the land is used for residential buildings, the state allows individuals to lease land for seventy years due to the fact that up to now the state has total ownership of land. In other words, although people may buy houses from developers, they do not legally own the land where the houses are built; and the state can confiscate land if it deems necessary.

2. The Land Law Enforcement and Monitoring Bureau in the Ministry of Natural Resources and Land (MONRAL) is the China's land law enforcement agency responsible for collecting information on land law violations. It uses several methods to monitor land law violations. One major method is to use satellite images to monitor large-scale land violations and send these images to its local branches at provincial, city, and county levels. 2007 is the seventh year that MONRAL has used satellite images to monitor land law violations. MONRAL focuses its resources on large metropolitan areas where rapid urbanization is more likely to erode farm land. Local branches use the satellite pictures as a starting point of investigation to determine whether observed land changes have obtained appropriate official approval.

3. We should caution our readers that the data is incomplete, and likely to lead to an underestimation of land law violations. The data presented are only known land law violation cases as many cases are likely to be unreported. Also the number of land law enforcement staff is extremely limited, with restricted authority in conducting investigations. This is especially true when cases involve high-level government officials. Moreover, official data not only capture violations of the law, but may also involve data collection agencies' recording behavior. It is reasonable to assume that a substantial amount of land violations and corruption may go unnoticed. However, according to Chinese sources, information about land is reasonably reliable since large areas of occupied land can be monitored or verified through various means of observation, including satellites. The data were taken from *China Land and Resources Almanac*. Unfortunately, no detailed data are available for further analysis in terms of the categories of common violations.

4. The World Bank's definition of poverty is US$1 per day that is higher than China's official definition of poverty. We use this number to calculate the average annual income of poor people.

References

Boston Consulting Group. 2007. Tapping human assets to sustain growth: 2007 Report. Available at: http://www.bcg.com/impact_expertise/publications/files/Tapping_Human_Assets_GW_Sept_2007.pdf (accessed November 15, 2007).

Brandt, L., S. Rozelle, and M. A. Turner. 2004. Local government behavior and property right formation in rural China. *Journal of Institutional and Theoretical Economics* 160: 627–662.

Brenner, M. 2004. The evolution of land distribution in reform-era China. Political Economy Research Institute of University of Massachusetts. Available at: http://62.237.131.23/research/2004-2005/2004-2005-6/cip2/papers/brenner.pdf (accessed October 20, 2007).

Chan, N. 2003. Land acquisition compensation in China: Problems and answers. *International Real Estate Review* 6: 136–152.

Chen, J. H. 2006. When Ren Zhiqiang defends excessive profit in real estate, What does it reveal? The black-hole in the housing cost. *Shanghai Securities Daily*. October 24. Available at: http://www.chinanews.com.cn/estate (accessed October 20, 2006).

Chen, W. 2002. Warning signs of increasing rural vs. urban inequality. *China Youth Daily* November 1.

Cheung, S. 1996. A simplistic general equilibrium theory of corruption. *Contemporary Economic Policy* 14: 1–5.

Clarke, S. 1982. *Marx, marginalism and modern sociology: From Adam Smith to Max Weber*. London: Macmillan Press.

The Constitution of the People's Republic of China of 1975 and 1982.

Ding, C. R. 2003. Land policy reform in China: Assessment and prospects. *Land Use Policy* 20: 109–120.

———. 2007. Policy and praxis of land acquisition in China. *Land Use Policy* 24: 1–13.

Editorial Office of China Land and Resources Almanac. 1999–2006. *China Land and Resources Almanac 1999–2006*. Beijing, China: Editorial Office of China Land and Resources Almanac.

Guo, Y. K. 2007. Government's dilemma: The investigative report on Longquan land conflict. China Lawyer Observation Network March 5. Available at: http://www.ccwlawyer.com/center.asp?idd=936 (In Chinese) (accessed November 24, 2007).

Hu, Yi. 2007. The central government investigates the collaboration between officials and business: Major shock for Shanghai real estate industry. *New Century Weekly*. Available at: http://www.dzwww.com/synr/jdxw/200705/t20070523_2176175.htm (In Chinese) (accessed October 28, 2007).

Jin, H. H., Y. Y. Qian, and B. R. Weingast. 2005. Regional decentralization and fiscal incentives: Federalism, Chinese style. *Journal of Public Economics* 89: 1719–1742.

Keidel, A. 2006. China's social unrest: The story behind the stories. *Carnegie Endowment Policy Brief* Number 48, September. Available at: http://www.carnegieendowment.org/files/pb48_keidel_final.pdf (accessed November 12, 2007).

Kremzner, M. T. 1998. Managing urban land in China: The emerging legal framework and its role in development. *Pacific Rim Law and Policy Journal* 7: 611–654.

Kreuger, A. 1974. The political economy of rent-seeking society. *American Economic Review* 64: 292–303.

Larson, K. M. 1998. A lesson in ingenuity: Chinese farmers, the state, and the reclamation of farmland for most any use. *Pacific Rim Law and Policy Journal* 7: 831–857.

Lei, A. X. 2005. *It is high time for more complete marketization of land transaction.* Land Resource Utilization, Department of the Ministry of Natural Resources and Land. Available at: http://www.mlr.gov.cn/zt/2005tudiriluntan/leiaixian. htm (In Chinese) (accessed August 16, 2007).

Li, H. 2004. *From revolution to reform: A comparative study of China and Mexico.* Lanham, MD: University Press of America.

Li, W. W., K. Li, and D. K. Xie. 2004. Farmer without land, work without job, minimum insurance without Qualification. *Ningbo Daily* March 3: A4.

Lu, M. and C. Wiemer. 2007. Social equity in China: Building a *Xiaokang* society in an all-round way. *Outreach Development* November. Available at http://www1.worldbank.org/devoutreach/textonly.asp?id=354 (accessed November 16, 2007).

Lu, X. B. 2000a. Booty socialism, bureau-preneurs, and the state in transition: Organizational corruption in China. *Comparative Politics* 32: 273–94.

———. 2000b. *Cadre and corruption: The organizational involution of the Chinese Communist Party.* Stanford, CA: Stanford University Press.

Ministry of Natural Resources and Land. 2007. *No one should attempt to lift the gate of land resource illegally.* Ministry of Natural Resources and Land's Web site. Available at: http://www.mlr.gov.cn (In Chinese) (accessed July 8, 2007).

Nee, V. 1992. Organizational dynamics of market transition: Hybrid forms, property rights, and mixed economy in China. *Administrative Science Quarterly* 37: 1–27.

Olofsgård, A. and Z. Zahran. 2007. *Corruption and political and economic reforms: A structural breaks approach.* Economics Department, Georgetown University. June 1. Available at: http://www9.georgetown.edu/faculty/afo2/papers/corrjune12007.pdf

Oi, J. C. 1995. The role of the local state in China's transitional economy. *China Quarterly* 144: 1132–1149.

Palomar, J. 2004. Land tenure security as a market stimulator in China. *Duke Journal of Comparative and International Law* 12: 7–74.

Phan, P. N. 2005. Enriching the land or the political elite? Lessons from China on democratization of the urban renewal process. *Pacific Rim Law and Policy Journal* 14: 607–657.

Pils, E. 2005. Land disputes, rights assertion, and social unrest in China: A case from Sichuan *Columbia. Journal of Asian Law* 19 (Spring): 235–292.

Ping, X. Q. 2006. *Evaluation of effectiveness of China's local budget system and design of indicators.* Working Paper Series No. C20006018. Center for Economic Research, Beijing University. Available at: http://www.ccer.edu.cn/download/7184-1.pdf (In Chinese) (accessed May 28, 2007).

Ravillion, M. and S. H. Chen. 2004. *China's (uneven) progress against poverty.* World Bank Policy Research Working Paper No. 3408.Washington DC.

Shao, D. S. 2007. Corruption in real estate and corruption of power capital in China. In *The issue of corruption during the drastic social change in China.* Available at *Guang Ming Daily*: http://guancha.gmw.cn/show.aspx?id=4702 (accessed October 30, 2007).

Solnick, S. L. 1996. The breakdown of hierarchies in the Soviet Union and China. *World Politics* 48: 209–238.

Southern Daily. 2007. Hu Xing's corruption case in court: More than 10 million bribery in a single transaction. July 9. Available at http://www.southcn.com/news (In Chinese) (accessed November 15, 2007).

Svendsen, G. T. 2003. *Social capital, corruption and economic growth: Eastern and Western Europe.* Working Paper 03–21. Aarhus, Denmark. Available at http://www.hha.dk/nat/wper/03-21_gts.pdf (accessed July 28, 2007).

Walder, A. 2003. Sociological dimensions of China's economic transition: Organization, stratification, and social mobility. The Asia/Pacific Research Center of Stanford University. Working Paper. Available at http://iis-db.stanford.edu/pubs/20208/Walder_Sociological.pdf (accessed December 5, 2007).

Wang, F., T. O. Tai, and Y. J. Wang. 2006. *A decade of rising poverty in urban China: Who are more likely to fall under.* Working Paper 06–14. Center for the Study of Democracy, University of California, Irvine. Available at http://repositories.cdlib.org/cgi/viewcontent.cgi? article=1132&context=csd (accessed June 20, 2007).

Wang, X. L. 2007. *The current status of national income distribution and "grey" income.* Research Report of National Economy Research Institute of China Reform Foundation. Available at http://bbs.people.com.cn/ postDetail.do?view=1&id=2529141 (In Chinese) (accessed June 20, 2007).

Weber, M. 1988. *The agrarian sociology of ancient civilizations.* Trans. F. R. I. Verso: London.

Wright, M. 1951. The Chinese peasant and communism. *Pacific Affairs* 24: 256–265.

Zhang, X. B. 2007. International and urban affairs: Asymmetric property rights in China's economic growth. *William Mitchell Law Review* 33: 567–589.

Zhao, X. 2005. *Comment on China's contemporary land tenure system.* State Asset Management and Monitoring Commission of the State Council. Available at http://www.ccrs.org.cn (In Chinese) (accessed August 14, 2007).

Zhou, T. Y. 2004. Protecting farmers' rights in land transactions. *China Economic Times* February 10. Available at http://news.xinhuanet.com/house/2004-02/10/content_1307434.htm (In Chinese) (accessed November 5, 2007).

CHAPTER SIX

CONTESTING URBAN SPACE: DEVELOPMENT OF *CHENGZHONGCUN* IN CHINA'S TRANSITIONAL CITIES

Li Zhang

> *"Space is fundamental in any form of communal life" and "fundamental in any exercise of power"*
>
> —Foucault 1984, 253.

For social scientists, urban space, which represents a multiplicity of socio-material concerns (Gottdiener 1994), is both the geographical site of social action and the social platform for engaging in action. According to Lefebvre (1991), urban space is a "site" for contesting relations of domination and subordination. In the course of economic restructuring and urbanization, urban space is economically and socially (re)constructed by various forces. Although many empirical studies have been devoted to illustrate the powerful influence of globalization, macrolevel economic restructuring, and interaction among government agencies, firms and individuals, in transforming urban space in the Western context (e.g., Davis 1992; Gilbert 1998; Gotham and Brumley 2002; Gotham, Shefner, and Brumley 2001; Hutchison 2000; Logan and Molotch 1987), relatively little has investigated how different social groups produce and contest different meanings, imagery, and interpretations to spaces in the Chinese city.

In China, growing number of rural migrants in cities since economic reforms has led to the contestation of urban space centered in some highly selected neighborhoods, in particular *chengzhongcun*. The term *chengzhongcun*, literally meaning "a village within the city," refers, ontologically, to such settlements that are administratively classified as rural areas but are located in the inner-city or peri-urban areas. These "villages," formerly in suburban areas, have been swallowed up by urban expansion. Functionally, *chengzhongcun* are a de facto migrant enclave where migrants outnumber local residents significantly in many cases. When numbers of rural migrants have flooded into cities where public housing provided by government was predominant for decades, what they encounter is that urban public housing does not open to accommodate them and their living conditions are never on the government's agenda. They are forced to seek affordable accommodation oriented by the market. Largely financed by the rural land-use right and freed by falling outside the scope of city planning control, indigenous villagers develop *chengzhongcun* into a cluster of low-rent housing through "illegitimate" processes and by unregulated ways to reap financial benefit from the opportunity of increasing demand for housing resulted from migration. As *chengzhongcun* can provide inexpensive, albeit often substandard housing, *chengzhongcun* are seen by rural migrants as a secure source of material for their survival in cities. Nonetheless, the emergence of such urban space has been viewed by those intending to discipline space as a chaotic site of land use and fertile ground for the growth of social vices. City governments intend to rebuild *chengzhongcun* into an orderly space where standard planning procedures and governance regulations must be established. However, the redevelopment of *chengzhongcun* proposed by government conflicts with the existing way that indigenous villagers and migrant residents think about and use *chengzhongcun* and therefore faces various kinds of confrontation and challenge.

There is a large body of literature documenting migrant settlements in general and *chengzhongcun* in particular. In addition to general description on the physical setting and living conditions there, special attention has been paid to the particular role of *chengzhongcun* as migrant communities. Most scholarly works view *chengzhongcun* as a social place, focusing on the processes of radical social change occurring in such space (e.g., Beja and Bonnin 1995; C. G. Wang 1995; Liu and Liang 1997; Ma and Xiang 1998; Piante and Zhu 1995; Xiang 1993, 1999; Zhang 2001). Both Lan (2001; 2004) and Li (2004) addressed the formation of unique social structure found in *chengzhongcun* where simultaneously experienced both the end of rural organization and the persistence of rural identity when the city encroached on the countryside. Zhang (2001) and Ma and Xiang (1998), respectively, provided ethnographic investigation on the creation of social networks based on migrants' places of origin and the formation of non-state spaces produced in the interaction between migrants and government. Fan and Taubmann (2002), as well as Gu and Liu (2002), offered case studies of migrant enclaves in Shanghai and Beijing, giving greater emphasis to emerging social inequality and spatial segregation in the Chinese city. By examining the housing and settlement patterns of migrant households, Wu (2002) pointed out that migrants were excluded from the formal housing distribution system and, as a result, agglomerated in the fringe of the city. Zhu (2004) regarded the formation of *cheng-zhongcun* as rent-seeking processes driven mainly by local developmental state as well as by non-state economic forces. In general, the literature acknowledges the role of rural-urban dualism in constructing the physical and social landscape of *chengzhongcun*. What remains understudied is how *chengzhongcun*, as urban space having a distinctive built environment, economic function, social configuration, and social meaning, are contested by different social groups for their vested interests.

This chapter takes *chengzhongcun* as a case to study the contestation of urban space in transitional China. I will ground my analysis of *chengzhong-cun* development in sociomaterial practices. Specifically, *chengzhongcun,* functioned as a chaotic migrant settlement, will be examined as a microsite of social interaction and the exercise of power. Moving beyond seeing *chengzhongcun* as a spatial form simply evolved from urban expansion, *chengzhongcun* development will be analyzed as a space of mediating link between macro socioeconomic constraints and rational actions of affected social groups, for example, municipal government, indigenous villagers, and village committee, migrant residents, and developers. I will show how different social groups read *chengzhongcun* in different spatial metaphors, which made *chengzhongcun* to be evaluated differently in terms of its existence and utility function. The chapter will suggest that, being migrant settlements generating a wide range of conflicts of interest and confrontations between city government and the user groups there, *chengzhongcun* represent a good example that can illustrate the relational interplay of the systemic legacy and market forces under the socioeconomic transformation. It examines how different user groups in *chengzhongcun* grapple with recent reconfiguration of spatial politics embedded in the previous socialist dichotomous rural-urban divide. I first document the background and ways in which *chengzhongcun* is developed as a migrant settlement. This integrates my analysis of *chengzhongcun* development with macro socioeconomic and institutional changes. I then articulate how different social groups intend and resist *chengzhongcun* redevelopment, which highlight a dimension of changing state-society relationships in contesting urban space. Discussions in this chapter are based on interviews and ethnographic data collected in field research in Beijing, Shenzhen, Shijiazhuang, Nanjing, Zhuhai, Wuhan, and Guangzhou metropolises from 2000 to 2005. The fieldwork, with assistance from local colleagues, included field observations, informal and semistructural interviews with different user groups in *chengzhongcun*. Though the fieldwork covered several metropolises, many cases and materials cited were from Guangzhou and Shenzhen. This is mainly because these two cities were at the forefront of *chengzhongcun* redevelopment.

Institutionalized Exclusion and
Housing Choice of Rural Migrants

Better understanding of urban space contestation in China should begin with reference to the social exclusion of rural migrants in cities, which is conditioned by the household registration (*hukou*) system. The *hukou* system, established in the early period of socialist China and with the power to restrict population mobility and access to state-sponsored benefits, designates two spatially demarcated and socially exclusive classes based on the rural-urban divide within the same country (Chan and Zhang 1999; Cheng and Selden 1994; F. Wang 2005; Tian 2003). Two classes enjoy contrasting and unequal entitlements that are confined to a specified locality and cannot be transferred across spatiality without official approval to change one's *hukou* registration. In today's transitional China, the *hukou* system, though considerably eroded in its migration control function, has continuously produced the schismatic and exclusionary effect at both societal and individual levels in locally specific terms (F. Wang 2005).

The rural-urban divide becomes blurring with the initiation and perpetuation of massive rural-to-urban migration when China departs from its centrally planned economy since 1978. Multiple factors and changes seriously challenged the base of a rigid rural-urban divide and create an uprooted, mobile rural population. Huge, persistent rural-urban disparities in many respects and a large supply of poorly productive labor from the agricultural sector presented tremendous rural pushing and urban pulling forces and tended to trigger enormous and endless rural-to-urban migration. The implementation of the decollectivized household responsibility system in the countryside institutionally rearranged the division of rural labor and effectively released rural surplus labor from the limited farmland. Economic growth created certain better-paid and less-arduous jobs that attracted a more educated urban labor force. The unwillingness of urbanites to take jobs that were particularly strenuous, dirty, or monotonous caused a structural shortage of urban labor even when there was considerable unemployment and underemployment in cities. The disintegration of the socialist "urban public goods regime" and graduate liberalization of urban labor market enable rural-to-urban migration largely out of state control (Solinger 1995). Urban employers had a strong incentive to take advantage of the pool of cheap rural labor. The growth of export-based and labor-intensive manufacturing in coastal cities by the penetration of the global economy created strong demand for low-skilled workers. In combination, those forces made rural-to-urban labor transfer a profound feature of Chinese economy.

Yet, the urban presence of rural migrants has not necessarily translated into substantive rights in the city. Rural-to-urban migration seems inevitable, but social exclusion based on the socialist rural-urban divide continues. Most of rural migrants move spontaneously without an official permission for the transfer of their *hukou* status. In the Chinese context, these migrants are commonly known as "temporary," "floating," or non-*hukou* population. In essence, the "temporary population" is not so much defined by restriction on the maximum period of stay as by concomitant economic and social rights in the destination. No matter how long they have lived in the current place, temporary population is considered as outsiders and transients who are supposed not to (and are legally not entitled to) stay at the destination permanently. They do not have a full right of abode in substantive terms under the existing socioeconomic institutions. Accordingly, rural migrants are excluded on the basis of their rural *hukou*, which bars them from enjoying equal job opportunities to those of the state-designated urban locals and limits their entitlement to social services. As rural migrants have encountered various types of exclusion in cities, they are usually held up by marginalized working and living conditions (F. Wu 2004; Wong, Li, and Song 2007). Even though rural migrants are now allowed to enter into cities, they are deprived of their fundamental rights to settle there.

It is within this institutionalized social exclusion that we can understand the housing choice of rural migrants in cities. Table 6.1 presents data that show the housing types of temporary population, who are largely composed of rural migrants staying in cities. The data suggest that the accommodation of rural migrants presented strong low-rent and temporary characteristics over time. First, those people who came to work

Table 6.1   Housing types of temporary population

Year	Dormitory provided by employers (%)	Rental house (%)	Construction site (%)	Hotel or guest house (%)	Relatives' or friends' house (%)	Others (%)
1997	30.36	27.75	17.16	9.44	11.24	4.05
1998	29.30	28.05	15.80	11.91	11.00	3.93
1999	29.56	31.06	16.13	9.21	10.22	3.82
2000	29.90	32.37	15.70	8.48	9.36	4.20
2001	31.64	35.52	14.27	5.91	8.72	3.94
2002	30.28	38.36	13.34	6.26	8.08	3.67
2003	30.11	41.05	12.59	4.33	7.39	4.53
2004	27.89	44.07	11.72	4.34	7.36	4.62
2005	26.96	45.66	10.44	5.23	7.32	4.39

Source: Ministry of Public Security (various years).

consistently opted for accessible and cheap accommodation. Although temporary population employed in manufacturing and construction sectors often lived in dormitories provided by employers or on construction sites, those in low-wage service-sector jobs were accommodated by private rental houses. Second, the tenure of temporary population accommodation was mainly temporary by nature. A dominant proportion of temporary population was tenants. This implied that rural migrants had a very low degree of attachment to the urban property market, and they had almost no urban home ownership. This concurred with results of housing surveys carried out in Shanghai and Beijing, which found that among migrants, housing ownership was lower than 1 percent (W. P. Wu 2002, 100). Although dormitories and construction sites provided temporary and inexpensive accommodation, rental housing made it easier for footloose tenants to move in and out with less binding financial liability.

Habitat choice of rural migrants should be referenced to their low affordability and limited urban citizenship caused by institutionalized exclusion already noted. First, rural migrants, who faced many uncertainties in cities with the right of residence and job security and who were generally employed in more disadvantaged labor market position, did not intend to or simply could not spend much on their housing. In the expenditure list of rural migrants, housing cost as part of their surviving needs had to be given a low priority. They sought cheap but usually substandard housing that was perceived only as a secondary and transitional place necessary for earning money. Second, the alien status of rural migrants left them without the possibility of claiming any right to low-income affordable housing heavily subsidized by government for the urban poor (Huang 2003; Y. P. Wang 2000). The remaining viable options were living at the workplace or living in private rental houses.

Chengzhongcun is a cluster of private rental quarters as well as a migrant community that displaces a substantial number of migrants living there. *Chengzhongcun* attract rural migrants to stay by several place-based factors. Location is one of the factors. Many *chengzhongcun* are geographically closer to the employment opportunities that demand for migrants. My interviews found that migrants usually moved into *chengzhongcun* after they were employed. This means that location of employment set a spatial limit on migrants' daily lives and that *chengzhongcun* can make residents living not far away from their jobs. Being a part of the city, *chengzhongcun* are well connected with workplaces and shopping spots with convenient transportation. This highlights that residents in *chengzhongcun* can make their lives within the confines of public transport routes and that *chengzhongcun* have potential to increase the spatiality of migrants' everyday lives. There is an active housing rental market in *chengzhongcun* that can provide accommodation with comparatively lower rental rates that meet the financial capacity of rural migrants. In addition to shelter space, an array of services, specifically targeting for migrants, is also readily available in service spots within or adjacent to *chengzhongcun*. These service spots are often in a corner of small grocery shops and food vendors in the building's ground floor. The service items include rental assistance, moving help, repairs and maintenance of household goods, and the buying and selling of second-hand goods. The significance of such services is to provide practical assistance for migrant residents and to make *chengzhongcun* not only migrants' living space but also a migrant community. In *chengzhongcun* migrants can learn about job opportunities, housing rental information, develop community-based contacts, and expand their social networks through routinized activities and daily contacts.

Migrant residents as a group in specific *chengzhongcun* are not always homogenous in terms of geographic origins and occupations. Although some *chengzhongcun* housed people originating from the same place and engaging in one or two specialized occupations, not all *chengzhongcun* were necessarily ethnically based and employment-specialized. Many of them were in fact loosely structured socially, lacking dominant ethnic connections comparable to other native place-based migrant enclaves such as Zhejiang village or Wenzhou village in Beijing. The fieldwork indicated that migrants living in many *chengzhongcun* came from different parts of the country (Zhang, Zhao, and Tian 2003). It was hard to find a predominant portion of migrants who were from the same county or even the same province. Occupations of migrant residents also covered a wide range of categories from low-end service sectors to those casual employments that were hard to be classified. There was also a certain degree of diversity in income levels. The diversity of demographic and social characteristics of residents suggested that *chengzhongcun* can be socially heterogeneous and broken into existential fragments.

Chengzhongcun as a Space of Speculation and Irregularities

The emergence of *chengzhongcun* as a popular home for rural migrants is largely related to the rural status of *chengzhongcun*, which makes it possible to develop substantial number of low-rent housing there through unregulated processes. First, housing construction in *chengzhongcun* is dependent on the property rights of rural land. Land is not only a prerequisite for building houses, but also a resource to finance housing construction. The rural status of *chengzhongcun* entitles indigenous villagers to a certain plot of collectively held land with unrestricted tenure on which they can build their housing at their own expense, according to the state's Land

Management Law (1998). Land for housing is allocated free (in some cases with a nominal fee). Having access to a piece of free land for housing constitutes a significant element to build houses at a substantially lower cost in *chengzhongcun* than in other parts of the city, as land cost represents the most costly item of housing construction expenditures. Second, the rural status links *chengzhongcun* into the rural administrative system and largely protects *chengzhongcun* from the intervention of city planning control. As a tradition, Chinese rural settlements usually develop without formal planning blueprint and regulations. Though there are governmental organizations in charge of rural housing development, land and housing development in *chengzhongcun* are in practice beyond the enforcement power of city planning authorities who are primarily responsible for providing planning services to and enforcing development control over the land that is state-owned, not the rural areas even within the city's administrative boundaries. Housing construction in *chengzhongcun* can easily evade planning regulations and indigenous villagers often build excessive floor areas at a very high density that is not allowed by the building codes. Unit cost of housing construction can be easily lowered by circumventing planning restrictions. In fact, the investment in rental houses in *chengzhongcun* is in large part reduced by a substantial reduction in the official minimal requirements concerning plot ratio, density limits, permissible road widths, and compulsory public infrastructure. It is not surprising to find in *chengzhongcun* that many houses were built by ignoring the legitimate procedures and planning regulations, resulting in chaotic utilization of land resources (Tang and Chung 2002).

To take economic benefits from growing number of rural migrants who are denied access to urban public housing, indigenous villagers are keen to fill *chengzhongcun* with housing estates for income. As housing demand is strong and renting is lucrative, indigenous villagers are intrinsic to build as many living units for lease as they can on their housing land. It is estimated that the total income from market-based leasing in *chengzhongcun* in Shenzhen was as large as RMB 20 billion (approximately US$2.5 billion) per year (*Southern Metropolitan Daily*, October 28, 2004). More housing is therefore developed on speculation through increasing housing density and the number of floors to maximize rent. By bypassing development control, housing construction in *chengzhongcun* is cost-saving and, on completion, can suppress rent levels. Thus many houses are available, at comparatively lower rental rates, for newcomers, survival in the city must depend on inexpensive accommodations.

Market forces have undermined government surveillance on the housing rental in *chengzhongcun*. For the sake of public security and social order, urban housing rental is codified in a series of municipal regulations.

However, government intervention in housing rental in *chengzhongcun* is not always effective, given the dominance of private housing there and the economic incentives of the landlords and tenants. Under existing official regulations, both landlords and tenants are required to register with the local police for urban housing rental within a certain period after the tenant moved in (Anonymous 2003). The detailed information of the tenant must be reported. To landlords and tenants, these requirements are perceived as costly and troublesome, because migrant tenants are very mobile and are substituted frequently. At the level of implementation, government administration and surveillance of rental housing in *chengzhongcun* are ineffective because of loopholes in the regulations and insufficient number of official security personnel. Landlords can easily get around the regulations. Most houses rented out are based on bilateral agreements between landlords and tenants but do not follow municipal regulations. The number of tenants without registration with the local police is substantial in *chengzhongcun*. As a result, rental market in *chengzhongcun* is outside the government's purview and an incipient migrant settlement is in the making.

At a local level, village committees (the legal representative of *chengzhongcun* administrations), indigenous villagers, and migrants are equally committed to making *chengzhongcun* work for their vested interests. To reap migration benefits, rural migrants need accessible and affordable urban accommodation. Though living condition is poor, field interviews suggest that migrant residents in general are satisfied with the living environment of *chengzhongcun*. Indigenous villagers have seen migrant tenants as an important source for broadening their income base. From the perspective of village committees, the presence of migrants, who can be easily subjected to various kinds of management fees and therefore financially exploited, has been regarded as a bonanza for expanding local revenues. More importantly, almost all members of village committees come from indigenous villagers who are also house owners. Their self-interest provides village cadres with a low incentive to follow and implement the legitimate procedures that are stipulated by the higher level of government and that deem jeopardize to their aggressive use of land. To accrue financial benefits and to attract more migrants, village committees in *chengzhongcun* may tacitly allow some illegal activities by not strictly enforcing central laws and municipal regulations. Nonetheless, from an economic standpoint, all parties in *chengzhongcun* are mutually beneficial. They act together as active agents to shape the use of space in *chengzhongcun*.

Table 6.2 corroborates some of the points just discussed. The table presents seven cases in several *chengzhongcun* in Guangzhou and reveals the factors—land, cost, and return of housing construction—that are crucial

Table 6.2 Housing construction costs and rental income in selected *chengzhongcun*, Guangzhou city

Case	Location	Land size (m²)	Land cost	House size (m²)	Construction cost Unit cost (yuan/m²)	Construction cost Total (yuan)	Financial source	Annual renting-out rate (%)	Estimate rental income Monthly unit rate (yuan/m²)	Estimate rental income Annual income (yuan)
1	City proper	40	Free	160	650	104,000	Family saving	70	10–12	16,000
2	City proper	40	Free	160	375	60,000	Family saving	60	7–8	86,400
3	City proper	20	Free	60	380	22,800	Family saving	90	35	23,000
4	Adjacent suburb	60	Free	390	620	241,800	Family saving & loan from relatives	50	36	28,800
5	Adjacent suburb	39	Free	252	550–650	151,200	Family saving & loan from relatives	60–70	6–8	17,000
6	Distant suburb	80	Free	80	n/a	n/a	Family saving	100	13.5	11,000
7	Distant suburb	100	Free	220	200	44,000	Family saving	75	5–6	14,400

Source: Zhang, Zhao, and Tian (2003).

for forming a functional migrant settlement in *chengzhongcun*. All houses were built on free land. As there was no cost for the land, the investment of housing construction (from as low as RMB 60,000 [approximately US$7,500] to no more than RMB 250,000 [approximately US$31,250]) was relatively low and was affordable for most indigenous villagers. By utilizing the free land as well as by mobilizing necessary resources (family savings and private loans), indigenous villagers successfully financed housing construction and rented out at a substantially lower rental rate than that of other parts in the city (usually 20–30 percent lower). As the renting-out rate was quite high (from 50 percent to 100 percent annually), investment in housing could be easily recovered by rental income. The high renting-out rate implied that housing in *chengzhongcun* was attractive by competitive rent rates. Rural migrants, as major tenants of the low-end of the housing market, made the housing market in *chengzhongcun* financially sustainable through their rental. Although the cost and the rent varied with *chengzhongcun* locations and housing structures, it was evident that the cost recovery of housing construction and financial gain through housing rental were promising for landlords in all cases. It took a very short time, even as quick as one or two years, for the landlords to recoup their investment.

As the space beyond the jurisdiction of formal planning regulations and a vacuum in urban administration, *chengzhongcun* can be seen as a kind of informal settlements. As part of the reality, many *chengzhongcun* are indeed plagued by insufficient facilities with poor maintenance, very narrow pathways between rows of terraced buildings, intensive use of space without appropriate master design, and high residential density that are beyond the capacity of infrastructure services (X. Wu 2003; Zhang, Zhao, and Tian 2003). Most structures in *chengzhongcun* are built without meeting the government requirements of building safety and fire control standards. There are also social problems such as pornographic activities, gambling, and drug abuses, in addition to unpleasant living conditions. To some extent, *chengzhongcun* share some of the worst features of shanty-towns in many cities of the developing world.

Being restructuring into enclaves of rural migrants, *chengzhongcun* adds a new dimension of spatial segregation in transitional urban China. During the socialist period, the spatial organization of Chinese cities was compartmentalized by uniform and self-sufficient urban cells. Urban space was often structured around large, independent, and walled work-unit compounds (Gaubatz 1999; Huang and Clark 2002). Nowadays, this work-unit based urban space has undergone restructuring. Changes in the spatial structure of Chinese cities have been characterized by specialization of land use and spatial segregation. Housing becomes increasingly separated from work places and newly developing residential districts have expanded outward toward the urban periphery. Although a fairly small number of old urban neighborhoods have been reconstructed into central business districts and luxury residential districts, many dilapidated and overcrowded ones within the city proper (including the inner suburbs) have not yet been scheduled for demolition and redevelopment. One general result of the restructuring process of these urban spaces is the creation of segregated residential districts for different classes, spatially separating luxury housing for the rich from the basic shelter of ordinary urban residents. The emergence of *chengzhongcun*, often portrayed negatively in government reports and in the media, represents the formation of a new slum-like space within the city's built-up areas or at the edge of the city in sharp contrast to the affluent districts in terms of living and social landscapes. For those intending to enforce the proper order of urban space, *chengzhongcun* were not only out of sync with those newly developed decent districts in terms of living environment, but also worse than those decayed old neighborhoods with respect to urban governance. Nevertheless, in the context of space contestation, such new urban space represents a profound aspect of socioeconomic transformation where civil forces from the bottom reshape the formal urban social and spatial relationships formerly fostered by the state in selected locales.

Chengzhongcun as a Space of Confrontation and Contestation

The function of *chengzhongcun* as migrant settlements appears to create interest conflicts between municipal governments and the user groups and has increasingly become a matter of policy concern. Though they are thought positively by indigenous villagers and migrants, many *chengzhongcun* now face a situation of government-imposed demolition and redevelopment. *Chengzhongcun* redevelopment is an attempt by city authorities to reorganize and beautify space, to restructure the social order, and to enhance its exchange-value through land-use right transfer and urban renewal while reducing its use-value for low-income migrants. This section discusses confrontation and broad shifts of the policy approach involving *chengzhongcun*.

As a disordered, unplanned socioeconomic space, *chengzhongcun* is never recognized by the city government as a legitimate community; rather, it is largely perceived by officials as a source of danger because of its potential to develop into an oppositional social force in competition with state control. *Chengzhongcun* are officially regarded as a problem because of their association with chaotic land use, inferior housing construction, severe infrastructure deficiencies, intensified social disorder, and deterioration of city scenery. Owing to their informal and illegitimate characteristics, *chengzhongcun* development is usually associated with bad images and social dysfunctions, making mainstream urban citizens (those with formal urban *hukou*) and urban authorities uncomfortable. The dissatisfaction of the mainstream citizens has frequently generated strong political pressure on city government, who is always sensitive to the social consequences of urban disorder and the image of its jurisdiction. Urban redevelopment is therefore adopted in part for the sake of political expediency.

In addition to political justification, the motivation of city governments to rebuild *chengzhongcun* also comes from an economic consideration. The rise in land value in *chengzhongcun,* particularly those in the inner-city location, offers city governments economic incentive for *chengzhongcun* renewal. Given that urban land is an important source of city revenue and land in *chengzhongcun* has high potential to be turned into higher-value development, city governments have strong interest to commodify land there through the transfer of land-use right in the name of repairing the incredible dysfunctional community currently in place. There has been a strong signal from city governments attempting to demolish *chengzhong-cun* with urban redevelopment projects (see *Beijing Daily,* June 19, 2004; *Southern Metropolitan Daily,* October 28, 2004). Practically, city governments tend to employ various rhetorical devices and imagery to define *chengzhongcun* as an undesirable area of overcrowding and social pathology. *Chengzhongcun* are often criticized as deficient with regard to abysmal living conditions and social disorder that should not be tolerated by the socialist ideology. Financially, investments from private and joint-venture developers are regarded as the main source to fund property renewal. Unavoidably, *chengzhongcun* has become the space of confrontation and commodification.

As early as in the 1990s, the incompatible views on the role of *chengzhongcun* already caused *chengzhongcun* itself to become an object of conflicts. Notwithstanding their role of making affordable housing and survival space available for low-income migrants, *chengzhongcun* were officially regarded as slums or shantytowns with shabby buildings and unsightly urban eyesore. Journalistic reports and Chinese scholarly works also tended to perceive *chengzhongcun* as undesirable, attributing to them the root of social and environmental problems that were seen as jeopardizing urban development. City governments believed that such slums would not go away without some sort of government intervention and massive renewal projects.

The earlier government action commonly taken in many cities was simply to cleanse and deport migrants from *chengzhongcun* while keeping housing there intact. The "cleansing-deportation" campaigns, though inhumane and even brutal methods, were carried out whenever city governments perceived such actions necessary. Under the slogan of "maintaining social order and cracking down on crimes," *chengzhongcun* in many cities had gone through rounds of "cleansing," and migrants without proper documents were forcibly deported, especially in the eve of big official events. One well-known case was an armed confrontation in November 1995 between rural migrants and officials of public security in Dahongmen District, the largest migrant enclave consisting of twenty-six *chengzhongcun* and with approximately 1 million temporary population (commonly known as Zhejiang village) in Beijing (for more detailed reports of the case, see Beja and Bonnin 1995; Gu and Shen 2003; Jeong 2002; Liu and Liang 1997). The bloodshed led to a citywide forced deportation of migrants who had no proper living documents. Like other cities, however, such cleansing and deportation could not stop the urban-bound flow of migration. Soon after the deportation, migrants returned in greater numbers (Cai 2001, 316; Gu and Shen 2003, 119). Some even brought their family members, friends, and fellow villagers. The migrant settlement soon resumed and became even larger.

The perennial failure of "cleansing-deportation" campaigns vividly expressed the firm resistance to the clearance effort and illustrated the confrontation between city governments and migrant communities. The resumption and expansion of migrant settlements represented the power of the alliance among indigenous villagers, local community administrations, and migrants, demonstrating the difficulty of effectively implementing municipal policies against local interests. For city governments, a full scale of redevelopment seemed to become an only solution to the problems of physical deterioration and social pathology (*Beijing Daily,* June 19, 2004; Liao 2005; Song, Zenou, and Ding 2008).

In the early 2000s, a new policy approach was initiated to deal with *chengzhongcun*, which could be summarized as the "demolition-redevelopment" approach (Yu 2005; Zhang, Zhao, and Tian 2003). Albeit varied in operational details, policy frameworks and strategies for *chengzhongcun* redevelopment were basically identical in nature across different cities.[1] The "demolition-redevelopment" approach has been elaborated in position documents issued by municipal governments (e.g., PCGM 2002; SMG 2002; SZMG 2004). According to those documents, the *chengzhongcun* will be gradually rehabilitated through a series of initiatives, including administrative reorganization, land-use regularization, and housing upgrading. This will consist of two phases. The first phase is characterized as institutional transformation of the rural status of *chengzhongcun* into the urban status. The rural *hukou* of indigenous villagers constituted by village committees will be converted into the urban *hukou* and this population will be administrated under urban residents' committees. The significant implication of such institutional transformation is that all former collectively owned land in *chengzhongcun* will be nationalized. Indigenous villagers are no longer entitled a land-use right for housing as before. In the second phase, in compliance with municipal regulations and city planning, *chengzhongcun* will be demolished and rebuilt through real-estate development. Management of land development will be unified in terms of development applications and land transactions. Construction of housing property will be formalized with respect to building technocratic standards and on-site densities. Existing precarious housing will be replaced by decent apartments. Some of newly built apartments will be allocated to the indigenous villagers free as a form of compensation for their demolished properties. The others will be sold at market prices. Redevelopment programs will be financed in accordance with the principle of "beneficiaries pay." Developers are encouraged to invest in the renewal projects in accordance with government planning (Cheng 2003).

Under this newly proposed policy approach, *chengzhongcun* redevelopment will be carried out by both administrative and market forces, without offering redevelopment choices to indigenous villagers and replacement choices to current migrant residents. The key to the "demolition-redevelopment" approach is to change the rural status of *chengzhongcun*, which was decisive in producing the existing social and physical landscapes of *chengzhongcun*. Forcible urbanization of indigenous villagers by converting their rural *hukou* into the urban one will deprive them of their rights and capacities to develop housing for rent in the future. The land-use right in *chengzhongcun* will be first taken back by government and then be sold to developers. Although reconstruction can be facilitated through private real-estate projects, *chengzhongcun* redevelopment is under the full control of city planning. *Chengzhongcun* will be finally converted into an orderly and decent space.

Nonetheless, the initiatives under the "demolition-redevelopment" approach are not implemented smoothly and effectively. *Chengzhongcun* redevelopment is in different stages in different cities. For the time being, the institutional transformation of *chengzhongcun* is being undertaken in cities such as Guangzhou and Beijing. As a front-runner, Shenzhen went one step ahead and completed the process within the city's build-up area in 2003. All indigenous villagers were granted an urban *hukou* and village committees were reorganized as urban street committees. Although Shenzhen finished the first phase of *chengzhongcun* redevelopment and the city authorities decided to redevelop all *chengzhongcun* in three or five years, it achieved no real progress in the second phase—demolition and redevelopment. The city government had difficulties coming up with the timetable for the commencement of housing rehabilitation in its *cheng-zhongcun* whose status had already been urbanized, because of resistance from different user groups.

Resistance to the "demolition-redevelopment" approach took several forms. For indigenous villagers, *chengzhongcun* redevelopment is not an attractive proposal even with compensation. To maintain their existing chance of rent-making, which was anticipated to be lost after redevelopment, and to negotiate for more compensation, indigenous villagers tried to postpone the redevelopment on the one hand and hastily built more housing on the other. Indigenous villagers well understood that by law no redevelopment can make before appropriate compensation and replacement had been settled. Using their own calculation of the market value of their property, indigenous villagers asked for indemnification to a high level that may be unacceptable by city government and developers involved. Rounds of negotiation became unavoidable and the date of redevelopment therefore hard to be scheduled. Anticipating that they should get monetary compensation for their relinquished property according to housing space, indigenous villages conducted rush construction by either expanding their current structures or simply erecting more housing with speculation to receive more compensation. Even under surveillance of city government, new illegal dwellings were found every day (*Southern Metropolitan News*, October 28, 2004). Government could not find a manageable way to stop illegal construction in *chengzhongcun*. Snowballing of illegal construction certainly created more challenges for compensation negotiation, generated extra cost, and slowed the process of redevelopment.

Chengzhongcun redevelopment was also hindered by developers. Developers, whose involvement was essentially profit-driven, were cautious about redevelopment projects taking place in areas like *chengzhongcun* with high-density housing and population. A feasibility study conducted by Shenzhen Institute of Real Estate Appraisers showed that *chengzhongcun* redevelopment was a costly exercise (SIREA 2003). It was estimated that RMB 22.4 million (approximately US$2.8 million) of compensation was required for redevelopment of one small *chengzhongcun*, which was located within the center of Shenzhen and had 110,340 square kilometers of housing on 70,396 square kilometers of land. Total investment of RMB 105 million (approximately US$13 million) was needed for a full scale of redevelopment. Table 6.3 shows the standards of compensation for *chengzhongcun* redevelopment in Shenzhen at the 2004 price. The standard for public housing in other parts of the city was also given for reference. Certainly the compensation cost was high and was a big concern of developers. In addition to resettlement compensations to house owners and construction costs, developers had to pay for various charges and

Table 6.3   The standard of compensation for redevelopment in Shenzhen city, 2004

Housing type	Resettlement compensation (yuan/m²)	Housing decoration compensation (yuan/m²)	Moving allowance (yuan/m²)	Total (yuan/m²)
Private housing	1,028	420	12	1,512
Public housing	288	—	—	288

Source: Interviews with scholars from the Shenzhen Institute of Real Estate Appraisers, February 2005.

administrative fees, such as land transfer fee, environmental sanitation fee, and construction taxes. They also needed to provide certain public infrastructure and facilities to improve the overall amenity of *chengzhongcun*. Therefore, one *chengzhongcun* renewal project requires significant investment, depending on the actual dwelling density of the *chengzhongcun* in question and the renewal scale. For instance, one *chengzhongcun* redevelopment, which was located in the northeastern corner of Shenzhen's city center, involved a RMB 6 billion (approximately US$750 million) investment (*Yangcheng Evening News,* August 6, 2007). In Guangzhou, it was estimated that it would require more than RMB 200 billion (approximately US$25 billion) for redevelopment of 139 *chengzhongcun* (Yu 2005). Many developers perceived *chengzhongcun* projects economically unattractive (even unfeasible) and did not respond positively to the projects. To make *chengzhongcun* projects profitable, the developers usually bargained with the city government in an increase in plot ratio and floor areas, waiver of some charges, or granting of land-use rights in other places of the city. Developers' concern on financial return made redevelopment projects more complex. Negotiation between government and developers often ended up in deadlock, and the redevelopment plan has to be postponed or even suspended.

Rural migrants, who were major tenants of *chengzhongcun* but were politically and economically powerless, would be most likely to adopt a passive form of resistance toward *chengzhongcun* redevelopment—geographically shifting disordered spaces. Redevelopment was likely to have significant exclusion impact by reducing the supply of affordable housing for migrants. It inevitably meant an amelioration of housing qualities, a decrease in inexpensive housing stock, and an increase in rent at the renewal sites. Low-income migrants would not be able to afford new houses produced in absence of government subsidies. For now, there is no sign that the government intends to remove the differentiation in housing provision policy between rural and urban populations and provide affordable housing for rural migrants who are working in cities. Beyond the political imperative that the physical and social environment of *chengzhongcun* must be improved, the policy approach of "demolition and redevelopment" is much less explicit as to how the millions of migrant tenants should be relocated. The growing housing need of rural migrants is left unattended. In the absence of any policy consideration for migrants' housing needs, the renewal of *chengzhongcun* into more orderly urban spaces will no doubt be at the expense of rural migrants whose immediate homes have been destroyed. While a fairly small number of the rich migrants can afford to live in the redeveloped districts, most of the poor will be forced to face new financial burdens and to move out to search for alternative inexpensive housing. Though rural migrants may not have bargaining power to mobilize themselves openly against *chengzhongcun* redevelopment, they are most likely to reproduce slum-like settlements elsewhere in or around the city, undermining the government's effort to regularize urban space.

Intention and resistance to *chengzhongcun* (re)development as discussed earlier are an essential constituent of space contestation. It showed that *chengzhongcun*, as a distinctive urban space, can be viewed as a realm of spatial metaphors: a means of production, and an object of confrontation, and a microsite of social and spatial contestation. *Chengzhongcun* (re) development is an interesting case to illuminate our understanding of the inseparability of spatial and social relations, interconnectedness of power and space in the city, and the association of space with social stratification and marginalization.

Concluding Remarks

The underlying process of *chengzhongcun* (re)development discussed in this chapter can be referred to the range of social activities that various social groups engage in to create, present, and sustain a particular identity (agglomeration of low-rent housing and concentration of migrants) attached to specific locales. *Chengzhongcun* is a particular sociophysical space that is involved in the production and reproduction of social structures, social conflict, and relations of power and resistance under the existing institutional arrangements. Different social groups, who possess different powers to shape and transform urban space, read *chengzhongcun* in different spatial metaphors. Their interpretations were in turn used to guide their actions toward *chengzhongcun* redevelopment. Indigenous villagers interpreted *chengzhongcun* as a means of production, where they can mobilize their individual land-use rights and resources to develop a market of housing rental. Marginalized rural migrants viewed *chengzhongcun* as a survival place that provided the only means of affordable shelter available to them against the risk of homeless in a new place. By emphasizing the most extreme and pathological dimensions of life in *chengzhongcun* environment, city governments delimited *chengzhongcun* as a hotbed of disorder and criminality and labeled it as a thorn of potential danger that the city sought to destruct. In comparison, the designation of production and safe places were part of a range of actions that indigenous villagers and migrants used to deny that irregularity and crime pervaded the entire development of *chengzhongcun*, and they attempted to disavow the stigmatized identity of a criminal spot that were assigned to *chengzhongcun*. Collectively, user groups tended to view space for the advantage it might bring, especially as a means to financial and social gains.

Contestation and reordering of urban space in transitional China are in line with respective changes in the role of the state (including the central and local governments) in association with the transformation of the regime of urban accumulation from the "developmental" state, which emphasizes the use of centralized economic policies to direct national growth, to the "entrepreneurial" city, which commodifies "place" as a space of commodity (Wu, Xu, and Yeh 2007). In the prereform period, to finance state-centered industrialization, the fiscal system was highly centralized, in which almost all taxes and profits generated in the economy were collected by local governments and then remitted to the central coffer while financial expenditures at the local level were covered by the central budgetary plan (Zhao and Zhang 1999). City governments functioned as economic puppets and executors of the orders emanating from the central government, as the central state took full responsibility for initiating developments and providing public goods at the local level. With the introduction of market forces in shaping the economy and society in the transitional period, the early regime of urban accumulation has experienced a transformation alongside decentralization of the financial system. This transformation has involved the functional transition of city governments from economic puppets of the central government to financially more independent and behaviorally more entrepreneurial entities. Although greater fiscal power has been granted to the locality, some of the central state's obligations have also been transferred to city governments, resulting in the increasing importance of local revenues and obvious tension between development promotion and the need to provide social services. Every city government seeks to manage and maximize urban accumulation by emphasizing economic growth and by escaping its financial obligations whenever possible. One unavoidable implication of such transformation is that urban governance is more reactive to economic growth than it takes into consideration increasing demands of social services in the process of urbanization. Although city governments generally put greater efforts on disciplining and beautifying the city to attract capital investments from outside, they aim to shift the responsibility of providing social services (such as affordable rental housing for low-income rural migrants) to the market and individuals. The success of *chengzhongcun* in providing cheap rental housing suggests that it has been the absence of government involvement that has provided the opportunity. However, a price has to be paid for this entrepreneurial governance in terms of uncontrolled development and lack of social "formality." Policy solution toward formalizing *chengzhongcun* is the reflection that the focus of urban redevelopment is more concerned about physical quality than the role that such settlement plays in the process of urbanization.

Note

1. There are many reports on the policy of *chengzhongcun* redevelopment in different cities. For the case in Shenzhen, see Cheng 2003; for Zhuhai's case, see *People's Daily,* July 5, 2002; for the case in Xi'an, see *China Construction Daily,* November 6, 2007; for Guangzhou's case, see *Southern Weekend,* October 31, 2002; for Qingdao's case, see *Qingdao Daily,* April 8, 2006.

References

Anonymous. 2003. *Chengshi gongzuo juzhu guiding (Stipulations on working and living in cities).* Beijing: Zhongguo fazhi chubanshe.

Beijing Daily. 2004. *Beijing huanjing jianshe guihua: san nian nei xiaomie liangbai ge chengzhongcun (Beijing environmental construction planning: Demolishing 200 villages within the city by 3 years).* June 19.

Beja, J. P. and M. Bonnin. 1995. The destruction of the Zhejiang village. *China Perspectives* 2: 21–25.

Cai, F. (ed.) 2001. *Zhongguo renkou liudong fangshi yu tujing 1990–1999 (Forms and ways of population movements in China, 1990–1999).* Beijing: Shehua kexue wenxian chubanshe.

Chan, K. W. and L. Zhang. 1999. The hukou system and rural-urban migration in China: Processes and changes. *China Quarterly* 160: 18–55.

Cheng, J. L. 2003. Shenzhen tequ chengzhongcun gaizao kaifa moshi yanjiu (Research of the reconstruction models of villages inside the city in the special economic zone of Shenzhen). *Chengshi guihua huikan (Urban Planning Forum)* 3: 57–60.

Cheng, T. and M. Selden. 1994. The origins and social consequences of China's *hukou* system. *China Quarterly* 139: 644–688.

China Construction Daily. 2007. *Xian duoxiang youhui zhengce licu chengzhongcun gaizao (Xian city vigorously promoted the redevelopment of villages within the city with a number of preferential policies).* November 6.

Davis, M. 1992. Fortress Los Angeles: The militarization of public space. In *Variations on a theme park: The new American city and the end of public space,* ed. M. Sorkin, 154–180. New York: Hill and Wang.

Fan, J. and W. Taubmann. 2002. Migrant enclaves in large Chinese cities. In *The new Chinese city: Globalization and market reform,* ed. J. R. Logan, 183–197. Oxford: Blackwell.

Foucault, M. 1984. Space, knowledge, power. In *Foucault reader,* ed. P. Rabinow, 239–256. New York: Pantheon Books.

Gaubatz, P. 1999. China's urban transformation: Patterns and processes of morphological change in Beijing, Shanghai and Guangzhou. *Urban Studies,* 36: 1495–1521.

Gilbert, M. R. 1998. Race, space, and power: The survival strategies of working poor women. *Annals of Association of American Geographers* 88: 595–621.

Gotham, K. F. and K. Brumley 2002. Using space: Agency and identity in a public-housing development. *City & Community* 1: 267–289.

Gotham, K. F., J. Shefner, and K. Brumley. 2001. Abstract space, social space, and the development of public housing. *Critical Perspectives on Urban Redevelopment* 6: 313–335.

Gottdiener, M. 1994. *The social production of urban space* (2nd ed.). Austin: University of Texas Press.

Gu, C. L. and H. Y. Liu. 2002. Social polarization and segregation in Beijing. In *The new Chinese city: Globalization and market reform,* ed. J. Logan, 198–211. Oxford: Blackwell.

Gu, C. L. and J. F. Shen. 2003. Transformation of urban socio-spatial structure in socialist market economies: The case of Beijing. *Habitat International* 27: 107–122.

Huang, Y. Q. 2003. Renters' housing behaviour in transitional urban China. *Housing Studies* 18: 103–126.

Huang, Y. Q. and W. A. V. Clark. 2002. Housing tenure choice in transitional urban China: A multilevel analysis. *Urban Studies* 39: 7–32.

Hutchison R. (ed.) 2000. *Construction of urban space. Research in Urban Sociology* 5. Stamford, CT: JAI Press.

Jeong, J-Ho. 2002. Shifting central-local relations in post-reform China: Case study of a migrant community in Beijing. *Development and Society* 31: 23–51.

Lan, Y. W. 2001. Chengzhongcun: cunluo zhongjie de zuihou yihuan (Villages inside the city: The last lap of the village ending circle). *Journal of the Graduate School, The Chinese Academy of Social Science* 6: 100–105.

———. 2004. *Doushi lide cunzhuang (villages within the city).* Beijing: Shenghuo, dushu, xinzhi sanlian shudian.

Lefebvre, H. 1991. *The production of space.* Oxford: Blackwell.

Li, P. L. 2004. Jubian: cunluo de zhongjie (Profound changes: The end of villages). *Zhongguo shehui kexue (Chinese Social Science)* 1: 168–179.

Liao, M. Z. 2005. Guanyu Shenzhen chengzhongcun gaizao de duice jianyi (Suggestive measures for chengzhongcun redevelopment in Shenzhen). *Naoku kuaican (Think-tank's Reference)* 93: 1–11. Internal report of China Development Institute (Shenzhen).

Liu, X. L. and W. Liang. 1997. Zhejiangcun: Social and spatial implications of informal urbanization on the periphery of Beijing. *Cities* 14: 95–108.

Logan, J. and H. Molotch. 1987. *Urban fortunes: The political economy of place.* Berkeley: University of California Press.

Ma, L. J. C. and B. Xiang. 1998. Native place, migration and the emergence of peasant enclaves in Beijing. *China Quarterly* 155: 546–581.

Ministry of Public Security (MPS). Various years. *Collection of statistical materials on temporary population in China*. Beijing: Mass Publishing House.

Party Committee of Guangzhou Municipality (PCGM). 2002. *Guanyu chengzhongcun zhuanzhi gongzuo de ruogan yijian (Suggestions for institutional changes of villages inside the city)*. Document no.[2002]17, issued on May 24.

People's Daily. 2002. *Zhuhai chengzhongcun chaichu xinluzi (Redevelopment of villages within the city in Zhuhai found new ways)*. July 5.

Piante, C. and H. B. Zhu. 1995. A law unto itself—Beijing's Zhejiang village. *China Perspectives* 2: 12–15.

Population Census Office. 2002. *Tabulations of the 2000 census of China*. Beijing: China Statistics Publishing House.

Qingdao Daily 2006. *Qingdao chutai chengzhongcun gaizao xinbanfa (Qingdao city implemented new measures for the redevelopment of villages within the city)*. April 8, 2006.

Shenzhen Institute of Real Estate Appraisers (SIREA). 2003. *Ludancun zhongjian xiangmu shouzhi fenxi baogao (Income and cost appraisal of ludan village redevelopment project)*. Unpublished internal research report.

Shenzhen Municipal Government (SZMG). 2004. *Shenzhenshi chengzhongcun (jiucun) gaizao zanxing guiding (Provisional regulations on redevelopment of villages [old villages] inside the city in Shenzhen)*. Document no.[2004]177, issued on November 1, 2004.

Shijiazhuang Municipal Government (SMG). 2002. *Guanyu jiakuai chengzhongcun gaizao de shishi yijian (Suggestions for implementation of accelerating the redevelopment of villages inside the city)*. Document no.[2002]14, issued on February 25, 2002.

Solinger, D. 1995. China's urban transients in the transition from socialism and the collapse of the communist "urban public goods regime." *Comparative Politics* 27: 127–146.

Song, Y., Y. Zenou, and C. Ding. 2008. Let's not throw the baby out with the bath water: The role of urban villages in housing rural migrants in China. *Urban Studies* 45: 313–330.

Southern Metropolitan Daily. 2004. *Shenzhen tiaozhan chengzhongcun (Shenzhen challenged villages within the city)*. October 28, 2004.

Southern Weekend. 2002. *Chengzhongcun kao shenme yongyou weilai? (What can villages within the city depend on for their future?)* October 31.

Tang, W-S. and H. Chung. 2002. Urban-rural transition in China: Illegal land use and construction. *Asia Pacific Viewpoint* 43: 43–62.

Tian, B. X. 2003. *Zhongguo diyi zhengjian: zhongguo huji zhidu tiaocha shougao (China's number one certificate: manuscripts on investigation of China's household registration system)*. Guangzhou, China: Guangdong People's Press.

Wang, C. G. 1995. Shehui liudong yu shehui zhonggou: jingcheng zhejiangcun yanjiu *(Social mobility and restructuring—A case study of Beijing's Zhejiang village)*. Hangzhou, China: Zhejiang People's Press.

Wang, F. 2005. Organizing through division and exclusion: China's *hukou* system. Stanford: Stanford University Press.

Wang, Y. P. 2000. Housing reform and its impacts on the urban poor in China. *Housing Studies* 15: 845–864.

Wong, Daniel F. K., C. Y. Li, and H. X. Song. 2007. Rural migrant workers in urban China: Living a marginalized life. *International Journal of Social Welfare* 16: 32–40.

Wu, F. 2004. Urban poverty and marginalization under market transition: The case of Chinese cities. *International Journal of Urban and Regional Research* 28: 401–423.

Wu, F., J. Xu, and A. G. O. Yeh. 2007. *Urban development in post-reform China: State, market, and space.* London: Routledge.

Wu, W. P. 2002. Migrant housing in urban China: Choices and constraints. *Urban Affairs Review* 38: 90–119.

Wu, X. 2003. Bianyuan shequ tancha: woguo liudong renkou jujuqu de xianzhuan touxi (Investigation of marginalized communities: Perspectives on existing characteristics of floating population' clusters in China). *Chengshi guihua (City Planning Review)* 27: 40–45.

Xiang, B. 1993. Beijing youge zhejiangcun: Shehui zhuangxingzhong yige zifa chengshihua quanti de chubu yanjiu (Beijing has a Zhejiang village—a preliminary study on a spontaneous urbanization group during the social transition). *Shehuixue yu shehui diaocha (Sociology and Social Investigation).*

———. 1999. Zhejiang village in Beijing: Creating a visible non-state space through migration and marketized traditional networks. In *Internal and international migration: Chinese perspectives*, ed. F. N. Pieke and H. Mallee, 215–250. Surrey, Canada: Curzon Press.

Yangcheng Evening News (2007). *Shenzhen tou liushiyiyuan gaizao quanguo zuida chengzhongcun (Shenzhen invested 6 billion to redevelop the national largest village within the city).* August 6, 2007.

Yu, J. 2005. Beijing, Zhuhai, Guangzhou chengzhongcun gaizao mianlin de kunnan ji gaizao banfa (Facing challenges and measures for redevelopment of villages inside the city in Beijing, Zhuhai and Guangzhou). *Naoku kuaican (Think-tank's Reference)* 94: 1–11. Internal report of China Development Institute (Shenzhen).

Zhang, L. 2001. *Stranger in the city: Reconfigurations of space, power, and social networks within China's floating population.* Stanford: Stanford University Press.

Zhang, L., S. X. B. Zhao, and J. P. Tian. 2003. Self-help in housing and chengzhongcun in China's urbanization. *International Journal of Urban and Regional Research* 27: 912–937.

Zhao, S. X. B. and L. Zhang. 1999. Decentralization reform and regionalism in China: A review. *International Regional Science Review* 22: 251–281.

Zhu J. 2004. Local developmental state and order in China's urban development during transition. *International Journal of Urban and Regional Research* 28: 424–447.

Chapter Seven

A State Creation? Civil Society and Migrant Organizations

Jennifer Hsu

In the previous chapter, we saw that migrants are changing the urban space. The emergence of civil society organizations (CSOs) across China since economic liberalization of the late 1970s is a significant indication of civil society development. This chapter examines a particular segment, namely the CSOs that work with migrant workers in Beijing and Shanghai. As we have seen in Li Zhang's chapter, rural-urban migration has contributed and shaped China's economic development tremendously, more acutely in the last thirty years. The discrimination and poor treatment, including hazardous working conditions and lack of social benefits as experienced by migrant workers in China's urban areas have prompted the emergence of many organizations seeking to represent and assist this vulnerable social group. As noted in the previous chapter by Li Zhang, the presence of migrants in the cities have not resulted in substantive rights in terms of access to decent and secure housing, and they are thus continually excluded in various ways. The organizations that have surfaced, by and large have sought to partner with the government to further expand their work. When referring to the term CSOs, it is deemed to primarily encompass a wide range of civil society actors whether non-state, nonprofit, and voluntary organizations among many others; nongovernment organizations (NGOs) are included in the term. Rural labor migrants arriving into both cities have produced not only new social dynamics, but also concerns for the state. Although there are some 200 million migrants working and living in Chinese cities, the focus of this chapter is on the organizations that represent and/or support these workers.[1] The prospects for social change will unlikely come from a relatively impassive political and social group, namely that of migrant workers who are more concerned with urban employment and incomes. Their concerns of the immediate, such as on time payment of wages and a safe working place are concerns that outweigh the need for political or societal change. Consequently, it would be the experiences and organization of the CSOs that have the potential to bring about change for migrant workers; and ultimately contribute to the growth of civil society. The chapter first outlines how civil society is conceived within the Chinese context as this provides an understanding of the space in which CSOs and the state are attempting to shape. While Paul Thiers will provide a more extensive review of the literature in the next chapter, this current chapter will seek to operationalize the concept of civil society, in that it becomes a concept that is useable and measurable. The second section provides a delineation of Chinese rural-urban migration within a timeframe of the last thirty years to the present that also seeks to present the government's stance in relation to migrants and migration. Section three provides an insight into specific Beijing and Shanghai migrant CSOs, their activities and strategies. Section four analyses the relationship between migrant CSOs and the state, and the potential for such relations to affect social change. The conclusion posits the future of civil society, and ultimately, state-society relationship in China within the context of migrant CSOs. An investigation of this relationship provides an insight into the future growth and factors that shape civil society in China.

Chinese Civil Society

The demise of communism in Eastern Europe in the late 1980s prompted scholars to use the notion of civil society to understand the sociopolitical changes (see Tismaneanu 1992). In the case of China, system change is of a much more gradual nature. Nonetheless, those concerned with China have used civil society to interpret the growth of social organizations and new interactions between state and society. Although the concept of civil society derives its roots from Western/European thought, its use to comprehend China must be employed with caution, it is however, an analytical tool. To grasp the changes that is occurring within China's urban areas, civil society provides the scholar the opportunity to observe the transformation from a bottom-up perspective—that is, individuals or social groups advocating for changes. Social transformation is most commonly seen from the standpoint of the state, given that the Chinese state is still so prominent. In attempting to operationalize the concept of civil society, we may consider the UNDP's very practical definition as "the space between family, the market and the state; it consists of non-profit organizations, and special interest groups, either formal or informal, working to improve the lives of their constituents" (UNDP 2002). According to scholars such as Hampton, this space between state and society, and the discourse that surrounds it is steered by the state. Hampton's case-study on the Uyghur people in Xinjiang, reveals that their attempts to claim to their own history and identity within the region are not mentioned in the official Han dominated discourse (2005). Rather the discourse on China's ethnic minorities is spoken on the lines of solidarity emphasized by the government due to the fear that an independent identity is a threat to national security (Hampton 2005). The space, in which social groups operate and converse with other actors within it, is therefore dominated and shaped by the state. Similarly Zhou notes the interference of the state in mediating conflicts between social groups. As there is a lack of institutional mechanisms to settle disputes, the state is called upon to intercede and thus the process and the issues at stake becomes politicized (Zhou 1993). The state may then seize on the opportunity to initiate action along its agenda. Zhou observes there are opportunities afforded to individuals and groups who participate in state-initiated campaigns, as it provides the space for those groups to pursue their own agenda. For unorganized groups and individuals it mobilizes them. Zhou refers to this as institutionalized collective action where the state initiates the action (1993, 61). Social groups in China are therefore constrained by the state and its agenda, hence reinforcing the idea that the state is still so pervasive in all areas of society, including civil society. However, this should not discount any attempts to understand social change using civil society as an analytical tool.

Using civil society to understand China accentuates the social changes that have occurred since the introduction of economic reforms in 1978. It also helps the observer to comprehend how the actors within civil society are engaging with each other. Béja in his study of Chinese academics as forces of change has highlighted the interaction and partnership between the state and academics and its affect on civil society development. Academics have utilized CSOs as an indicator of change and development of civil society, whereas the government believes that academics are an important element in the development of civil society and in designing new policies. Nonetheless, academics "intervene as experts inside the system" (Béja 2006, 67). Although academics have advocated for social policy change in some areas, and also with many CSOs requesting their assistance in the hope of being represented in the eyes of the government, many have not pushed for further policy changes relating to CSOs. Many have remained silent or voiced their opposition against social organizations in their quest for an autonomous voice, as they are well aware of the government's intolerance of such actions. With such assessment of China's civil society, one that is partially being represented by academics and consequently without an independent voice, it leads to the question of whether China's civil society and CSOs can be effective in negotiating with the government for social changes.

Rural-Urban Migration

Rural-urban labor migration since China's economic reforms has taken on new meanings for state and society relationships. The intensification of migration has pressed the state to engage with CSOs. The state's engagement is attributable to the decline of its ability and resources to exert full control over the society that it governs.[2] Authors such as Mallee (2003) have viewed the development of the rural-urban migration since 1978 as an indication of the erosion of state power, because of its inability to maintain a stranglehold of the rural population as it did pre-1978. However, as seen in the previous section on Chinese civil society, the state is not automatically retreating from society due to lack of resources, it has capitalized on segments of society such as academics to maintain its authority within the social realm. The decline of rural income coupled with huge amounts of foreign direct investment on the eastern seaboard has contributed to the continuous flow of rural to urban migration, although destination cities for migrant workers now include areas closer to their villages.[3] However, Beijing and Shanghai have prevented migrant workers from entering a range of jobs, primarily those located in the white-collar sectors. Thus migrant workers are relegated to "the bitter, dirty, arduous, and low prestige work denigrated by urban residents" (Solinger 1995, 129). Nonetheless, it is without doubt that migrant workers have contributed to economic growth and wealth of China's cities. The state however has been slow to recognize the contribution of migrants to China's economic development. It is only in the last two years that the government has taken positive outlook and measures in dealing with migrants. The State Council Office issued Document No. 1 in 2003 to ensure fairer treatment for migrant workers, including greater legal protection; better social security; more attention to safety at work sites; training of migrants in terms of providing information on laws applicable to migrant workers with a reasonable fee; and provision of education to children of migrants, among other stipulations. The National Plan of Training of Rural Migrants is one of the projects to have emerged and complements the State Council Office Document. The seven year project, 2003–2010 aims to focus on vocational and skills training such as job-seeking skills. In March 2004, the Ministry of Agriculture launched the Sunshine project involving the sending areas to provide training to the labor migrants. The 2003 State Council document realigned the government's position on internal migration, a position that focuses on the positive effects of migration rather than the burdens. To further reiterate improving conditions and environment for migrant workers, the government's 2005 (and further consultation in 2006) *Notice on Further Strengthening Employment and Reemployment Efforts* Circular 36, emphasizes the rights of migrants to minimum wage, timely payment of wages, the enforcement of labor contract system among other items. With such weight given to ensuring the legal employment rights of migrants, CSOs that are seeking to work in this area are encouraged by the government as will be evident in the following sections.

The process of migration has generated institutional change and compelled the government to rethink its cooperation strategy with new social groups, including migrant CSOs. Rural-urban labor migration over the last decade has contributed to China's urbanization and within this urbanization a new set of social relations has emerged between state and society.

Consequently, labor migration has hewed new social dynamics and contributed to the changing face of China's urban areas. An assortment of CSOs has emerged over the past decade to address the social problems that have beset China's development. Whether the CSOs in Beijing or Shanghai have emerged in direct response to migrants in the city or not, the contribution of migrants and the organizations that serve and/or represent them, to the changing relationship between the state and CSOs is noteworthy for analysis.

State and Migrant CSOs Relationship

Migrant CSOs relationship with the state is not homogenized across the cities of Beijing and Shanghai. The focus on Beijing and Shanghai provides an indication of where the future of state and society relationship is heading. The proliferation of CSOs in Beijing in various sectors, including environment, HIV/AIDS among others affords an insight into the social and civil society terrain, juxtapose against the seemingly rigid state. Shanghai with its dynamic economic activity sees much more municipal government management across society and economy in terms of migrants, contrasting that of Beijing. Recent interviews conducted with migrant CSOs in Beijing and Shanghai indicates that engagement with the state varies across cities and organization type. This section provides an insight into the variety of relationships and engagement between state and migrant CSOs in Beijing and Shanghai.

Beijing

Two categories of CSOs emerge from the nine interviews conducted with Beijing's local migrant CSOs, and thus different forms of connection with the state. The first category is that of three organizations undertaking a service delivery role providing for the social needs of the migrants. Three organizations fall into this first category. The second category consists of legal and advocacy organizations representing migrant workers to the government. It is the first category of CSOs that show the most robust ties with the state or with the Beijing Municipal government. The Beijing Legal Aid Office for Migrant Workers (BLAOMW) may have the strongest ties to the government of all nine interviewed CSOs. The Beijing Justice Bureau granted BLAOMW permission to legally represent migrant workers. It has received a total of 1 million yuan (US$140,000) in financial support from the China Legal Aid Foundation and All-China Lawyers' Foundation. These foundations are part of the state apparatus. As such, it would suggest that the Legal Aid Office is directed by the state, leading to questions of autonomy. The interviewee of BLAOMW candidly describes that its responsibilities are to solve problems of migrant workers by providing legal advice and represent them but not to oppose the state (Personal communication September 26, 2006). The organization is further courted by state institutions such as the All-China Federation of Trade Unions (ACFTU) to conduct legal training workshops for migrant workers. BLAOMW's cooperation with the government implies complicity with the state's agenda to "manage" migrant workers. However, such relationship with the state has allowed BLAOMW to replicate its services in Hebei province and Ningxia Hui Autonomous Region. The governments of these regions have permitted similar organizations to be established in their provinces. This denotes that BLAOMW has the strongest ties to the state and may actually have greater success in scaling up their services or at least replicate them in other parts of China. What this organization demonstrates is its ability to work under the instruction of the state, simultaneously taking a significant step in addressing the legal rights of migrant workers and representing them in the eyes of the law, signifying a move toward incorporating migrants into the urban environment.

Xiaoxiao Niao (XXN), another organization working in the legal advocacy area for migrant workers has received approval from the Beijing Justice and Labor bureau. One of its main activities is broadcasting a half hour weekly program on the Beijing People's Broadcasting Station. The program allows migrant workers to call into the program and share their thoughts and experiences. Such program would not be permitted without the approval of Beijing's authorities due to the sensitive nature of the issue. However, in publicizing the issues that affect migrants, including delayed wages, health and safety on the worksite, the media according to the staff at XXN has been an indispensable partner. Nonetheless, the interviewed representative of XXN stressed that their work is endorsed by the government, not restricted (Personal communication October 9, 2006). Like the Legal Aid Office, XXN has managed to establish branch offices in Shenzhen and Shenyang. Despite being influenced by the state or local authorities, both organizations have managed to extend their services beyond Beijing.

Facilitators, the third organization of the first category has collaborated with both the central government and at the very local level, the *juweihui* or the local residents' group. At the local level, it is encouraged by the *juweihui* to partake in some of the activities of the neighborhood such as festivals and cultural events. Such activities according to the interviewee, occurs regularly due to the organization's desire to incorporate migrant workers into the local community (Personal communication October 12, 2006). Facilitators' 2004 conference on work safety and migrant workers attracted several key members of the central government's National Work Safety Administration. More recently, the Ministry of Labor and Social Security has solicited Facilitators input into the Ministry's training program for migrant workers. The government is willing to listen to new thoughts and suggestions relating to the well-being of migrant workers as advocated by CSOs. However, the state is currently only willing to actively listen to CSOs' suggestion within set boundaries, primarily work safety and legal rights of migrant workers. As discussed in the previous section, the government directives have focused heavily on the protection of workers' employment rights. Hence, to be a party at the table, all three organizations have framed their work and advocacy within acceptable language that is being promoted by the government.

In comparison, the six organizations that are in category two have more informal and localized relationship with the government. Tongxin Xiwang (TXXW) has received support from its local residents' group but this may in part be driven by economic reason, as suggested by the interviewee (Personal communication September 26, 2006). The office that TXXW occupies is rented from the group and the rent from the organization provides the group with an extra source of income. In addition, the group has also assisted TXXW by providing equipment for its performances organized and planned by migrant workers within the community. Other than such interactions, TXXW has no other sustained interactions with other levels of government. The situation stands as it is limited by TXXW's own inclination to serve its immediate community of migrant workers, thus restricting its impact at the very micro level. To an extent this type of approach is shared by the Migrant Women's Club, Gongyou Zhijia (GYZJ) and Worry Assistance Hotline. The Migrant Women's Club has sought to expand its range of services to its members ranging from legal counseling to English and computer classes. Through its work, it has sought to engage with both relevant government department and academics. The interviewee voiced her hope that academics could be the bridge between CSOs and the government. The focus of GYZJ came across as confident in that the confined approach of its work, at the micro and community level is sufficient. The interviewee of GYJZ while acknowledging the role of various stakeholders in the migrant issue, scorned at the idea of trying to put GYJZ's in the macro picture, primarily their relationship with the government and ultimately their impact on social change. Worry Assistance Hotline is equally localized in its approach and focus. However, the inability to attract sufficient funding has meant that it is unable to expand its current service of providing a hotline for migrant workers. The interviewee for the Hotline has nonetheless, organized informal events such as a "salon" within the Xiaojiahe migrant community where migrant workers gather regularly to discuss and chat about issues of concern. The localization of these organizations' work is in part affected by its size and access to funding. It is a shared belief that until the organization has "proven" itself and obtained some level of success in its work with migrant workers, they will unlikely be party at the table with the state to suggest changes and improvements for its constituents.

The Shining Stone Community (SSC) and Compassion for Migrant Children (CMC) while service delivery focused are more actively pursuing the government to carry out its programs. SSC is in negotiations with the *juweihui* of one particular area in Haidian district to set up similar community project as the one it has in Ningbo. The local officials from Haidian while receptive to their work in Ningbo, they have generally resisted the idea of implementation in their own community. Its activities in Ningbo of incorporating migrant workers into the community by supporting the new terms of *xinjumin* (new resident) and *laojumin* (old resident) is seen by the Haidian officials in Beijing as stepping into official and political realms, where these new terms are playing on the terms that are encoded by the government. CMC is also courting government officials to expand its work. CMC focuses primarily on migrant workers' children by working with local migrant schools. Local migrant schools across Beijing are under constant pressure from the Municipal Government because of the grey area that they operate. Many do not meet the regulations as set out by the government. Thus, the migrant schools that CMC works with are pressured by the local authorities to cease their engagement with the organization for fear of potential difficulties. It is currently an unregistered organization in China but is seeking to localize its work by registering as a Chinese CSO. Hence, its status creates this tension between CMC's partners, the local schools, and the schools' relationship with the government. CMC has directly sought to meet with local education officials to explain its activities and also negotiate future projects. Hence, the first category of organizations suggests that only certain types of CSOs are able to engage with the state in a constructive way to advance the interests of migrant workers. CSOs in Shanghai are not as polarized as those in Beijing, thus its homogeneity is an advantage for CSOs wishing to engage with the government.

Shanghai

Of the nine organizations interviewed in Shanghai, all had sustained relationships with some level of Shanghai's Municipal Government. Unlike Beijing, the CSOs in Shanghai are not exclusively dedicated to serving or focusing on migrant communities. For some CSOs, the organization's target group may include migrants or for other CSOs they may have one program exclusively for migrants. All CSOs interviewed concentrated on delivering education related services and almost all to children of migrant workers. These organizations rely heavily on volunteers to conduct the activities and programs for migrant children. Two organizations, Roots and Shoots (RS) and Hands on Shanghai (HS) are international organizations but RS has obtained local nonprofit status in Shanghai and HS is in the process of seeking local status. RS has recently ventured into the provision of services to migrant children. It has initiated a sports development program with the aim of encouraging children in migrant schools to be more active and also to develop their leadership skills. As most migrant students lack health education, RS believes the sports program would not only assist them physically but it would also teach them team building and leadership qualities. For RS its relationship with the government is perhaps one of the most amicable and trouble free of all organizations interviewed in Shanghai and Beijing. It is one of a handful of international organizations to have received nonprofit status in China and is thus highly supported and praised by the Shanghai Municipal Government (Personal communication March 1, 2007). HS differs in that it works with local organizations to develop programs and acts as a placement service for volunteers. For these two organizations, they have attracted volunteers and also sponsorship from expatriates and international companies. Relationship with the local government and its institutions for HS is based on per project, while this may not be the desired situation, its government partner found it difficult to comprehend the need to sustain a long-term program for the migrant children. The interviewee of HS suggested that the government is more enthusiastic about supporting large events such as a fund raiser rather than the day to the day running of the programs (Personal communication March 5, 2007). However, it is the long-term programs rather than the one-off fund raiser that will create the biggest impact on migrant children and thus meeting their needs.

This source of support allows both organizations to extend and expand their programs for migrant children. Other local organizations depend largely on university students and/or young professional Chinese to assist with programs.

For Reai Jiayuan (RAJY), Xishou Tongxin (XSTX), and Loving Heart Association (LHA) their programs with migrant children involve the assistance of volunteers, where they provide the students with extra tuition to help them in their studies. RAJY is conducting their program in a migrant community. They have rented two rooms from the local residents' group for their weekend programs for migrant children of the community. Despite this liaison with the residents' group, RAJY does receive complaints from the group due to the noise created by children. Thus, this type of relationship would suggest that it is more out of necessity on both sides, rather than a mutual one. Nonetheless, as RAJY is a community development organization with official registration status with the department of Civil Affairs, which enables the organization the space to conduct their work. In comparison, XSTX is a new and small CSO without the resources or capital of other organizations. Nonetheless, it is working with one migrant primary school located in Pudong, where students of four to six years receive the opportunity to attend extra-curricular activities such as art classes. According to the interviewee of XSTX, access to the school would have been difficult if it had not partnered up with the local Communist Youth League (Personal communication March 1, 2007). This cooperation has meant that the work of XSTX is fully funded by the league. The organization's relationship is suggestive of a government agency that is willing to partner with small local CSOs to assess the possibility of such a project and the likelihood of expanding such involvement.

For Loving Heart Association (LHA), migrant children are not its primary target groups. The goals of LHA are to improve the quality of education and pedagogy methods across schools in Shanghai. However, its adhoc activities in 2006 did include a partnership with a local international school to raise funds for two migrant schools, one in Minhang District and the other in Huangpu. LHA has received substantial support from Shanghai's Municipal Education Bureau and is registered as a research institution that comes under the bureau. Thus, migrant children are not specific target groups of the organization.

In terms of government relations, Lequn was on the brink of shut down in 2004 due to the lack of government support (*Shanghai Star* February 26, 2004). Although it is operating to the tunes of favorable government policies, the lack of finances from the government created great uncertainties for its operation. For those organizations operating under government auspices or established under its guidance, financial support is essential to their survival. Despite, the precarious situation for Lequn it is similar to LHA in that it does not specifically target migrant children. Nonetheless, in working in the two Putuo district schools, they have encapsulated migrant children in its program. The work of the CSO in the schools concentrates on skills and leadership development.

Project Integration (PI) a small organization established by German speaking expatriates also directs its energies to migrant children. It differs to the other organizations in that its main activity is to raise sufficient funds to support as many disadvantaged migrant school children as possible. At this point, it has enough funds to finance twenty-two school children, and it aims to provide continuous educational support for the same children. Its ability to liaise with education officials has ensured the continuation of its program. This can be in part understood within the context of power relations. PI has given the school and education departments of relevant districts to determine the students who are in need of funding.

Haikeyi and the Fudan University Student Volunteers' Association (FUSVA) are the two Shanghai organizations that do not work with migrant children. Haikeyi is in an unusual position to work with migrant workers because it is a university student association. The association's main aim is to provide free seminars and workshops to students on sexual health and HIV/AIDS. However, since its inception in 2003 it has worked with the Family Planning Association of Minhang District to assist and deliver similar seminars to migrant workers of the area. FUSVA, another university association works in collaboration with its sponsoring organization, Sunrise Library and has produced a manual for newly arrived migrant workers into the city, covering topics from transportation to health. The production of this manual was delegated to the group by Sunrise Library. It is only with the distribution of the manual, that FUSVA has had to contact local government agencies to gain their permission for distribution in areas such as train stations. Although the government agencies concerned were obliging with the group's request just before Spring Festival in February 2006, subsequent requests were denied. The organizations presented here indicate that there is perhaps greater willingness on the side of the Shanghai government to work with CSOs on the issue of migrant workers than Beijing. Nevertheless, the range of activities conducted by Shanghai's CSOs lack diversity as almost all focus is on migrant children education.

Discussion

The interviews reveal that migrant CSOs or organizations working with migrants, whether in Beijing or Shanghai, are more likely to partner with the government if they are operating within the agenda as set by the government. CSOs that are dealing with legal issues concerning the employment rights of migrant workers are particularly in favor with the government. Recent government documents have highlighted the need to protect migrant workers' rights and their health and safety within their workplace. Consequently, CSOs such as the Beijing Legal Aid Office for Migrants that seek to advocate for migrant workers within this realm have successfully established and maintained collaborations with the government. Aside from partnerships with various government departments, the Legal Aid Office has also received substantial funding from the government. The government is more responsive and willing to work with CSOs if there is a level of certainty that the organizations will not challenge the government in their wisdom or authority. This is especially noticeable in Shanghai, where all but two are involved in working with migrant school children and accordingly, local Shanghai authorities have been willing to cooperate with CSOs. Nonetheless, there are disparities in Beijing and Shanghai CSOs' relationship with the government. The three organizations in Beijing working primarily in legal presentation (BLAOMW, XXN, and Facilitators) have relatively robust ties to the central government compared to the Shanghai CSOs, where all are connected at the local level. Such ties with the central government can also be attributed to the fact that the CSOs in Beijing are within close proximity to the seat of the government. Thus, it would be more likely for these CSOs than its counterparts in Shanghai to engage with the central government on policy reform and pilot projects affecting migrant workers. With a top-down system, government policies will take some time to filter down into the local regions.

CSOs working in the service delivery realm are experiencing greater room than ever before to undertake their work due to greater government understanding of the CSO sector rather than perceive it as a threat. The threat of SARS in 2003 has strengthened the role of CSOs in society and regarded as a partner to that of the central government's efforts in delivering social services:

> In the current fight against SARS, an effective approach to avoiding a crisis of social fragility would be to allow a mature, autonomous society to support an effective government. Encouraging civic participation and consciousness, encouraging the development of social self-organization and participation; the support of such a social force in the struggle against SARS can take over some of the government's load of concerns. (*21st Century Economic Herald* May 15, 2003)

The six social services-oriented organizations in Beijing, while working in the accepted realms of service delivery, their partnership with the government is of a much more restricted or adhoc nature. This can be attributed to the government's gradual move away from social services. Consequently, there does not seem to be room for the government to do or collaborate more, precisely because the government is retreating from the provision of social welfare. Nevertheless, the six Beijing organizations in category one do have more significant ties with local levels of government. This connection is observable at the *juweihui* level as these community bodies are now assigned with the task of governing the local community, which includes the management of social welfare issues as well as matters pertaining to migrant workers living and residing in the area. Despite the tasks delegated to these bodies, many are reluctant to fulfill their responsibilities as financing of programs and events that benefit the community are often not widely available. As a result, many *juweihuis* have utilized the existence of CSOs within their area to carry out their duties but at the same time are hesitant to relinquish control to the CSOs. One Beijing academic with her own migrant CSO reiterated her difficulty in working with the *juweihui*. The academic and her organization had intentions of approaching the program for migrant workers in a more participatory way but the *juweihui* objected to such a process (Personal communication November 7, 2007). In addition, the division of responsibilities also became a problem in their cooperation with the *juweihui*. This is most demonstrable in the SARS example, where the *juweihui* objected to its own staff handing out face masks to community members, but it did not object to the organization in doing so. Although *juweihuis* may be responsible for the social welfare of its community members and have partnered with local CSOs to realize their tasks, the question of power relations deeply complicates the relationship between CSOs and local levels of authority and government.

Although the SSC and CMC are service delivery-oriented and also cooperating with local Beijing authorities, they are at the same time being proactive in terms of engaging with higher levels of the government. They have sought to follow-up with district government agencies in the hope of furthering their work and expanding their services for migrant workers. In the case of SSC, the organization has escorted local Beijing officials to their program sites in Ningbo on a study tour. It is therefore possible to consider SSC and CMC as transitioning toward more like Facilitators and BLAOMW, where government departments have actively sought their services and suggestions.

Relationship between the interviewed Shanghai's CSOs and the government is at the municipal level or lower. Although the interviewed CSOs in Shanghai are not migrant organizations per se, the majority of these organizations have sustained relationship with government agencies. This may be attributed to the fact that these CSOs focus on a general belief of promoting community development through volunteerism. Organizations such as HS essentially recruit volunteers who are then matched with suitable projects conducted by other organizations. The publication of the migrant manual by Sunrise Library was completed solely by a group of university students, dedicating their time to the various tasks associated with its production. The dedication of such students reinforces the notion of government's perspective on volunteerism and youth of China:

> The development of society is now to an extent reliant on the youth who have a different perspective than the older generation. They are more willing to be adventurous, to be avant-gardes. For example, volunteering is one way for them to realize themselves and what they can contribute to society. (Personal communication, Ministry of Civil Affairs September 21, 2006)

Although various ethical issues arise in the use of volunteers, the point that is most pertinent is that government forces see this as a positive and tangible contribution to the "harmonious society," the current socioeconomic ideology of the Chinese state. By promoting community development and the volunteer spirit, it is well in align with the state's desire for social equity and justice (see *People's Daily Online* June 27, 2005). In addition, as the majority of the Shanghai's CSOs interviewed are working in the area of migrant children's education, the Shanghai government has shown that it is willing to work with such organizations. The partnership between XSTX and the local branch of the Communist Youth League clearly indicates that the government is receptive to CSOs working in the area of migrant children's education and the utilization of volunteers as a way of harnessing the energies of society. The area of education is seen as a "safe" entry point for many organizations that are trying to enter and work with the migrant community. The fact that the central government has demonstrated its concern for migrant children's education in urban areas and extensive media coverage has almost neutralized this topic for the Shanghai government.[4] With the nine year compulsory education across China, education is deemed as a right, thus primary school aged migrant children in urban areas have started to benefit from a more favorable government stance. Accordingly, organizations in Shanghai have found a niche for their work with the migrant community.

What does all this mean for China's civil society? Whether in Beijing or Shanghai, the government has exerted in its influence when it comes to CSOs working with migrants. The state has marked areas that they are open to cooperation with CSOs. Hence, those wishing to make an impact need to work within these preset boundaries and ultimately, it is a civil society that is shaped by the government. The situation is further reinforced by CSOs actively courting government agencies. Strategies adopted by migrant CSOs show that they are willing to be flexible in their programs and focus, to work with the government, thereby ensuring that the organization has as much influence across migrant communities as possible. CSOs that have opted to maintain a low profile and work at the grassroots level, show that such strategy is optimum given the size and capacity of their organization. As in the case of TXXW and GYZJ, the immediate needs of their constituents in the migrant community are far more pressing than engaging with the government. The interviewee for TXXW clearly notes that the organization has not achieved sufficient results to promote themselves either to the government or to the media (Personal communication November 9, 2006), as many other organizations have done to gain the support of the public and the government. Nonetheless, the room for civil society and organizations within to develop is greater than before with the possibility of more CSOs emerging in the future. Perhaps for the government it is not about civil society development as such, rather it is about the management of society. To achieve this, the government is encouraging CSOs to assist migrant workers to pursue their grievances such as unpaid salaries through legal means. Through CSOs, the state is attempting to achieve a harmonious society where there is greater social equity. What this indicates is that the end goal is to utilize CSOs in the government's development and modernization drive. As a result, the near self-censoring nature of CSOs and the strength of the state will prove difficult for China's civil society to affect the government in its engagement with migrants and CSOs.

Conclusion

Recent fieldwork with migrant CSOs suggest that the work of these CSOs in Beijing and Shanghai is shaped not only by the government but also by the CSOs own desire to partner with the government. From the perspective of migrant CSOs, civil society is a space in which they can engage with the community in building a just society, although we must remember this is part of the current government ideology. Nonetheless, in terms of engaging with the community, Shanghai's CSOs prove to be ahead of Beijing, where it is not just migrants that these CSOs are trying to connect with but the greater Shanghai community, from university students to professional workers. Migrant workers will continue to influence on their urban host areas, whether CSOs will successfully address their various concerns is uncertain. In the case of Beijing, CSOs are addressing a greater range of issues than Shanghai. The relative narrow focus of Shanghai's CSOs, mostly on migrant children education, signifies that the range of issues experienced by migrant workers are neglected by the CSOs in their attempts to work with the government. This leads to the question of whether we will see diverging forms of state-society relationship emerging that is specific to its location. If we use migrant CSOs as the case-study, the case of Shanghai would suggest that those actors within society are relatively homogenous, given that almost all organizations work on migrant children's education. For Beijing, we see diversity, different CSOs working on various matters and engaged with more levels of government than Shanghai. As a result, state-society relationship in Shanghai will be relatively consistent with the government maintaining an overall control on the work of CSOs. State-society relationship in Beijing maybe much more diversified as the circumstances of migrant CSOs indicate. The range of CSOs in Beijing and the types of relationships with the government point toward a rapport that will be equally varied as various levels of government and CSOs are involved. The potential of China's migrant CSOs to represent migrant workers is visible. However, it is a question of whether the representation would be sufficient to truly reach the goal of equity and justice for the marginalized of China and indeed whether state-society relationship will change due to their existence.

Notes

1. However, as a caveat, not all organizations interviewed focus entirely on migrants or migrant communities, particularly the organizations located in Shanghai.
2. The decline in state control is in one part accredited to the state giving local and regional governments' greater power or decentralization. The other part is the redistribution of resources to areas such as the economy and military and less on social welfare.
3. As part of the rural development strategy, the Chinese government is seeking to rebuild the countryside. Migration has caused the decline of rural villages. Hence, the government is seeking to urbanize the rural with the dual aim of attracting migrants back to their homes to develop these new regions and also ease pressure on the existing urban areas. See for example "Rural development strategy boosts urbanization," *Xinhua News Agency*, January 1, 2006.
4. See for example "Educational opportunities open up for migrant population in Shanghai," *English People Daily*, January 9, 2004 and "Schooling vital for migrant children," *People's Daily Online*, June 29, 2007.

References

Béja, J-P. 2006. The changing aspects of civil society in China. *Social Research* 73: 53–74.

Editorial. 2003. *21st Century Economic Herald* (trans. by D. Kelly) May 15.

English People Daily. 2004. Educational opportunities open up for migrant population in Shanghai. January 9. Available at http://english.peopledaily.com. cn/200401/09/ eng20040109_132247.shtml (accessed November 4, 2007).

Hampton, A. F. 2005. Unlocking the hegemonic power of "The People's Democratic Dictatorship": An analysis of civil society and the state in the PRC. *China Report* 41: 255–266.

Mallee, H. 2003. Migration, hukou and resistance in reform China. In *Chinese society: Change, conflict and resistance,* ed. E. Perry and M. Selden, 83–101. London: Routledge.

People's Daily Online. 2005. Building harmonious society crucial for China's progress: Hu. June 27. Available at http://english.people.com.cn/200506/27/eng20050627_192495.html (accessed November 9, 2007).

———. 2007. Schooling vital for migrant children. June 29. Available at http://english.people.com.cn/200706/29/eng20070629_388722.html (accessed November 4, 2007).

Shanghai Star. 2004. Answering social needs. February 26. Available at http://app1.chinadaily.com.cn/star/2004/0226//fo5-1.html (accessed November 9, 2007).

Solinger, D. J. 1995. China's urban transients in the transition from socialism and the collapse of the communist urban public goods regime. *Comparative Politics* 27: 127–146.

Tismaneanu, V. 1992. *Reinventing politics: Eastern Europe after communism,* New York: Free Press.

UNDP. 2002. *Essentials UNDP practice area: Democratic governance synthesis of lessons learned,* 8. Available at http://www.undp.org/eo/documents/essentials/CivicEngagement-Final31October2002.pdf (accessed June 6, 2006).

Xinhua News Agency. Rural development strategy boosts urbanization. January 1. Available at http://www.china.org.cn/english/2006/Jan/153923.htm (accessed November 6, 2007).

Zhou, X. G. 1993. Unorganized interests and collective action in communist China. *American Sociological Review* 58: 54–57.

Chapter Eight

Stretching Away from the State: NGO Emergence and Dual Identity in a Chinese Government Institution

Paul Thiers

Decades of dramatic economic reform and struggles for political change have led to speculation and research on the emergence of civil society and pluralism in China. The establishment of autonomous nongovernmental organizations (NGOs) would mark a significant milestone in this process. However, assumptions inherent in non-Chinese concepts of NGOs and civil society do not fit easily within the Chinese state-society context. A number of scholars have argued that the study of emerging pluralism in China must not assume a zero-sum, oppositional model of state-society relations and that even the distinction between state and nonstate itself should be drawn lightly.

This study attempts to build on this scholarship by considering the fragmented state itself as one possible source of pluralism. The case of a governmental research institute that, over more than a decade, established an identity as an internationally connected NGO is used to argue that the distinction between state and nonstate organizations is not simply ambiguous. State and nonstate identity is dynamic and intentionally blurred as institutions stretch away from the state, balancing the benefits of state authority with the desire for greater autonomy. Both domestic economic reform and opening up to foreign institutions have played a significant role in shaping this process. In particular, international NGOs, as alternative sources of funding, information, and authority, provide incentives and strategies for organizations to maximize their autonomy from the state.

I begin with a review of the literature focusing on those scholars who have questioned the appropriateness of assumptions inherent in Western concepts of civil society and NGO. I then present a case study of the Nanjing Institute of Environmental Sciences (NIES), a state research institution that developed an alternative NGO identity. In analyzing this case, I propose that a state/nonstate dichotomy be rejected in favor of a continuum, with organizations attempting to move in either direction in response to specific tasks or interactions.

NGOs and the Search for Civil Society

The first decade of reform made it clear that the Post-Maoist state-society relationship would not follow patterns of North America, Western Europe, Latin America, or even late-socialist Eastern Europe. A recognizable civil society became the subject of a "search" in the Chinese studies literature (Chamberlain 1993; Gu 1993; Huang 1993). The relationship between civil organizations and the state itself proved to be particularly complex. Several authors questioned the utility of pluralist and corporatist foci on civil organizations as a threat to the state or as the objects of state control and cooptation. Instead they asked directly what both state and civil organization might be gaining from a negotiated relationship.

At a relatively early date, Susan Whiting (1991) rejected assumptions that NGO emergence will be resisted by the state, arguing instead that NGOs are sometimes encouraged as an alternative means of meeting state administrative goals. "The NGO phenomenon in China reflects an attempt on the part of the government to divest itself of some of the burdens of socio-economic development without at the same time sacrificing significant political control" (Whiting 1991, 17). Shifting instead to questions of degrees of autonomy, among "truly non-governmental," "semi-governmental," and "quasi-governmental" organization, Whiting noted that NGOs themselves may prefer to maintain some connection to state institutions and often rely on the state for funding, staff, and other resources. She expected that the further development of a market economy would create new opportunities for non-state sources of funding and labor.

Elizabeth Knup (1997) further developed the ideas of state encouragement and varying degrees of autonomy, noting the importance of government-organized nongovernmental organizations (GONGOs). GONGOs often share the same leadership, staff, offices, funding, and housing as the state institutions with which they are associated. But they perform functions for which a state identity is problematic, including interaction with foreign NGOs looking for nongovernmental partners in China. Although GONGOs represent the lowest degree of autonomy from the state, Knup adds that "this closeness, while limiting, also allows these groups to operate effectively within the current Chinese context" (1997, 9). Clearly, NGOs have more complex relational goals than a simple maximization of autonomy from the Chinese state.

Fengshi Wu (2002) finds evidence that some GONGOs, ostensibly state controlled organizations, are developing autonomy, not only in terms of funding and other resources, but also as advocates for alternative policies and representatives of non-state constituencies. However, increased autonomy does not automatically constitute a severing of the state relationship. Wu argues that GONGOs have become a bridge between government agencies and NGOs, including international NGOs. Wu expands and disaggregates the types of organizations described as GONGOs, including both those formally registered as social organizations with governmental affiliation, and the more clearly state-identified public mission institutions (*shiye danwei*[1]) devoted to government sponsored research and public education, such as the All-China Women's Federation discussed in the Currier chapter. She also notes the creation of secondary GONGOs by which a state affiliated GONGO can create a subunit with even greater institutional autonomy from the state. Wu finds that the ability of these various organizations to increase actual autonomy depends most significantly on two factors, internal potential to build administrative capacity and connections to the international community.

It is significant that Wu did not find that the actions of the state itself were directly responsible for increased or decreased GONGO autonomy. The term *government organized,* NGO is somewhat misleading, not because it depicts organizations as simultaneously governmental and nongovernmental. (As the case in the following text illustrates, this dual identity may be quite real and intentional.) The most problematic aspect of the term is the assumption that GONGOs are always organized by the government and therefore continue to lack their own institutional agency. Although a date of formal establishment by a state organization is frequently referred to, some GONGOs, including some described by Wu and the one described in this chapter, emerged and develop through their own internal agency and through the influence of those outside of the state, including international actors. Wu's concession, that GONGOs are of course "creations of the state" (2002, 56) may be technically true, but misleading in the light of her own empirical evidence.

Without specifically referring to GONGOs, Tony Saich (2000) takes the complex agency of social organizations one step further, arguing that the relationship with the state is negotiated and therefore subject to reconfiguration and specialization. Again, a zero-sum conception of the state-society relationship is rejected in favor of a focus on the benefits social organizations gain from state association. These include not only material benefits such as funding, staff, and housing, but also levels of legitimacy gained through state connectedness. Organizations pursue a level of autonomy that is "strategically optimal for them" (Saich 2000, 139).

Like Whiting, Saich predicts that organizations will increase their autonomy as the economic reforms make non-state sources of funding and other resources available. He also notes that the vertical relationship between social organizations and the central government may be less important than the horizontal relationship with the local government where the contours of state connectivity can be even more complex.

The ambiguous identity of GONGOs, and the pursuit of a "strategically optimal" level of autonomy through negotiations with various levels of the state, points toward the utility of a *fragmented authoritarian* model for analyzing the state/NGO relationship. This established model of Chinese bureaucracy focuses on the fragmentation of state power among bureaucratic elements in vertical and horizontal relationships with each other (Lieberthal and Oksenberg 1988). State policy emerges through a process of struggle, negotiation, and appeal to authoritative elites by subunits of ministries and local governments. To the extent that these state fragments articulate differing interests in opposition to each other, the fragmented state itself may play a direct role in the development of pluralism. Xin Gu (1998) explicitly applied the fragmented authoritarian model to the civil society debate using the term "plural institutionalism" to argue that a fragmented state structure creates public space for intellectual debates and new organizational forms in reform era China as alluded too by Hubbert's chapter.

The mechanisms by which state fragmentation might facilitate pluralism have been understudied and undertheorized. Two hypotheses could serve as the basis for additional study. First, social organizations that originate without state involvement may *plug-in* to like minded state fragments as a means of gaining resources and legitimacy from the state. Second, state fragments may *spin-off* from the state to cultivate a non-state identity. While both possibilities are worthy of attention, this chapter focuses on the latter, considering the emergence of nongovernmental identities from within the fragmented state.

Before presenting the case study, it is useful to consider one other source of literature on ambiguity in state and non-state identity, studies of business associations in contemporary China. While business associations are not typical NGOs, they are ostensibly non-state organizations representing a segment of society in relationship with the state. Therefore, their degree of autonomy and state versus non-state identity can shed light on the question of NGOs and the emergence of pluralism.

Christopher Nevitt (1996) found that the assumed confrontational relationship inherent in the pluralist concept of civil society did not accurately describe private business associations in Tianjin. Instead, a state institutional approach reveals that even these private associations remain closely integrated with state institutions, including a prevalence of current and former state bureaucrats in association leadership. From this perspective, the development of private business associations has less to do with state weakness than it does with increased opportunities for entrepreneurial state officials to pursue business activities. Nevitt stresses that local bureaucrats responding to new institutional incentives may develop state and societal strategies simultaneously.

> This is not to say that officials are abandoning their careers to pursue private business; private enterprise remains a politically risky venture. Rather, economic reform has caused careers within the party-state to become bifurcated, offering the ambitious local official the opportunity to become a "big fish in a small pond" rather than simply to follow the traditional "ladder of advancement" up the Party-state hierarchy. (Nevitt 1996, 38)

From an overtly corporatist perspective, Margaret Pearson (1994) comes to a similar conclusion, that private business associations maintain a "Janus-faced" dual identity, serving both the state, from which they emerge, and the sector of society they represent. Focusing on associations representing foreign invested enterprises, where she expects autonomy to be most pronounced, Pearson finds that state ties persist even as associations advocate alterative policies on behalf of the foreign business community. Thus, the China Association for Enterprises with Foreign Investment receives from the state, not only staff, but also monopoly rights to represent foreign business. At the same time, the association "appears to enjoy significant autonomy in its realm of expertise" (Pearson 1994, 43). Pearson sees considerable stability in this duality that clearly benefits the association. Significantly, the only scenario she sees leading to greater autonomy would come from its "base of authority in foreign companies, and hence outside of the state" (Pearson 1994, 45).

Jonathan Unger's (1996) study of semi-state business associations provides further insights into how associations continue to use state identity as a source of resources and authority. Unger shows that the Self-Employed Laborers Association, which represents market vendors, remains firmly tied to the Bureau of industry and Commerce through interlocking leadership, staff, and office space. The leader of a district branch of this nongovernmental association even patrols the market in his governmental uniform. The association uses state authority to advance its interests, rewarding cooperative vendors with reductions in taxes or stall fees, while using the threat of taking away licenses or stall space to control vendor behavior. The association serves as a bridge between the purely governmental Bureau of Industry and Commerce and "non-state" entrepreneurial behavior by spinning off for-profit organizations providing wholesale marketing and insurance to vendors. "As a government organ, the Bureau is not permitted to establish its own enterprise; but the district Association, as a so-called 'non-governmental organization' can. Any profits that it can generate through this business activity can go towards supplementing the salaries and perquisites of Association/Bureau employees" (Unger 1996, 805).

The business association literature shows that there are advantages to maintaining state connectivity even as NGOs pursue autonomy. Semi-state institutions perform a complex balancing act between the desire to both maximize autonomy and maintain the benefits of association with the state. To return to Tony Saich's phrase, the challenge for NGOs is to pursue a "strategically optimal" level of autonomy. As the following case shows, this is not simply a matter of negotiating a static relationship, but an ongoing process of stretching away from and back toward the state depending on specific needs and opportunities.

Case Study: The Nanjing Institute of Environmental Sciences

Similar to many small *shiye danwei* of the early Deng era, The Nanjing Institute of Environmental Sciences (NIES)[2] was unambiguously established, funded, and controlled by the state. But that control was tempered by the urgency of the state's modernization and open door programs and by the fragmentation of authority within the bureaucracy. As a research institution without direct responsibility to educate students, NIES enjoyed some degree of academic freedom. As a *shiye danwei*, NIES could interact with the international nongovernmental community with somewhat greater flexibility than could a formal ministerial bureau. As an attempt by one state agency to create a policy outpost in the established turf of another, NIES had some institutional incentive to put forth alternative policy arguments within the state system. All three of these factors creating opportunities for autonomy were accentuated by the institute's location away from Beijing. However, NIES did not pursue these opportunities in an intentional rush for autonomy. Rather, the non-state elements of NIES identity grew logically in response to the sequence of events and shifting institutional realities of the next twenty-five years.

State Origins and International Support

NIES was founded in 1978 as a research institute of the State Environmental Protection Agency (SEPA).[3] While the Ministry of Agriculture (MOA) fought to maintain its hegemony over questions of agricultural development, the emergence of environmental problems in agriculture allowed NIES to carve out a small research niche over the course of the 1980s.

In 1983, NIES formally established a Rural Ecosystems Division, the first SEPA affiliated unit to address questions of pollution and sustainability in agriculture. In the following ten years, this division became an important center (the only one outside of MOA control) in the development of the Chinese Ecological Agriculture Movement (CEA). Under the leadership of Professor Li Zhengfang, the Rural Ecosystems Division became known nationally and internationally for the systems oriented on-farm research that characterized CEA.

In terms of agricultural development policy, Li Zhengfang and NIES represented the radical wing of the CEA movement, advocating that "China's agricultural development can't go the same way as the western developed countries have done, the so-called petro-agriculture with high input, high investment, high consumption and high output" (Li 1993). This position, at odds with the agricultural development mainstream within MOA, brought Li to the attention of international organizations interested in fostering sustainable agriculture in China. In the mid-1980s, Professor Li was invited to several international meetings that exposed him to the increasingly social and political (as opposed to purely biological) orientation of sustainable agriculture research in the developing world. By the early 1990s, the Rural Ecosystems Division of NIES was contracted by the United Nations Environmental Program to provide training sessions on sustainable agriculture for participants from across China and other parts of Asia.

In 1986, the Rockefeller Brothers Fund (RBF) began to support NIES' Rural Ecosystems Division financially in an effort to promote an integrated approach to sustainable agricultural development. Over the next ten years, RBF gave NIES three grants totaling US$240,000, more money than the Rural Ecosystems Division received from the Chinese government in the same period.[4] This money was important because it allowed the division to survive and expand at a time when financial support from the central government was being cut. In the late 1980s and early 1990s, the central government began pushing NIES (and many other research institutions) to find alternative sources for more and more of its budget. The government reportedly cut the national contribution to the NIES research budget from US$50,000 in 1992 to US$17,500 in 1993. Without RBF support, NIES, and particularly the Rural Ecosystems Division, would not have been able to continue its level of research during this period. This money, and the status associated with international support, was also important in surviving the turf battle with the MOA.

RBF money and contacts provided NIES staff with access to alternative ideas at odds with the orthodox view of agricultural development in China. In 1987, RBF arranged and sponsored a U.S. tour for Li Zhengfang and other NIES staff that included visits to important centers for agro-ecology and organic agriculture such as the Rodale Institute in Pennsylvania and the Agro-ecology Program at the University of California, Santa Cruz. Later that year, representatives from Rodale and from Santa Cruz followed up by conducting agro-ecology training workshops in Nanjing. NIES interest in organic agriculture, including organic certification appears to have originated through these contacts. In the following years, Li and others from NIES spent several months in Santa Cruz collaborating on a research project to compare the ecological and economic implications of organic farming in Mainland China, Taiwan, and California. During these visits to Santa Cruz, NIES staff were exposed to the heart of the organic farming movement. In 1989, NIES joined the International Federation of Organic Agriculture Movements (IFOAM), an international association of NGOs involved in organic production, certification, and marketing. IFOAM functions as an institutional voice of the organic movement and as a regulatory body for the international organic industry by producing basic standards and accrediting nongovernmental certification organizations. In 1993, RBF sponsored an important trip to Germany and the Netherlands where Li and others met with IFOAM officials and visited organic farms, processors, retail stores, and certification organizations. Thus, within a span of only seven years, NIES became closely familiar with an organic movement and industry that had been developing in the United States and Europe for several decades.

In 1994, the entire Rural Ecosystems Division of NIES was converted into the Organic Food Development Center (OFDC) with the expressed purpose of becoming an organic certification organization for China.[5] This apparently abrupt shift from an ecosystems-oriented research institute to a regulatory body for Chinese organic food production was actually a gradual response to domestic and international pressures and opportunities. As mentioned, SEPA contributions to NIES budgets were falling during the late 1980s and early 1990s. Although RBF grants made up for these declining budgets, RBF staff made it clear to NIES during the second funding cycle (1989–1993) that the upcoming third grant would be the last and would be specifically contingent on NIES proposing a long-term strategy for its own self-sufficiency. The first indication of what that strategy might be came in 1990 when a Dutch tea trading company asked NIES to assist a European organic certification organization in inspecting and certifying naturally organic[6] tea production areas in Anhui and Zhejiang Province. By facilitating this and other inspections in 1991 and 1992, NIES saw that foreign trading companies would pay for inspection and certification services. This potential source of income was reinforced during Li's 1993 trip to the Netherlands and Germany, which specifically included visits to certification organizations. By late 1993, NIES had made a clear decision to pursue fee for service organic inspection and certification as a long-term funding strategy for its Rural Ecosystems Division.

It is important to note that the decision to develop OFDC as a certification organization was initiated by NIES in Nanjing, not by SEPA leaders in Beijing.[7] As a state agency, NIES had to justify this decision to SEPA and receive SEPA's formal approval. In particular, NIES needed central government permission to develop standards that would be backed by national authority. SEPA consented to NIES' proposal and officially justified the establishment of OFDC on the grounds of national policy goals (Zhuang 1995). Yet this justification and formal endorsement came only after NIES had cleared the establishment of OFDC with its most important financial backer, the RBF.

Developing an International NGO Identity

NIES' shift from sustainable agriculture field research to organic certification took place in negotiation with a number of international actors. RBF did not immediately consent to the plan, preferring that NIES take on an identity more consistent with a developing world, developmental NGO. In 1991, Li Zhengfang repeatedly requested permission to use RBF funds to pay for a study tour of Germany and the Netherlands with the goal of establishing relations with the international organic community. The RBF officer in charge of the grant responded that any funds not used for domestic research should go toward cooperation with "regional" institutions such as the International Institute for Rural Reconstruction in the Philippines.

What was actually in debate here was the future identity of NIES, and of China, in the international sustainable agriculture community. By pushing NIES to confine its activities to regional cooperation in Southeast Asia, RBF was maintaining an image of Chinese sustainable agriculture as part of the "sustainable agriculture and rural development" paradigm prevalent among poor countries of the south.[8] By pursuing organic agriculture certification, Li Zhengfang was taking NIES toward that segment of the sustainable agriculture movement most clearly associated with the rich nations of North America and Western Europe. Thus, in addition to the potential financial benefits, NIES' transition from agro-ecology research to fee for service organic certification can be seen as an attempt to resolve China's ambiguous position in the north/south dichotomy in favor of the more attractive identity.

This debate was resolved in 1993 when a new RBF program officer took responsibility for overseeing the NIES grant. The new officer was an advocate of market based solutions to environmental problems and was also focused on the fact that the coming grant cycle would be the last RBF would offer to NIES. He endorsed the OFDC proposal as a way of simultaneously developing Chinese sustainable agriculture and of achieving financial self-sufficiency for NIES. He did encourage NIES to focus OFDC on the domestic and regional markets, a strategy to which OFDC paid lip service while actually increasing their cooperation with Europe and North America.

To solidify its international identity, NIES formed an alliance with another international NGO, this time not seeking funding but legitimacy and authority. The Organic Crop Improvement Association (OCIA) is one of the dominant nongovernmental organic certification organizations in North America and is also active in Central and South America and in Asia. OCIA certifies both through a central office in the United States and through chapter organizations, a flexible and relatively decentralized structure that allowed it to grow from four chapters certifying just more than 100 farms in 1986 to 79 chapters in 28 countries certifying more than 35,000 "grower members" on 1 million hectares 10 years later. NIES staff met OCIA President Tom Harding in 1993 when they toured Germany and the Netherlands where Harding was also serving as an official with IFOAM. In 1994, Harding visited NIES and trained two individuals to be OCIA inspectors, one who was officially on the OFDC staff and one who was from another division of NIES. In 1995, OFDC, while maintaining its status as a unit of SEPA, formally became the Chinese national chapter of OCIA. OFDC was now simultaneously a subunit of a Chinese state ministry and a chapter of an international NGO, accountable to the bylaws and policy decisions of that NGO.

The new identity as the Chinese branch of OCIA gave NIES a shortcut to international legitimacy and authority. Giving Chinese organic producers access to internationally recognized certification through a Chinese institution was a major boost to organic agriculture in the country.[9] But joining the international community carried its own complexities and risks. In 1996, OCIA itself suffered a crisis of legitimacy as a conflict of interest scandal led to the resignation of OCIA leader (and NIES mentor) Tom Harding. In 1997, OCIA lost its accreditation under the IFOAM. While the OCIA label could still offer Chinese producers legitimacy among some American buyers, loosing IFOAM accreditation closed access to the important European market. This crisis also coincided with the end of the final grant from the RBF. Clearly, NIES needed some new international patrons.

To regain legitimacy among international buyers (especially Europeans), NIES began actively pursuing direct IFOAM accreditation for its own OFDC certification label. OFDC's new director Xiao Xingji obtained a seat on the influential IFOAM Standards Board. Certification procedures and institutional arrangements, which had been modeled on OCIA, were modified to meet IFOAM and European expectations. In December 2002, after many years of effort, OFDC received formal IFOAM accreditation, an important level of acceptance into the international organic movement.

NIES' efforts to find a replacement for RBF funding reinforced the transition away from the U.S. connections and toward IFOAM and Europe.[10] A German international development worker in China helped NIES write a successful grant proposal to the German development agency GTZ. The multiyear grant was not as lucrative as the relationship with RBF had been, but it did provide staff and equipment (including computers and cars) to help OFDC complete its transition away from international donor funds to a sustainable fee-for-service, NGO model. The GTZ grant also provided technical assistance for institutional capacity building with the specific goal of obtaining IFOAM accreditation, including bringing German experts to China to educate OFDC staff into global norms and requirements. OFDC officials cited GTZ help as essential in the accreditation effort.

One IFOAM requirement posed a specific difficulty for OFDC and NIES. To be accredited, OFDC had to be established as a separate legal entity, an identity hard to reconcile with OFDC's state origins and continued connection to SEPA. In 2002, OFDC registered with the local government as an independent certifier, a spin-off company whose stock was owned by NIES, a state institution. This level of independence satisfied IFOAM while allowing OFDC to maintain elements of its state identity. Domestically OFDC is now a for-profit company owned by a state research institution. Internationally, it is an NGO accredited by IFOAM. While this dichotomy may seem untenable from a western prospective, it is actually in OFDC's interest to maintain it as long as possible.

Maintaining State Identity

NIES and OFDC's continued maintenance and use of state authority illustrates that state and nongovernmental identity is not an either/or proposition in China. Even as NIES was pursuing international sources of funds and legitimacy, its links to the state were essential and not to be given up lightly. The IFOAM requirement for separate legal personhood caused NIES/OFDC staff the greatest concern. As the OFDC director put it "we want to wear the IFOAM hat but we can't give up our SEPA hat." OFDC's state identity is an essential source of material resources, authority, and protection within the domestic political and economic environment.

Regardless of the portion of operating capital coming from foreign donors or certification fees between 1994 and 2004, state housing and other benefits have always been important. As OFDC has had to expand its staff beyond NIES capacity (paying their salaries with OFDC's own fee for service revenues), finding decent housing for new workers has been a limiting factor. OFDC cannot afford to find housing for the longtime staff who still occupy apartments provided through the NIES work unit.

But material resource dependency is only the most obvious reason why the link to the state is maintained. More important has been NIES and OFDC's use of state structure and state authority to pursue developmental and political goals. From the Rural Ecosystems Division's first establishment of organic agriculture research sites, to the recruitment and inspection of new organic farming clients for OFDC, NIES has relied extensively on its connection through SEPA to provincial and county level Environmental Protection Bureaus or other SEPA institutions. Some of the land used for organic production is also connected to the SEPA system through state designated Natural Protection Areas. Other lands are converted to organic production under the direction of local government officials for whom OFDC's state identity is an important symbol of legitimacy. The connection to SEPA, which appears prominently on OFDC's certification label, is also an important tool for gaining consumer trust, especially in the domestic market. Although a nongovernmental certification label is accepted (and even preferred) among many North American and European consumers, a state affiliated seal of approval is seen by OFDC staff as essential for domestic marketing. In written and verbal discourse with domestic producers, consumers and state organs at any level, OFDC always presents itself as a state institution.

OFDC used a combination of its international NGO and domestic state identities to triumph over its more powerful institutional rival. In 1990, the MOA established a "Green Food" program to assure domestic and foreign consumers that food bearing the Green Food label had been tested and found not to contain excessive pesticide residues. As MOA became aware of the lucrative premium organic certified food received on the international market, they made an extensive effort to convince foreign buyers that the Green Food label was equivalent to organic. Like NIES, MOA spun-off a "Green Food Development Center" that joined IFOAM (though it was never accredited) and used MOA's extensive network of county agricultural bureaus and state farm offices to convert agricultural bases to Green Food certified production. However, Green Food did not establish an autonomous NGO identity or conform its definition of organic to accepted international standards.[11] At a 1995 IFOAM meeting in Seoul, South Korea, OFDC officials publicly challenged Green Food's claims to organic status, a charge OFDC has continued to press in the international NGO community. This undermined Green Food's international legitimacy making it impossible for them to gain access to most foreign markets. MOA officials reportedly appealed to the central government to shut down OFDC. Nonetheless, SEPA, as a separate ministerial system, was able to protect OFDC from MOA attacks. Without its international connections, OFDC could not have credibly challenged Green Food's authenticity. But if OFDC had only been a non-state entity within the domestic political environment, it would not have survived the MOA backlash. Maintaining both identities has been a key element of OFDC success.[12]

Policy Advocacy and Public Mobilization

OFDC's success at establishing connections to the global organic community in combination with its continued connection through NIES to the state has allowed it to exert influence on national policy on organic agriculture. Beginning in 2002, OFDC and NIES staff drafted national organic standards for the China National Certification and Accreditation Supervision Committee, a national level body tasked with regulating and accrediting the growing number of domestic certifiers of green products. In this way, NIES and OFDC have played a role in bridging two worlds; the NGO dominated global organic community and the state-centered domestic regulatory environment. In doing so, they help to ensure that the organic farming movement in China will be accepted and supported by both national elites and the global industry.

NIES has continued to establish ties with various international donors and NGOs to support specific research and development projects throughout China. It has also ventured into direct policy advocacy at the national level, again with support from global NGOs. The most important example is its work with Greenpeace to open up public debate on biotechnology and the regulation of genetically modified organisms (GMOs). Greenpeace began its relationship with NIES in 2001 by supporting organic and ecological agriculture research through OFDC. The relationship quickly expanded to include cooperation on GMO policy. Greenpeace Hong Kong (which operates an office in Beijing) and NIES jointly publish a monthly *International Biosafety Newsletter* consisting mainly of GMO critical news from around the world collected, translated, and edited by Greenpeace. The two organizations also copublished an important report critical of the environmental impacts of GMO cotton, the only GMO crop widely adopted in China (Xue 2002). The report received considerable media attention and sparked a high-profile debate with pro-biotech scientists who had dominated government policy discussions until that point.

The significance of NIES/Greenpeace cooperation is multifold. The MOA and Ministry of Science and Technology have claimed dominion over the GMO issue, maintaining a focus on research, development, and questions of commercialization and competition. SEPA's formal role has been limited to duties outlined in the Cartagena Protocol on Biosafety. SEPA/Greenpeace cooperation on biosafety publicity campaigns has put the biosafety of GMOs on the public agenda, thus opening a door for SEPA involvement in the domestic policy debate (Newell 2003). At the same time, NIES, as a state institution, provides political cover for Greenpeace whose standing in domestic policy discussions, and very existence in Beijing, is tenuous. By working together, both the global NGO and the state institute strengthen their position and create greater pluralism in a significant area of environmental policy.

Analysis

NIES and OFDC's gradual adoption of an international NGO identity was not only opportunistic, but also purposeful and strategic. A sequence of international NGOs served as an alternative source of resources, helping NIES develop an autonomous institutional profile. RBF and later GTZ provided direct financial and technical assistance. Just as importantly, OCIA and eventually IFOAM were sources of legitimacy in the international community. IFOAM accreditation in particular increased the international attractiveness of OFDC's fee for service organic certification activities, advancing the organizations financial stability. While the implications of the new relationship with Greenpeace are still playing out, Greenpeace is, at a minimum, a source of alternative information about the global biotechnology debate. Cooperative activities such as the copublication of the *Biosafety Newsletter* and anti-GMO reports indicate that Greenpeace is also introducing its state partner to public education and mobilization tactics common in more liberal political environments.

The impact of this case on Chinese environmental politics and policy is also an unfolding story. The existence of an internationally recognized organic certification organization lays the foundation for organic agriculture to be part of China's search for sustainable agricultural development in the context of economic reforms. Such an outcome would not have been possible if organic certification had been left to the MOA through its Green Food program. OFDC's survival and triumph in the face of MOA pressure is a significant political event, not only in the promotion of globally integrated organic agriculture, but also in the broader turf battle between the production-oriented MOA and the regulatory SEPA. Representation in the state council level China National Certification and Accreditation

Supervision Committee, and the establishment of biosafety as an issue in the domestic biotechnology debate are further examples of NIES' continued potential to influence both bureaucratic and public politics.

It is important to recognize, however, that the transition to a non-state identity is partial and dynamic. NIES remains a formal state institution and even OFDC has protected its capacity to project an image of state authority when it serves specific purposes. Clearly state and non-state identity is not a zero-sum game. Susan Whiting's degrees of autonomy approach to NGO identity is useful, provided the designations are not seen as static or central government imposed. Tony Saich's analysis of "strategically optimal" levels of autonomy correctly puts the focus on institutional agency. The relationship between state and social organization is not only blurred, it is flexible and manipulated.

Both Whiting and Saich predict that economic reforms, by making available non-state sources of funding, will allow organizations to pursue greater levels of autonomy from the state. The NIES case bears this out as fee for service revenue has allowed OFDC to hire new staff and pursue its own developmental goals. Yet, it is important to recognize that money is not the only benefit an institution may gain from state affiliation. In the NIES/OFDC case, the authority to certify products is also essential. Although OCIA affiliation and IFOAM accreditation provided alternative sources of authority in the international arena, state authority is still important domestically. At various times, and in various contexts NIES and OFDC reassert their state connection to claim the authority of state actors.

The search for emerging civil society in China must recognize that there are incentives for organizations to move away from and back toward the state. Dependency on the state for resources such as housing may well decline as the market rationalizes. Nevertheless, state authority will continue to be a valuable asset. Rather than putting organizations into formal and static categories (state, NGO, GONGO, etc.) it might be more analytically useful to place organizations temporarily on a continuum with full autonomy at one end and state authority at the other. Rational organizations will seek both the freedom of non-state autonomy and the safety and power of state authority, moving back and forth along this continuum as constraints and opportunities arise.

The decision by NIES to spin-off OFDC as a quasi-independent company exemplifies this effort to stretch toward autonomy while maintaining state authority. To twist a Chinese phrase, this process might be described as stepping far into the non-state sea while keeping one foot on the firm ground of state identity.[13] Such a dynamic has important implications for the development of political pluralism in China. NGOs can be a source of pluralism even as they maintain some affiliation to a seemingly anti-pluralist state. Institutions may simultaneously pursue state and non-state channels to advocate alternative policies. Overtly public political activities may be opportunistic and temporary, followed by a reemphasis of state connectedness.

The role of global NGOs in facilitating and shaping NIES and OFDC's emergence from the state parallels the role of global capital in China's economic reform. International corporations were an important source of capital, technology, managerial capacity, market connectivity, and ideas for business ventures early in the reform era. Their Chinese joint venture partners were, in one form or another, state institutions that subsequently spun-off for-profit corporations with varying degrees of autonomy from the state. In this context, global NGOs and Chinese state fragments might be seen as joint ventures creating a foundation for social and political reform.

Conclusion

In this chapter, I have argued that the fragmented authoritarian state itself may be a source of pluralism in China. The case presented here illustrates how a state institution can take on an NGO identity as a matter of choice and opportunism. It also shows that full autonomy from the state may not be the sole institutional goal. The pursuit of autonomy may be balanced with a strategic maintenance of state designated authority. A bifurcated conception of the state/civil society is less useful than a dynamic continuum approach.

International NGOs can facilitate this pluralism to the extent that they understand the significance of state fragmentation. An insistence that Chinese partners come from a clearly defined civil society recognizable to Western NGOs, may cause those NGOs to overlook appropriate partners. A willingness to cooperate with state and semi-state institutions may be more productive in the near term. By providing such state institutions with alternative sources of resources, information, and legitimacy, the international community may do more to advance political reform than it can by concentrating on a western civil society model.

Further systematic research into this phenomenon might start from two parallels to China's economic reform experience: (1) the spin-off corporation and (2) the joint venture. Spin-offs enabled state entrepreneurs to begin the transition to private sector companies without sacrificing the security and market advantages of state identification. Joint ventures allowed Chinese industry to make use of foreign capital and technology while maintaining some state control. As the economic reform process matured and the state gained confidence, spin-offs and joint ventures were eclipsed by a more autonomous private sector (although state entrepreneurial involvement continues to be a significant factor in officially private enterprises as we will see in the following chapters). A working hypothesis for further study might be that a similar process of semi-state pluralism is underway marking the early stages of meaningful political reform. As with the economic reform process, one would anticipate periodic accelerations and retrenchments as the central government is encouraged or alarmed by the course of events. As with the mixed economy, we should expect a *mixed politics* to be characterized by new organizational forms and relationships that contradict traditional state-society assumptions.

Of course the parallels with economic reform are limited. Political pluralism directly threatens one-party authoritarianism, even if this version of pluralism is linked to state institutions. The role of international NGOs is also more complex than that of foreign capital. Future theoretical and empirical study is needed to determine whether pluralism emerging from state fragmentation is a dead end or a transition to something new.

Notes

1. Wu translates *shiye danwei* simply as "public enterprises," a term that I believe does not adequately illustrate the public interest mission of these research institutions and centers. Although there has been increasing pressure on these institutions to find creative ways to cover their own expenses, the term *shiye danwei* still implies a level of public investment in the generation of public goods rather than an entrepreneurial generation of profit.

2. The following case study was compiled based on field data collected from 1997 to 2004, including interviews with SEPA, NIES, and OFDC staff, with farmers, local government officials, and business people, and with staff members from international foundations and NGOs. Published and unpublished documents at NIES and at the Rockefeller Brothers Fund were reviewed.

3. Before government restructuring in 1998, SEPA was officially the National Environmental Protection Agency. To avoid confusion, I use the acronym SEPA throughout.

4. Budget comparisons are problematic because the substantial contributions made by the government in the form of housing subsidies and other benefits are impossible to calculate meaningfully. NIES staff estimated that RBF grants constituted 75 percent of the Rural Ecosystems Division's budget during this period.

5. The Rural Ecosystem Division continued to exist on paper but all of its staff, offices, laboratories, and research sites, even its business cards, were converted to OFDC.

6. Naturally organic refers to lands that are thought to have been continuously farmed without chemical inputs. Some certification organizations will certify such lands without requiring conversion or transition

periods (one or more years of documented chemical free farming) although soil testing for chemical residue may still be required. In the case mentioned here, the Zhejiang site was certified while the Anhui site was rejected.

7. Both NIES staff and the SEPA official in Beijing most familiar with the sequence of events confirm that the proposal to establish OFDC came from NIES in Nanjing, not from SEPA.

8. Sustainable agriculture and rural development is a common phrase in the development community. It connotes an emphasis on poverty alleviation, appropriate technologies and, in some cases, participatory approaches to third world development.

9. Without the NIES/OCIA connection, Chinese organic producers must obtain certification from foreign certification organizations before they can sell to the international market. This is expensive and logistically difficult.

10. IFOAM is not only headquartered in Germany, it has a much tighter relationship with EU and member state agricultural ministries than it does with the U.S. Department of Agriculture.

11. Identity and standards are related issues. A core requirement in the global organic community is that certification must be performed by a "third party" that has no economic ties to production or marketing. Since Green Food and MOA are directly involved in these activities, it is probably structurally impossible for them to ever satisfy global expectations.

12. By 2002, producers with institutional ties to MOA and Green Food began switching to OFDC for organic certification because the IFOAM accredited label was accepted by foreign buyers. For a more extensive description of the bureaucratic and entrepreneurial struggle between OFDC and Green Food see Thiers 2002.

13. The Chinese phrase *xiahai* (to jump into the sea) is frequently used in reform era China to describe going into business.

References

Chamberlain, H. B. 1993. On the search for civil society in China. *Modern China* 19 (2): 199–215.

Huang, P. C. C. 1993. "Public sphere" and "civil society" in China. *Modern China* 19 (2): 216–217.

Gu, X. 1993. A civil society and public sphere in post-Mao China? An overview of Western publications. *China Information* 8 (3): 38–52.

———. 1998. Plural institutionalism and the emergence of intellectual public spaces in contemporary China: Four relational patterns and four organizational forms. *Journal of Contemporary China* 7 (18): 271–301.

Knup, E. 1997. Environmental NGOs in China: An overview. In *China environment series 1*, ed. A. Frank. Washington DC: Woodrow Wilson International Center for Scholars.

Li, Z. F. 1993. Briefing of organic agriculture in China. Nanjing: Rural Ecosystems Division, Nanjing Institute for Environmental Science

Lieberthal, K. G. and M. Oksenberg. 1988. *Policy making in China: Leaders, structures and processes.* Princeton, NJ: Princeton University Press.

Nevitt, C. E. 1996. Private business associations in China: Evidence of civil society or local state power. *China Journal* 36: 25–43.

Newell, P. 2003. *Domesticating global policy on GMOs: Comparing India and China*. Brighton, UK: Institute of Development Studies.

Pearson, M. M. 1994. The Janus face of business associations in China: Socialist corporatism in foreign enterprises. *Australian Journal of Chinese Affairs* 31: 25–46.

Saich, T. 2000. Negotiating the state: The development of social organizations in China. *China Quarterly* 161: 124–141.

Thiers, P. 2002. From Grassroots Movement to State Coordinated Market Strategy: The Transformation of Organic Agriculture in China. *Government and Policy* 20 (3) June, 357–373.

Unger, J. 1996. 'Bridges': Private business, the Chinese government and the rise of new associations. *China Quarterly* 147 (September): 795–819.

Whiting, S. 1991. The politics of NGO development in China. *Voluntes* 3 (2): 16–48.

Wu, F. S. 2002. New partners or old brothers? GONGOs in transnational environmental advocacy in China. In *China environment series 5*, ed. J. L. Turner, 45–58. Washington DC: Woodrow Wilson International Center for Scholars.

Xue, D. Y. 2002. *A summary of research on the environmental impacts of Bt cotton in China*. Hong Kong: Greenpeace.

Zhuang, G. T. 1995. China national EPA taking measures to promote OA development. *IFOAM Asian Regional Network Newsletter* (6): 3–4.

Chapter Nine

Red Capitalist: The Rising Chinese Private Entrepreneurs

Jing Yang

In the past half century, the private economy in China has grown from the marginal and supplementary element of the socialist construction, to a crucial and integral part of the state economy.[1] Accordingly, the total registered capital of private enterprises has increased from approximately US$1.5 billion in the early 1990s to approximately US$150 billion in 2000. The period since the early 1990s has been one of extraordinary economic growth, particularly in the private sector, and the opening of new job and investment opportunities in the market.[2]

Along with the subsequent economic growth, the Chinese class structure has also experienced transformation from a simple, bounded, and rigid occupational hierarchy under Mao, to an open, modernized, and evolving system in the early industrialization period of the nation (Lu 2002, 2004). The increasing material basis led to an expanding new middle class in China and among which, some scholars have drawn particular attention to private entrepreneurs, since private economy is an increasing influential element toward government policymaking. Moreover, private entrepreneurs with their rising social status, their close ties with other elite groups, political prospects, and their concerns about policymaking, have intensified the interest of many scholars. The implementation of market mechanism has not only granted the private sector a certain degree of autonomy, but also invigorated the local government's incentives on coordinating and managing the market-oriented activities. The shift from institution of central planning to market economic and the extraordinary growth of private economy also produced side effects that rocked the traditional base of the Communist Party of China (CPC). Evidently, the departure from command economy has weakened the centralized party-state apparatus (Tsui, Bian, and Cheng 2006, 254–58; Oi and Walder 1995).

Some scholars observed that the continued economic growth and increasing privatization of state enterprises in scale and scope will ultimately lead to a political change. The rise of private entrepreneurs was regarded as a potential driving force for the process of democratization in pursuit of the civil society (Moore 1966). At the same time, the other widely held viewpoint that also prevailed was that under the booming private economy and decentralization of the state's management power, there has been the corresponding transition from "top-down" state corporatism to a "bottom-up" societal corporatism within the realms of the local economy (Unger 1996, 814–819). Although the current generation of private entrepreneurs may perform similar economic activities and share common interests on business, the differences still remain in their social and political background (Chen 2005, Tsai 2005), which further affects their behavior and perceptions on achieving their economic goals, geared at protecting their own benefits (Holbig 2002, 52–54). Moreover, given the relative youth and short life span of the majority of private enterprises, it is not surprising that there is a lack of common basis for identity and interaction within the entrepreneurs group (Tsai 2005, 1131–1133). Therefore, class formation has not occurred within this group, and it is unlikely for private entrepreneurs to take up the mission of pursuing democracy in China in the near future (Ibid, 1152–1153). Furthermore, some empirical studies (Ao 2005; Dickson 2003, 2007) have shown that the current Chinese entrepreneurs have established close ties with the local government officials that essentially prevents them from being a force of change (Chen, Li, and Matlay 2006; Dickson 2003, 2007; G. J. Chen 2005; Unger 1996; Unger and Chan 1999; Wank 1996, 2002). As long as private entrepreneurs share the same interests in promoting economic growth, many will "rely heavily on government patronage for their success in making profits" (A. Chen 2003, 157) and "they are among the party's most important bases of support" (Dickson 2007, 827–828). Consequently, both sides in this debate are in general agreement on the party's embrace of the private sector and the social impact of entrepreneurs as a new social group.

Among the entrepreneurs of various backgrounds, who have joined the party before starting their own business, what are the characteristics of the targeted candidates of co-optation of the party? Are they distinctive from the rest who are not party members in some ways? In this chapter, I examine the common factors that determine the entry of CPC members into the private sector and the entry of private entrepreneurs into CPC, and demonstrate how the patterns of entry in both directions vary over time. In the following sections, I first briefly review the development of government's co-optation strategy and some theoretical debates that surrounds this research. Second, I describe the survey data and the variables used for the empirical analyses. Lastly, I examine the difference and common factors on the CPC and private entrepreneurs' entry into private entrepreneurship. Results are also compared with previous research.

Embracing the Private Sector into the State Economy

The development of Chinese private economy has gone through several stages since the late 1980s. The debate over promoting economic growth while upholding the socialist regime, however, has been a main concern of the CPC government since 1949. During the economic restoration and socialist transformation period from 1949 to 1957, the government eliminated bureaucratic capitalists and landlords by confiscating capitalist corporations in the cities and land reform in the rural areas. As a result, eliminating the market economy and ushering in a centrally planned economy through the first Five Year Plan with focus on the expansion of heavy industry. During the Great Leap Forward and three-year natural disaster from the late 1950s to the early 1960s, the CPC government allowed people to operate small individual businesses, also known as *getihu* (self-employed), which fostered the beginnings of a *ziyoushichang* or free-market.

By the time of the Third Plenary Meeting of the Eleventh Central Committee of CPC (1978), after the events of the Cultural Revolution, no private enterprise existed aside from some 150,000 *getihu* (Wank 1995a, 156). The Third Plenum marked the official revival of private business within the limits prescribed by law and under controlled by the local government. The economic-oriented reform was initiated from the countryside, replacing the collective production with household responsibility system, accompanied with leasing the land to the individual household. During the first decade of market reform, therefore, the debates on private economy issues were mainly focused on the legitimization of small-scale individual business.

The high unemployment rate among the youth who were sent to the rural areas for education placed great pressure on the labor market in late 1970s (Ibid, 19–24). To tackle this problem, as well as to increase commodity supply to the cities, the State Council approved the first statement on supporting the individual economy, which essentially gave permission for individual businesses (*geti jingji*) to operate without employees. At the Fifth section of Fifth National People's Congress (NPC) in 1982, Article 11 of the Constitution confirmed the complementary position of the individual economy to the socialist public economy and its operation under state protection. At that time, most people who ran privately owned businesses were from the "grassroots" class, such as peasants, the self-employed, and the unemployed in the city who had limited options for making a living (Chen, Li, and Matlay 2006, 150–155). From 1982 to 1984, the State Council gradually loosened the marketing restrictions on nonessential goods and released a series of guidelines that allowed traders and peasant producers to engage in long-distance wholesale and retail trade. Corresponding to the initial success of the private sector, contracting (*chengbao*) or leasing (*zulin*) the small and unprofitable state- and/or collectively owned (SOEs and COEs) to individuals in return for a certain proportion of the profit was initiated in the countryside and was further formalized by the State Council in 1984, with the practice spreading to the cities (Young 1995, 98–102). The government's major concern in this period mainly focused on whether to allow the owners of the small individual businesses to hire employees, as such "exploitation" is against the spirit of Marxism-Leninism and Maoist thought. Accordingly, the government has reluctance toward the growing private sector due to the seemingly contradictions to traditional political thought, hence adopting a "wait and see" approach before further condoning and supporting private entrepreneurs.[3]

In April 1988, the first section of the Seventh NPC approved an amendment to Article 11 of the Constitution, which declared that the existence of the private economy was growing within the limits as prescribed by law. In addition, it was noted that the private economy was a complement to the socialist state public economy. This was the first official confirmation of the lawful status of the private economy and its supplementary function to the state economy. The State Council further encouraged professionals and administrative personnel from SOEs and COEs to start contracting out small- and medium-sized ailing SOEs and COEs in the countryside or to start township and village enterprises (TVEs) to divert the surplus rural labor force and resolve some of the unemployment issues in the cities. However, many privately owned firms established in the countryside, mostly TVEs, were registered as COEs, a prevalent strategy known as "wearing a red-hat" to ensure the entrepreneur's business (Ao 2005, 4; Holbig 2002, 35–37; Tsai 2005, 1135–1136; Young 1995, 95–111). Confronted with changes brought on by the market economy, since late 1988, societal corporatism emerged as a strategy for the CPC to recruit new members to the political arena, particularly entrepreneurs and those with scientific and technical expertise, thus entrepreneurs were for the first time co-opted into the party in large numbers (Dickson 2003). However, the ban was again applied in 1989, due to some private entrepreneurs' support for the student movement (Dickson 2003, 34–37; Wank 1995b, 56–58).

In early 1992, Deng Xiaoping advocated the importance of preserving the private economy and market reform during his tour of southern China. In October 1992, the Fourteenth Party Congress signified the acceptance of Deng's ideas by making a socialist market economy a national goal. The former cadres and administrative personnel in SOEs and COEs, professionals, and intellectuals were either "pushed" or "pulled" into the sea of private sector, which was well-known as the wave of *xiahai* (to jump into the sea) among the elites in China (Ao 2005, 6), also noted by Thiers in the previous chapter. Accordingly, the private entrepreneurs and the self-employed were encouraged to join organizations established by the central or local governments, such as the Federation of Industry and Commerce (FIC)[4], which was dissolved during the Cultural Revolution, but revived at the beginning of the economic reform. As organizations of the state, business associations registered with the government and sponsored by the state organizational units have become regular channels for local officials and businesspeople to communicate on various issues. The party continues to play a leading role in the private economy by monitoring these associations from central to local levels.

As mentioned earlier, 1992 can be considered as the second phase of establishing private business, advanced primarily by people who had already occupied privileged positions in business. As the market has become mature, the competition among enterprises has been enhanced and upgraded to competition on the control over social resources, such as capital for further investments, technology required for industry, and networks for business information. The less privileged "grassroots" class who started their own businesses at the earlier stage of market reform, have founded it increasingly difficult to survive during this period of intense competition.

The Fifteenth CPC Congress in 1997 elevated the private economy from the constitutive position to a more significant one. From this point, enormous numbers of private enterprises that were either unregistered or under the cover of COE obtained official registration status, thus "throw away the red-hat" characterized this period. By the time 1999, the private ownership was fully legitimized by the constitution.

In May 2000, Jiang Zemin proposed the "Three Represents" theory,[5] and called for lifting the ban in the CPC constitution that officially prohibited private businesspeople from joining the party and serving the government.[6] Since 2003, the CPC government has undertaken a determined and extensive effort to recruit entrepreneurs into the party, a key dimension of the inclusion policy that allows CPC to adapt, and it is an important factor for promoting organizational change. Some subset of the cadres in the party, however, warned that the growing numbers of red-capitalists, especially the private entrepreneurs who were co-opted into the party were weakening the party's cohesiveness and betraying its original class nature. The conservatives and observers further asserted that the red-capitalists are leading agents to promote political change if the interests and policy preferences of the business elites are substantially incompatible with the party and government officials (A. Chen 2002, 420–422). Some reformers, on the other side claimed that even though there are serious ideological barriers toward the red-capitalists, encouraging party members to *xiahai* and recruiting entrepreneurs into the party can also be interpreted as a rational strategy to secure the CPC's leadership. Furthermore, on March 16, 2007, the enactment of the first Private Property Law of the People's Republic of China (PRC) at NPC in Beijing finally assured formal and legal protection to Chinese private enterprises declaring: "The property of the state, the collective, the individual and other obliges is protected by law, and no units or individuals may infringe upon it." In addition, it guarantees that people can own and sell assets such as land-use rights for as long as seventy years in the cities. Accordingly, the criteria for recruiting CPC members shifted between "redness and loyalty" and "expertise and elitism" along with fluctuations in the government's goals on balancing political legitimacy and the logic of market economy. Economic reforms have not only created enormous material benefits for many Chinese people, but also new challenges to the socialist regime and the dictatorship of the CPC.

The Rising Red Capitalists and Alliance with the Local Government

For the last three decades, the CPC government has been slowly whittling away the institutions that defined the planned economy and embracing market mechanisms. This has reinforced the transaction of property relations between the central and the local governments, and further engendered the cooperative relationships between local officials and businesspeople. The central government have restored the concept of property rights through five processes (Holbig 2002, 35–38; Oi and Walder 1999, 10–12): the contracting or leasing of public assets since late 1980s; the expanded sale or outright "privatization" of those assets since early 1990s; the illicit transfer of ownership to elites since the late 1980s; further investment by state entities in private enterprises, and the massive establishment of new private businesses since the late 1990s. In accordance with these changes and gradual privatization all around the country was the central government's strategy for granting greater autonomy over the arrangement of local economy to local governments. This transformed the relationship between local officials and private entrepreneurs from critical to an interdependent patron-client relationship.

Several empirical studies in cities and township revealed that under the decentralized fiscal system patron-client relationships between the local government and private enterprises have evolved and changed. For example, Wank's (1996) fieldwork in Xiamen proved that the private entrepreneurs seek the support of local officials. The support comes in the form of access to all kinds of resources crucial to production that are under the control of public enterprises. Other forms of support include favorable bank loans, trade opportunities with overseas business and other public units, and opportunities to cooperate with large-scale public enterprises. Another crucial form of support sought by private entrepreneurs from local officials is access to protection from the bureaucratic processes. In return, government officials or personnel who are involved may expect pay-offs from the entrepreneurs, or being assigned with to positions within the company. Moreover, with the intensification of business competition, private entrepreneurs have gradually developed relationships with officials at senior levels and seeking far more enduring ties (Wank 1995a, 160–175). However, this is more likely to be found between large-scale enterprises and the government in most empirical research (Bruun 1995, 186–189).

Tsai (2005) and A. Chen (2002; 2003) investigated the issue by the systematic assessment of the perspective of "class" and "civil society" postulated by structural theory. Both agreed that given the growing contribution of the private sector to the local economy, and the government's gradual co-optation of the entrepreneurs into the party, the mutual interdependence between party and entrepreneurs has been strengthened. This not only divided the entrepreneurs into different positions in the operation of local economy and politics, it further removed the desire and ability of entrepreneurs to claim more autonomy in doing business (Tsai 2005, 1145–1153).

The empirical research that most recently focused on embryonic co-optation strategy of the party toward private economy and entrepreneurs are mostly regional (Dickson 2003; 2007) or based on case studies (You 1998). My own empirical research is largely in the same vein as Dickson's (2003; 2007) studies on CPC's adaptation strategies in the face of the growing private economy and the changing criteria in recruiting the candidates from entrepreneurs. Dickson's two surveys of private entrepreneurs in eight counties[7] compared the political attitudes and behaviors between the two main actors in the discussion: local officials and entrepreneurs. He found the support toward maintaining cooperative relationships between the two sides and recruitment of entrepreneurs, owners of large-scale business in particular, to the party. At the same time, the red-capitalists' shared similar perceptions on policymaking, and behaviors with the local officials further proved their lack of motivation in achieving a democratic future (Dickson 2007, 847–853).

Moreover, he found distinctive characteristics among *xiahai*, co-opted, and non-CPC member entrepreneurs, more specifically, in terms of their backgrounds, *xiahai* entrepreneurs are typically older, better educated, and have settled longer in their counties than nonparty members. *Xiahai* entrepreneurs are also less likely to come from a *getihu* background, and they are more likely to be FIC members than non-CPC member.[8] The effects of gender, family income, and enterprise revenue were found insignificant, due to the gender biased existed in the private sector and the nature of the sample. The characteristics of co-opted entrepreneurs have shown slight differences, such as the effects of age, business revenue, and family income have faded away, and more surprisingly, the *getihu* status was found positively related with the likelihood of being the target of co-optation. He also found narrowing gaps between the party and the entrepreneurs on their political preferences and the increasing efficiency of the government-run business associations. He further argued that although the entrepreneurs might have not formed a coherent class, their political perceptions do not pose as a challenge to the party-state dominance.

In this chapter, I use the data taken from a series of large-scale cross-sectional surveys on Chinese private enterprises and entrepreneurs based on the national representative sample and apply the hypotheses derived from the previous studies on the adaptive strategies of the government toward the private economy and the co-optation procedure of the entrepreneurs to the party. First, *xiahai* entrepreneurs, owing to their previous working experience and political background, are usually better educated. Second, the business networks gained from previous *getihu* experiences may help private entrepreneurs start or expand their own business, but it does not help them join the party (Dickson 2003; 2007). Third, in the region of higher bureaucratic level (i.e., capitals, big cities, etc.) the linkages between government officials and private entrepreneurs appear to be weaker. This is reflected in the empirical analysis, the more developed the region where the business headquarter is located, the less likely it is for CPC member to be a *xiahai entrepreneur*, or for private entrepreneurs to be co-opted. Lastly, the scale of the business is positively correlated with the likelihood of being led by the *xiahai* entrepreneur or the possibility of the owners to be the targets of the party to incorporate. In addition, by including the data of different survey years I hope to sketch the changing characteristics as well as the self-perceptions of private entrepreneurs with different political identities.

Data and Variables

Data for the empirical analysis is taken from the project *Survey on Private Enterprises and Entrepreneurs in China* (SPEEC).[9] The multi-stage, stratified, national probability sampling was applied on a selection of samples from domestic, private enterprises registered with the State Administration of Industry and Commerce at year end, before each survey was conducted. The number of entrepreneurs interviewed ranges from approximately 2,000 in 1997 to approximately 4,500 in 2006, with an average response rate of more than 80 percent. The purpose of the SPEEC project is to study the development strategy of private enterprises as the Chinese government has been incrementally releasing control over the private economy. The survey covers the private entrepreneur's family background, work history, political attitudes, income, current family information, housing condition, and the operation of the enterprises. A specific part of the questionnaire is designed in relation to political events, with specific reference to policy changes occurring at the time of inquiry, which will be the main focus of my empirical study. Since the design of the questionnaires are not entirely consistent, for example, the date of joining the CPC was not included in the questionnaires of surveys completed before 2002, technically it is not possible to identify the types of private entrepreneurs from *xiahai*, co-opted, and non-CPC in the surveys conducted in previous years. Therefore, in this chapter, only data from surveys conducted in 2002, 2004, and 2006 will be used.

Table 9.1 presents the major information of the private enterprises operated by the respondents interviewed in the surveys. The first panel shows the decreasing proportion of private enterprises registered before 1997. The total proportion of private enterprises registered during the early stages of economic reform, before 1992, and from 1992 to 1996, has decreased from approximately 57 to 30 percent from 2002 to 2006. The proportion of private enterprises registered from 1997 onward has increased from 40.4 percent in 2002 to 66.7 percent in 2006.

Figures in the second panel indicate that the majority (more than 70 percent across the 3 surveys) of private enterprises have lasted no longer than 10 years, which further indicates the immaturity of Chinese private businesses. The distribution of registered industry, however, has been stable. Approximately 45 percent of private businesses are located in the secondary industry[10] and the tertiary industry comes second at approximately 35 percent. Similarly, the distribution of where business headquarters are located does not show much change from 2002 to 2006. Approximately one-third of the headquarters of the private businesses are located in small and middle cities as indicated across the three surveys. Meanwhile, business headquarters located in big cities first increased from approximately 25 to 29 percent in 2004, followed by a sharp decrease to 17 percent. Conversely, the proportion for the headquarters located in township first decreases from 24 to 20 percent, followed by an increase

Table 9.1 Information of enterprises in the survey: 2002, 2004, 2006

	2002(%)[a]	2004(%)	2006(%)
Registration year			
1992 or earlier	22.3	12.6	10.6
1993 or later	74.6	83.0	85.0
Years registered as private enterprise			
5 years or less	40.4	42.7	37.7
6–10 years	38.7	35.7	34.2
More than 10 years	17.9	17.2	23.7
Industry at time of inquiry			
Primary	5.3	6.3	5.6
Secondary	44.0	43.5	46.3
Tertiary	36.3	35.2	35.7
Others[b]	9.9	10.1	—
Location of the headquarter of the enterprises			
Development zone	6.1	8.3	9.9
Big city	24.8	28.7	17.0
Mid/small city	34.5	33.2	33.7
Township	23.5	19.7	26.1
Countryside	10.3	8.5	9.9
Total N	3,258	3,593	4,315

Source: Survey on Private Enterprises and Entrepreneurs in China (See Note 10 [or 9 in updated version]).

[a]Columns may not sum to 100 due to rounding and the missing cases.

[b]Others: Either the industry is hard to classify, or might fall in the "quaternary sector," which consists of intellectual activities associated with government such as research and education. This is loosely defined in China. However, this category is not included in 2006 Survey.

of 6 percent in 2006. An exception is that there is a slight increase of approximately 4 percent of the proportion of business headquarters located in development zone from 2002 (6.1 percent) to 10 percent in 2006 (9.9 percent). The bureaucratic level of the locations is classified as: the countryside (set as reference category); township; small- to middle-sized city; big city; and development zone (DZ, *kaifaqu*). From the figures we observed that approximately two-thirds of privately owned businesses are located in small- to middle-sized cities and townships. The proportion of businesses located in development zones also increased from 6.1 to 9.9 percent, while the proportion of business headquarters located in big cities decreased from 24.8 to 17.0 percent.

Table 9.2 is the summary of principal background information of the private entrepreneur respondents included in the empirical analyses. Of the entrepreneurs participated in the survey, the quantity of male entrepreneurs is overwhelmingly superior to female entrepreneurs across three surveys. In terms of political status, the proportion of CPC members

Table 9.2 Background information of entrepreneurs in the merged data

	Registration year of business	
	before 1993(%)[a]	1993 onward(%)[b]
Sex		
Male	90.3	86.5
Female	9.3	13.2
Level of education		
Under/graduate school	22.0	25.2
Vocational school/college	14.9	23.3
High/vocational school	38.7	36.5
Middle school	20.6	13.2
Primary or lower	3.4	1.4
Political identity: Member of		
Communist Party of China (CPC)	27.3	33.7
Chinese Communist Youth League (CCYL)	1.6	5.1
Democratic Party (DP)	8.8	5.0
Membership of business associations		
Federation of Industry & Commerce (FIC)	13.4	54.1
Trade of Same Industry (TSI)	5.1	40.3
Types of entrepreneurs		
Xiahai	13.5	25.4
Co-opted	12.4	6.4
Non-CPC	67.2	59.6
Age of 40 or younger		
Xiahai	0.9	4.9
Co-opted	3.4	2.7
Non-CPC	16.5	26.7
Older than 40		
Xiahai	12.4	20.4
Co-opted	9.0	3.7
Non-CPC	50.2	32.5
With higher educational qualification (vocational school/college and higher)		
Xiahai	6.5	14.5
Co-opted	4.8	2.5
Non-CPC	22.9	27.8
Total N	1639	9,077
With Getihu experience		
Xiahai	9.9	13.3
Co-opted	10.9	8.2
Non-CPC	79.2	78.5
Total N	395	1,784

Source: Year Book of Private business, 1989–1999. Report on Private Economy (From Chinese Academy of Social Science) in 2003, 2005, and 2006.

[a]Columns may not sum to 100 due to rounding and missing cases.
[b]Vocational school qualifications are not classified in 2002 survey.

among male respondents rose from 31 percent in 2002 to 38 percent in 2006. We also observe the increasing proportions of Chinese Communist Youth League (CCYL) members for both male and female entrepreneurs. Accordingly, the corresponding proportions of CPC members of total Chinese population in 2002, 2004, and 2006 are 5.16, 5.35, and 5.54 percent respectively.[11] Overall, the proportion of entrepreneurs without any political affiliation has decreased by approximately 18 percent for both male and female respondents across the three years, from 61 to 43 percent for males and from 68 to 49 percent for females.

The dependent variable for our analysis is the political status of the private entrepreneurs at the time of inquiry. Non-CPC members are set as the reference category for this research. The second category is *xiahai* entrepreneurs, who joined the party before "plunging into the sea of private business," hence the term *xiahai*. The co-opted entrepreneurs, who were recruited by the CPC after they started their own business in the private sector, make up the third category.

Independent variables included in multinomial logistic regression are Age (and Age^2); gender (female is set as reference category); total family income; and annual turnover of the enterprise the year before the time of inquiry.[12] The third panel of table 9.2 shows that, first, among the CPC members, the proportion of *xiahai* entrepreneurs is much higher than co-opted entrepreneurs in each survey. At the same time, they have also been the oldest group among the respondents. From the following two panels, it is possible to see that the proportion of *xiahai* entrepreneurs more than 40 years old has slightly decreased from 74.6 to 72.7 percent from 2002 to 2006; there has been a stable gap of approximately 18 percent between them and the corresponding proportion of co-opted entrepreneurs. The proportion of co-opted entrepreneurs more than 40 years old slight decreases from 58.0 to 54.7 percent, whereas the proportion of non-CPC members, the youngest and majority group is constant at approximately 54 percent across the surveys.

In terms of education level, we used highest qualifications the respondents held at the time of inquiry, among which the primary or lower education level is set as the reference group, followed by middle school, high school, and vocational school (*zhongzhuan*)[13], and vocational college (*dazhuan*), undergraduate, and higher. From table 9.2 we can see that approximately half of the entrepreneurs have obtained qualifications from college (including vocational college) or higher. Among the proportion of *xiahai* entrepreneurs holding a higher educational degree (46 percent with vocational and undergraduate/graduate degree in 2002; 62.2 percent in 2004; and 57.5 percent in 2006), it is relatively higher than non-CPC members (37.1 percent with vocational/undergraduate/graduate degree in

2002, 48.3 percent in 2004, and 48.7 percent in 2006). Conversely, the proportions of co-opted entrepreneurs appear to have the lowest education for all three surveys (29.9 percent in 2002, 45.9 percent in 2004, and 43.6 percent in 2006, respectively).

The household income is also included as respondent's background factor. Total annual turnover, year in business, and the location of the business headquarter can be interpreted as the measurements of the scale of the business (the countryside is set as the reference category).

The local government-entrepreneur alliance is also considered as an important factor on private entrepreneurs' political identity and the indicator of their political behavior and concerns. The questionnaires cover several associations of different nature and administrative levels, such as the first and most popular government organization for businessmen: the Federation of Industry and Commerce (FIC), Private Enterprises Association (PEA), Self-employed Laborers' Association (SELA), and specific Sector Industry Association (SIA). From the figures, more than two-thirds of the respondents have joined the FIC and SELA. However, to avoid the colinearity problems that may be generated from including too many variables of the same kind, only membership to FIC is included in the regression model.

The *getihu* experience is also included in the analysis. In general, from the surveys, it is possible to see that the proportion of entrepreneurs with *getihu* background has decreased from 23.5 percent to 18.1 percent. From the last panel of table 9.2, we found that although the proportion of *xiahai* entrepreneurs has increased from 8.9 to 13.6 percent, approximately 80 percent of respondents with *getihu* experiences are not the member of CPC in the 3 surveys.

Results

What are the characteristics that distinguish the political identities and characteristics among private entrepreneurs? Table 9.3 presents the summary of the results of multinomial logistic regression analysis on the factors that define entrepreneurs' entry into CPC: before (*xiahai* entrepreneurs) or after (co-opted entrepreneurs) entry into the private sector, in comparison with non-CPC entrepreneurs. Overall, the factors integrated into the analysis can explain the entry of *xiahai* entrepreneurs more efficiently than they do on co-opted entrepreneurs.

First, age, gender, and level of education are important factors that are positively associated with the likelihood of the entry into the private sector for CPC members. The regression coefficients of age reported in the tables decrease from 0.429 in 2002, to 0.301 in 2004, then slightly increases

Table 9.3 Attribute of CPC members among private entrepreneurs (Multinomial logistic regression)

	Xiahai vs. Non-CPC entrepreneurs		Co-opted vs. Non-CPC entrepreneurs		Xiahai vs. Co-opted entrepreneurs	
	before 1993	1993 onward	before 1993	1993 onward	before 1993	1993 onward
Survey year						
2006	1.107***	0.410***	0.149	−0.603***	0.957**	1.013***
	(0.263)	(0.087)	(0.250)	(0.131)	(0.328)	(0.143)
2004	0.183	0.359***	−0.335	−0.590***	0.518	0.949***
	(0.243)	(0.087)	(0.237)	(0.134)	(0.314)	(0.146)
Age	0.499***	0.326***	−0.016	0.060	0.515***	0.266***
	(0.124)	(0.037)	(0.098)	(0.055)	(0.147)	(0.062)
Age^2	−0.004***	−0.003***	0.000	−0.001	−0.004**	−0.002**
	(0.001)	(0.000)	(0.001)	(0.001)	(0.001)	(0.001)
Sex (Male)	0.567	0.507***	0.043	0.465**	0.525	0.042
	(0.357)	(0.108)	(0.329)	(0.188)	(0.450)	(0.206)
Educational Background						
Under/graduate degree	0.360	1.253***	0.291	0.168	0.070	1.085*
	(0.485)	(0.294)	(0.610)	(0.428)	(0.707)	(0.482)
Vocational college	0.447	1.270***	1.059	0.384	−0.613	0.885
	(0.496)	(0.292)	(0.612)	(0.430)	(0.708)	(0.483)
High/vocational school	−0.589	0.821**	0.305	0.565	−0.894	0.256
	(0.463)	(0.288)	(0.575)	(0.414)	(0.670)	(0.468)
Middle school	−0.567	0.393	0.066	0.155	−0.633	0.238
	(0.473)	(0.294)	(0.588)	(0.425)	(0.685)	(0.480)

	(1)	(2)	(3)	(4)	(5)	(6)
Total family income (log)	0.131 (0.090)	-0.167*** (0.032)	0.037 (0.091)	-0.139** (0.051)	0.095 (0.115)	-0.027 (0.055)
Annual turnover (log)	0.018 (0.056)	0.182*** (0.019)	0.057 (0.057)	0.211*** (0.031)	-0.039 (0.072)	-0.029 (0.033)
Year in business	-0.116** (0.038)	-0.090*** (0.011)	0.101** (0.033)	0.064*** (0.018)	-0.217*** (0.046)	-0.154*** (0.020)
Location of business						
Development zone	-0.081 (0.410)	-0.532*** (0.143)	-0.822* (0.391)	-0.691*** (0.230)	0.741 (0.511)	0.159 (0.221)
Big city	-0.712* (0.356)	-0.861*** (0.123)	-1.576*** (0.348)	-1.638*** (0.199)	0.865 (0.456)	0.776*** (0.214)
Middle city	-0.123 (0.303)	-0.557*** (0.113)	-0.803** (0.257)	-1.010*** (0.156)	0.680 (0.357)	0.452** (0.170)
Small city/township	0.329 (0.312)	-0.042 (0.113)	-0.243 (0.261)	-0.393** (0.150)	0.572 (0.361)	0.351* (0.163)
FIC member	-1.244*** (0.255)	-0.374*** (0.072)	-0.660** (0.253)	-0.226 (0.117)	-0.584 (0.313)	-0.148 (0.124)
Getihu experience	-0.534** (0.223)	-0.909*** (0.092)	-0.473* (0.211)	-0.123 (0.117)	-0.061 (0.283)	-0.786*** (0.138)
Intercept	-13.924*** (3.200)	-11.333*** (0.899)	-1.398 (2.380)	-4.311*** (1.272)	-12.526*** (3.740)	-7.022*** (1.459)
1973–1992 (N=1197)	LR $\chi2$ (36) = 222.347 P ($\chi2$) = 0.000		-2 Log likelihood = 1715.760		Pseudo R^2 = 0.170	
1993–2005 (N=6384)	LR $\chi2$ (36) = 1397.650 P ($\chi2$) = 0.000		-2 Log likelihood = 9310.859		Pseudo R^2 = 0.197	

Note: *$p<0.05$; **$p<0.01$; ***$p<0.001$

to 0.354 in 2006 (with $p<0.001$ across the survey year), which indicates that in the three surveys, one-year increase in the age increases the net odds of CPC members' engaging in private entrepreneurship by a certain percentage.

The odds of male CPC member getting into business are 1.79 times ($=e^{0.581}$) the odds of females in 2002, which increases to 2.22 times ($=e^{0.796}$) in 2004, then drops down to 1.37 times ($=e^{0.318}$) in 2006.

Higher level of education also facilitates the entry into business, however, the impacts prove to be significant only in the 2004 survey. In the 2004 survey, the advantages of holding vocational college or under/graduate degree over primary school education on turning into *xiahai* entrepreneurs are particularly prominent: for the former, the net odds are 4.81 times ($=e^{1.570}$) the odds of primary school education; for the latter, the corresponding figure is 4.82 times ($=e^{1.572}$). Conversely, although statistically insignificant, they are all negatively associated with the odds of entrepreneurs joining the party.

Meanwhile, the results obtained from 2002 and 2006 survey also suggest that, the higher educational qualifications do not bring significant differences on the odds of entrepreneurs' entry to *xiahai* or being co-opted compared with non-CPC member. Moreover, educational qualification, together with age and gender, are found not to be significantly associated with the likelihood of entrepreneurs to be co-opted into the party, except in the 2006 survey: the odds of male entrepreneurs to be co-opted into the party are 2.34 times ($=e^{0.850}$) the odds of female.

The personal income of entrepreneurs and the scale of their business have shown contradictory impacts on their political identity. The total household annual income is found negatively associated with the likelihood of the CPC members' entry to the private sector, and the entrepreneurs' admission to the party. Therefore, as total family income increases, the log odds of being a *xiahai* entrepreneur or being co-opted decreases compared to the non-CPC member entrepreneurs, and the results proved to be significant in the 2002 and 2006 surveys.[14]

On the contrary, in the three surveys, the total annual turnover of the businesses has shown a positive and significant impact on the likelihood of party members' entering business and entrepreneurs' achievement of party membership. The results further confirm our anticipation that the CPC would prioritize owners of larger business for party recruitment.

The scale of the business aside, we found that the longer the entrepreneurs have been in business, the more likely they are to be co-opted by the party: an additional year they engaged in business, the odds of being co-opted increases by 10.5 percent ($=e^{0.100}-1$) in 2002, 6.5 percent in 2004 ($=e^{0.063}-1$), and 14.3 percent in 2006 ($=e^{0.135}-1$). However, the effect is reversed for the case of *xiahai* entrepreneurs across the three surveys, which are also contradictory to what Dickson found from his surveys: an extra year in business, the odds of being *xiahai* entrepreneurs are reduced by 10.6 percent (=1−e$^{-0.112}$) in 2002, which increases to 13.8 percent (=1−e$^{-0.155}$) in 2004, but then decrease to only approximately 5.7 percent (=1−e$^{-0.055}$) in 2006. The results may be partly explained by the fact that most CPC members started their business at a later stage of the reform.

Similarly to what Unger (1996, 815–817) and Nevitt (1996) stated in their research, in the major metropolitan areas, the officials have a superior attitude toward entrepreneurs and their associations. In other areas, the relationship between officials and entrepreneurs is more symbiotic, and officials may be more tolerant of collective action on behalf of business interests. Therefore, the more developed the region where the business headquarter is located, the less possible for either CPC members to *xiahai* or to be co-opted to the party. This argument has been proven to be true by the current survey data. Business headquarters locations are negatively associated with the likelihood of CPC members to become private entrepreneurs. There is also strong negative association in the 2002 survey, where location in a development zone reduces the odds of party members' entry to business by 60 percent (e$^{-0.917}$, with $p<0.01$), the effect then becomes insignificant in 2004 and 2006. Meanwhile, for the case of co-opted entrepreneurs, the odds of joining the party is found significantly reduced by 69 percent (e$^{-1.174}$, with $p<0.001$) in 2006 survey if their business is located in a development zone, and the association is found insignificant in 2002 and 2004 surveys. Overall, the regression coefficients of locations of business indicate that, by and large, it is less likely for party members to get involved in the private sector as well as for entrepreneurs to join the party if the business is located in big cities, as shown across the three surveys.

The negative affect of *getihu* experiences on the likelihood of being both *xiahai* party members and co-optation of the entrepreneurs are found in our survey data.[15] The net odds of CPC members with *getihu* background going to business are 46.7 percent (=e$^{-0.762}$) of the odds of the one without such experiences in 2002, the net odds increases to 51.0 percent (=e$^{-0.674}$) in 2004, followed by a decrease to 35.3 percent (=e$^{-1.042}$) in 2006 survey, with p-value smaller than 0.001. In contrast, for the case of co-opted entrepreneurs, the negative affect of self-employment experience on joining the party is only found significant in the 2002 survey. The corresponding figure is 56.0 percent (=e$^{-0.579}$), which has become insignificant in 2004 and 2006.

Membership to the FIC, the largest mediating channel of government and businesspeople, is not a significant factor on explaining CPC member's entry to private sector or the entry of private entrepreneurs to the party in the 2004 and 2006 surveys. Most surprisingly, in the data from 2002 survey, holding membership to FIC actually reduces the odds of party members' entry into private business by 79.2 percent ($=1-e^{-1.570}$). Similarly, the odds of entrepreneurs of being co-opted by the party are reduced by 72.9 percent ($=1-e^{-1.305}$) if they are a member of FIC. Besides, being a member of PEA, SELA, or SIA organized by the local government does not explain the type of entrepreneurs in our data across the three surveys either.[16] From 1997 to 2006, the proportion of entrepreneurs who joined the Trade of Same Industry has increased from 5.8 percent to 61.0 percent. Meanwhile, the proportion of those joining FIC has also increased from 53.2 to 62.1 percent.[17] Given the overall increasing proportion of entrepreneurs' involvement in the organizational activities, and regional variances in the operation of the local business associations, being a member of a particular one would be helpful for business, but may not affect much on the entry to CPC as it was found in other surveys.[18]

Among the non-CPC member entrepreneurs in our survey data, in 2002, 15.9 percent stated their desire to join the party. The proportion increased to 16.7 percent in 2004 and further to 20.6 percent in 2006.[19] In addition, approximately 21.2 percent of the total non-CPC member entrepreneurs have already handed in the application in 2002, and the proportion has slightly dropped to 16.5 in 2004 and 15.1 in 2006.

In terms of current plans of highest priority, doing business and gaining social reputation of both their enterprises and themselves are inevitably the predominant initiatives of all the entrepreneurs across three surveys. Particularly, in 2002 survey, when entrepreneurs were asked to select three most crucial plans instead of rating them, 80 percent of them chose "business is business" (*zai shang yan shang*), and approximately 75 percent chose "establishing the social image and reputation," while the proportion did not exceed 25 percent for most of the other statements. However, co-opted entrepreneurs were slightly more concerned about developing the contacts with local party leaders among them (32 percent in 2002, 26 percent in 2004, and 30 percent in 2006). In 2004 and 2006, developing social harmony has also become one of the major concerns of entrepreneurs.[20] From the trends presented, we observe that the majority of entrepreneurs are mostly concerned with their social status. Not surprisingly, more co-opted entrepreneurs have shown their concerns on social harmony among entrepreneurs (10 percent higher than *xiahai* and non-CPC member entrepreneurs in 2004 and 2006 that rated it as "most important"), and they were more devoted to establishing contacts with local government and political organization.

Table 9.4 Proportion of private entrepreneurs who rank their economic, social, and political status higher than "average" and the correlation between the rankings (merged data)[a]

	Registration year of business	
	before 1993 (%)	1993 onward (%)
Self-ranking higher than "average"		
Economic	43.8	33.7
Social	51.9	38.0
Political	42.9	29.5
Total N	1,639	9,077
Correlation of the ranking		
Economic * Social	0.566	0.573
Total N	1,617	8,899
Economic * Political	0.428	0.428
Total N	1,611	8,851
Political * Social	0.626	0.628
Total N	1,612	8,852

Note: All correlations are significant at the 0.01 level (2-tailed)
[a]In 1997, 2000, and 2002 survey, the terms used in this "self-ranking comparing with other social groups" question particularly referred to: "income level," "social prestige," and "political participation." In 2004 and 2006 survey, they were replaced by more general terms: "economic status," "social status," and "political status." The entrepreneurs were asked to rank themselves from 1 (highest) to 10 (lowest) across all the surveys. Table 9.4 presents the proportions of entrepreneurs from the merged data who ranked themselves higher than average in these three aspects.

Entrepreneurs' perceptions on their economic, social, and political status from 2002 to 2006 are presented in table 9.4. Overall, the proportions of the entrepreneurs who rank their status higher than average have shown decreases, ranging from 14 (from 44 to 30 percent for the economic status) to 26 percent (from 57 to 31 percent for the social status). Moreover, although their self-ranking on the political status has been the lowest compared with their confidence in the economic influence and social image, the gap among them have diminished considerably across the surveys.

Summary and Conclusion

Beginning in the late 1970s with the contracting or leasing of public firms in villages and township, to the outright sale of government assets to private individuals or families especially in rural industry in the 1980s, most *xiahai* entrepreneurs emerged during this process of gradual corporatization of public firms under the control of local government. The massive integration of entrepreneurs into business organizations and the party, the CPC government has undertaken a long journey to deal with the pace of expanding private sector as well as adjusting to the newly acquired political status of private entrepreneurs. Until recently, a new generation of private enterprises, larger in scope and scale have been established entirely by individuals and families and contributed to the subsequent growth of entrepreneurs group (FIC 2007, 233–237). Although data from SPEEC prove that party members occupy less than one-third of the entire entrepreneurs group, they have become less divergent in personal, education, and occupational backgrounds, as well as their attitudes and concerns toward their own social status and policymaking of the government.

Conversely, along with the growing proportion of younger and better educated private entrepreneurs, the distinctions within the entire private entrepreneurs' class have become less obvious. They have been increasingly involved in the local business and trade organizations of various types, and recently in the formal and informal industry-specific groups were also formed at local level, which made the communication and cooperation of the enterprises more efficient and further enhanced the internal bonding of the entrepreneurs.[21]

White (1994; 1993) argued that the steps toward democratization could take place at least in three spheres. First, basic citizen and economic rights need to be guaranteed under the legal system. Second, there needs to be a redefinition of the position of the dominant party, and its relationship with other political institutions. Third, social democratization would involve an expansion of social space to allow for organization of group interests within civil society greater freedom of ideological and cultural expression and the establishment of more autonomous mass media. These factors can be seen taking in China today. However, the data obtained from the surveys show that private entrepreneurs have been continuously adjusting their status to a lower rank in society even though they are becoming more actively involved with their political duties and social activities.[22] Such actions are intended to maintain cooperative relationships with local officials for business dealings, as well as to establish a social reputation for themselves and their business. Consequently, they are continuously contributing to the completion of the rule of law regarding property rights and the reinforcement of more economic liberalization. Although there are indications of greater involvement of private entrepreneurs in policymaking procedures, it is mainly within the economic realms, thus reflecting the mutual interdependence between them and local government rather than a move toward advocating for democracy. Private entrepreneurs as a newly rising class have shown a growing integration in terms of background and political concerns, but they have not become a unified class. Meanwhile, they have retained or sought for closer contacts with local officials. Entrepreneurs are still at the initial stage of developing a class consciousness perhaps once beyond infancy, this group within society maybe better advocates for democratization.

My research is an exploration into the characteristics of the different types of private entrepreneurs and their growing political concerns. There are several constraints derived from the empirical analyses that I must acknowledge. First, since the empirical part of this chapter is based on the data taken from surveys that mainly focused on the development of private enterprises and entrepreneurs, the other social groups are not included in this project, which are supposed to be a reference groups for our empirical analyses. Therefore, my study is immediately restricted to the comparison of the attributes toward different political identities of private entrepreneurs at different time points. Second, since the SPEEC project has been implemented through a series of cross-sectional surveys, the sample was drawn from the pool of existing private enterprises at the time of inquiry. Thus, my study is further restricted to the entrepreneurs who successfully "survived" the intensive competition in market. Third, my study on entrepreneurs' is only a preliminary exploration of their political concerns and attitudes to policy concerns. The research at the present time should consider regional variations on the communication between private entrepreneurs and the local government at different administrative levels, which affects the type of industry and prominence of the local economic development plans. Along with the sequent pace of expansion, private entrepreneurs have been promoted from a marginalized and politically vague element to a much more defined new social status. To some extent, they have gradually developed an awareness of their social status and reputation, mainly reflected in their comparisons with other social groups outside the private sector, particularly with the more marginalized groups within society. However, some scholars have warned that there is no equivalent that represents the interests of the marginalized such as, peasants and laid-off workers (A. Chen 2003, F. Chen 2003). The slogan of "harmonious society" used by the CPC might outline an ideal society to pursue in the future; however, the reality is more challenging. How to handle employee-employer conflicts especially in the private sector, between the entrepreneurs and the underclass, between the new rich and poor, and how it will affect the cooperative relationship between the party and entrepreneurs in turn, these are questions that prevail. Given the pace of economic growth and escalating income inequality in what way Chinese political reform will evolve? All these issues will require further investigation as they are factors that will shape the future of China's development.

Notes

1. This can be reconfirmed from official data. From 1990 to 2000, the total number of registered private enterprises has increased from US $98,141 to $1,761,769; then tripled to $4,947,000 in 2006.

2. Data from 1990 to 1999 are from the *Year Book of Private Economy, 1986–1999*, which contains information regarding different types of privately owned businesses at the year-end of inquiry. However, the publication of the series stopped in 2000. Unfortunately, basic information on total value of product is missing from 1999. Given the amount of relevant reports and figures, I managed to find the total value product (TVP) for 2002 and 2005 in the reports released from Chinese Academy of Social Science (CASS) and other institutes. Above all, my point is to show the tremendous growth of private economy especially since 2000. In addition, the information regarding private enterprises before 1990 is excluded from the graphs because private enterprises and the self-employed were not distinguished in the year books before 1999.

3. When the first well-known self-employed vendor became a millionaire by selling the snack "Fool Watermelon Seeds" (*shazi guazi*), Deng insisted "wait and see" approach (Ao 2005, 2–4).

4. FIC was founded in 1953 as the repository for "national bourgeoisie." FIC is the umbrella organization for business associations across the country. By 2007, it claimed having around 21.4 million members.

5. That is, the CPC must always represent the requirements of the development of China's advanced productive forces, the orientation of the development of China's advanced culture, and the fundamental interests of the overwhelming majority of the people in China.

6. On July 1, 2001, at the celebration of eighteenth anniversary of CPC, Jiang again recommended that lifting of the ban of private entrepreneurs from joining the Party. In 2006, Hu Jintao, leader of the CPC advocated for a "harmonious society," further confirming the status of the private economy and granted opportunities to private entrepreneurs to join the government.

7. The surveys were conducted in 1997 and 1999 in eight counties (three in 1997, the other five in 1999): two each in Zhejiang, Shandong, Hebei, and Hunan. The advantages of these surveys are: first, the sites chosen were at different level of economic development and privatization. Second, it included both private entrepreneurs and government officials, and the comparison was done with detailed manners (Dickson 2003, 86–89).

8. But according to Dickson, the coefficients for these variables are less significant.

9. *Survey on Private Enterprises and Entrepreneurs in China* was sponsored by China United Front Association, China Work and Trade Union, and Private Economy Research Association, and it was conducted every two years from 1991 to 1997 and 2000 to 2006.

10. In China, primary industry refers to agriculture, agribusiness, fishing, forestry, and manufacturing industries that process raw materials. Secondary industry refers to mining, salt-making, manufacturing, energy, construction among others. Tertiary industry refers to service sectors such as transportation,

media, IT, wholesale and retail, hospitality, finance, real estate, environment and public service, education, health care among others.

11. From *Remin Ribao* May 24, 2005 and October 14, 2007, and the relevant documents released by CPC National Congress.

12. Logarithmic representation of income is used instead of its linear representation, because income has a diminishing marginal effect on behavior and attitudes. Log-income implies that the equal proportional change, rather than equal RMB changes, has equal effects on political identities.

13. Vocational high school or *zhongzhuan*, provides less general courses compared with normal high schools, but more concentrated skills training and internship mainly in the service sector, such as hospitality, tourism, IT, and telecommunications. When students graduate from a vocational high school, they can either enter vocational college or *dazhuan*, for further training, or start working. However, vocational high schools and vocational colleges cannot be distinguished in the 2002 survey, thus they are in the same category as high school. Therefore, the reader should bear in mind that the real proportion of respondents with higher educational qualification in 2002 should be slightly higher than what is shown in the table 9.2.

14. The negative coefficients for *xiahai* and coopted entrepreneurs are found across the three surveys, although it is only proven to be significant in 2006 for the former (e−0.204, p<0.001), and in both 2002 (e−0.169, p<0.05) and 2006 (e−0.153, p<0.05) for the latter.

15. Dickson also expected to find this in his survey data but failed. Instead, he found the positive impact of *getihu* status on the likelihood of cooptation.

16. In the 2002 survey, the respondents were asked about their affiliation with either Private Entrepreneurs Association or Self-employed Association (PE/SE Association) in one question; in 2004 and 2006 survey, the respondents were asked their affiliation with association of commerce or association of the same industry organized by FIC (FIC-COM/SIA), and association of same industry organized by local government (Government-SIA) separately. We chose to use the model that only includes the membership of FIC, since the effects of membership in FIC-COM/SIA may be largely duplicated with the effect of membership to FIC.

17. However, I did not include these figures in the main text due to the inconsistent definitions and various types of "Trade of Same Industry" defined across surveys.

18. More significant effects of business associations on the entry to different types of entrepreneurs may be found in region specific survey.

19. In the 2002 survey, one of the question asked respondents to choose three of eight statements best describing their plan at the time of inquiry. The statements include (1) Joining the Party; (2) Joining the NPC and Chinese People's Political Consultative Conference; (3) Developing contacts with local CPC leaders; (4) "Business is business"; (5) Establishing the social image and reputation of private entrepreneurs and enterprises; (6) Publicizing the business; (7) Competing for the leadership of the community; and (8) Others. In 2004 and 2006, option 7 was replaced by "Social harmony" and changed the three-out-of-eight selection into rating from 1 (most important) to 5 (least important). Therefore, the figure for 2002 is the proportion of nonparty members

who actually chose their top three plans, whilst the figures for 2004 and 2006 is the sum of the proportion of the respondents who rated the statements at the "important" level (at 1 or 2).

20. Fifty-eight percent of respondents in 2004 and 49 percent of respondents in 2006 rate "pursuing social harmony" as "important," which is among the top three plans in the surveys.

21. I visited around thirty private entrepreneurs in Yangzhou city, Jiangsu Province in the summer of 2006 and found some of them within the same industry would arrange a casual meeting once a week to exchange information, discuss, and negotiate business deals. Some also meet on a more regular basis even when not in the same industry, due to personal connections, such as through friends, relatives, or were former colleagues.

22. In the survey data from 2002 to 2006, more than 60 percent of total respondents contributed to the "*Guancai* program," which is an entrepreneurs-government and organizations-rural area collaborative poverty alleviation program initiated in 1995.

References

Ao, D. 2005. *Political participation of private entrepreneurs.* Guang Zhou: Zhong Shan University Press.

Bruun, O. 1995. Political hierarchy and private entrepreneurship in a Chinese neighborhood. In *The waning of the communist state: Economic origins of political decline in China and Hungary,* ed. A. G. Walder, 184–212. London: University of California Press.

Chen, A. 2002. Capitalist development, entrepreneurial class, and democratization in China. *Political Science Quarterly* 117 (3): 401–422.

———. 2003. Rising-class politics and its impact on China's path to democracy. *Democratization* 10 (2): 141–162.

Chen, F. 2003. Between the state and labour: The conflict of Chinese trade unions' double identity in market reform. *China Quarterly* 176: 1006–1028.

Chen, G. J. 2005. From elites circulation to elite reproduction: The changing mechanism for the formation of Chinese private entrepreneurs' class. *Study and Exploration* 1: 44–51.

Chen, G. J., J. Li, and H. Matlay. 2006. Who are the Chinese private entrepreneurs? A study of entrepreneurial attributes and business governance. *Journal of Small Business and Enterprise Development* 13: 148–160.

Dickson. B. J. 2003. *Red capitalists in China: The Party, private entrepreneurs, and prospects for political change.* Cambridge: Cambridge University Press.

———. 2007. Integrating wealth and power in China: The communist party's embrace of the private sector. *China Quarterly* 192: 827–854.

FIC. 2007. *The large-scale survey on private enterprises in China: 1993–2006.* All-China Federation of Industry and Commerce Press.

Holbig, H. 2002. The party and private entrepreneurs in the PRC. *Copenhagen Journal of Asian Studies* 16: 30–56.

Moore, B. Jr. 1966. *Social origins of dictatorship and democracy: Lord and peasant in the making of the modern world.* Boston: Beacon.

Nevitt, C. E. 1996. Private business association in China: Evidence of civil society or local state power? *China Journal* 36: 25–43.

Oi, J. C. and A. G. Walder. 1999. Property rights in the Chinese economy: Contours of process of change. In *Property rights and economic reform in China,* ed. J. C. Oi and A. G. Walder, 1–26. Stanford, CA: Stanford University Press.

Tsai, K. S. 2005. Capitalists without a class: Political diversity among private entrepreneurs in China. *Comparative Political Studies* 38: 1130–1160.

Tsui, A. S., Y. Bian, and L. Cheng. 2006. *China's domestic private firms: Multidisciplinary perspectives on management and performance.* New York: M. E. Shape, Inc.

Unger, J. 1996. "Bridges": Private business, the Chinese government, and the rise of new associations. *China Quarterly* 147: 795–819.

Unger, J. and A. Chan. 1999. Inheritors of the boom: Private enterprise and the role of local government in a rural south China township. *China Journal,* 42: 45–74.

Wank, D. L. 1995a. Bureaucratic patronage and private business: Changing networks of power in urban China. In *The waning of the communist state: Economic origins of political decline in China and Hungary,* ed. A. G. Walder, 153–183. London: University of California Press.

———. 1995b. Private business, bureaucracy, and political alliance in a Chinese city. *Australian Journal of Chinese Affairs* 33: 55–71.

———. 1996. The institutional process of market clientelism: Guanxi and private business in a south China city. *China Quarterly* 147: 820–838.

———. 2002. *Social connections in China: Institutions, culture, and the changing nature of guanxi.* Cambridge: Cambridge University Press.

White, D. G. 1993. *Riding the tiger: The politics of economic reform in post-Mao China.* London: Macmillan Press.

———. 1994. Democratization and economic reform in China. *Australian Journal of Chinese Affairs* 31: 73–92.

You, J. 1998. *China's enterprise reform: Changing state/society relations after Mao.* London: Routledge.

Chapter Ten

The Taiwanese Business Community: A Catalyst or Virus for Chinese Development?

Joshua Su-Ya Wu

In analyzing the Taiwanese business community (TBC) and its influence on China, much of the existing research has focused on economic effects, and how the TBC has facilitated Chinese economic modernization and development. However, a paradigm that only focuses on the economic realm cannot capture the full extent to which the TBC is emerging as a legitimate Chinese actor. As a growingly important actor in China, the TBC affects not only the economy, but also society and politics. In analyzing the transformative effects of the TBC's dynamic interactions with local Chinese communities, a more expansive substantive and empirical perspective should be adopted. Beyond a focus only on the interaction of economics, I argue that we need to also examine how such economic activity is changing social identities and norms. According to the social constructivist paradigm, an actor's norms, identities, and cultures are only expressed through interaction, and that it is through interaction that they are changed. This chapter demonstrates how the TBC is transforming the culture of state-business relations, changing social norms, and reinforcing the dichotomy of state and society roles in the Chinese identity.

To analyze the transformative effects of Taiwanese business engagement in local Chinese communities, traditional political economy analysis is insufficient. Instead, a constructivist methodology is necessary to analyze how state norms, cultures, and identities change. This analytical focus is based on the social constructivist axiom "that agents themselves are in process when they interact [as] their properties rather than just behaviors are at stake" (Wendt 1999, 366). Often used interchangeably, norms, cultures, and identities can be differentiated on a continuum of varying degrees of actor internalization. On the low end are norms, which are relatively easy to change, whereas identities, on the high end, are relatively difficult to change. Norms are behavioral constraints and rules, based on expectations that govern actions in given contexts. Cultures, which are more internalized than norms, are environments that determine the rules and constraints of behavior. Cultures constitute values that define the broader set of rules relevant in a particular context, while norms dictate when which rule is relevant in particular situations. The most internalized ideational structure, identity, refers to how actors view themselves, and how interests and values are prioritized. The objective of analyzing norms, cultures, and identities is, as Wendt summarizes, "to analyze the social construction of international politics [and] how processes of interaction produce and reproduce the social structures [which] shape actors' identities and interests and the significance of their material contexts" (1995, 81).

In this chapter, I juxtapose Chinese norms, identities, and cultures before and after interaction with the TBC. Empirical evidence, both qualitative and quantitative, demonstrates how the actions of the TBC impact the Chinese actors it interacts with. While the TBC also changes during interaction, the scope of this chapter is focused on Chinese actor transformation, and so, I take the identities, cultures, and norms of the TBC to be relatively stable. A key variable that determines what ideational structure, norms, and/or cultures are transformed is the level of Chinese-Taiwanese interaction. The transformation and redefinition of norms, cultures, and identities varies on the type of actor interactions, the frequency of these interactions, and the depth of engagement. While extended actor interactions allows for engagement of cultures and identities, limited interaction only significant affects normative behaviors.

Economic Interactions

On a national level, it is undeniable that the TBC has been one of the most important drivers of China's rapid economic modernization and transformation. A month after Deng Xiaoping officially launched his "Four Modernizations" campaign in December 1978, the Communist Party of China (CPC) Standing Committee released a memorandum entitled "Message to Compatriots in Taiwan" on January 1, 1979. This landmark statement urged the development of "trade between [Taiwan and China], each making up what the other lacks [to] benefit both parties without doing any harm to either" (Standing Committee of the Fifth National People's Congress 1979). Responding to a long-awaited opening up of China, Taiwanese firms creatively circumvented Taiwanese restrictions on cross-Strait commerce to be one of the first foreign investors in post-Mao China. The early focus on attracting overseas Chinese investors, especially from Taiwan, was instrumental in helping ease China into economic modernization. Indeed, it is clear that "from its beginning, the [Chinese] economic reform movement was dependent on the overseas Chinese community [as China] needed massive outside assistance—financial, managerial, and technical—in order to develop industries that could compete successfully" (Weidenbaum and Hughes 1996, 77).

Geographically, Taiwanese investment has focused in four provinces: Jiangsu, Fujian, and Guangdong, and the city of Shanghai. From 1991 to 2006, these four provinces received 80.52 percent of total approved Taiwanese investment to China (Mainland Affairs Council 2007). Today, Taiwanese firms are leading participants of China's most important export sectors. One such industry is the high-tech and computer electronics sector, where "the output value of Taiwan-invested computer hardware has accounted for 72 percent of the mainland's total output value of these goods" (Yu 2003, 136). Increasingly, Taiwanese high-tech firms are also helping to integrate Chinese engineering talent with the global engineering community. In Shanghai for example, the recently established Semiconductor Manufacturing International factory is heavily recruiting Chinese engineers, both trained overseas and in China, to work alongside Taiwanese and international scientists. As one scholar puts it, "the role of Taiwanese technology-oriented firms have [thus] been transformed from cheap-labor exploiter to high-tech broker and mediator" (Leng 2002, 234). Finally, as more capital-intensive Taiwanese firms move operations and production centers to China, they have also attracted secondary industries. Thus, as Taiwanese high-tech firms have settled around Shanghai, "financial- and property-sector investors [have followed] so that there are now several hundred thousand Taiwanese there, making a big contribution to the rapid improvement in the quality of [the] services [industry]" (Bowring 2003, 134).

Cultural Consequences of Economic Interaction

Given the tremendous volume of Taiwanese investment in China, an estimated US$100 billion since 1979, interactions between the TBC and Chinese government officials have been extensive. The TBC has been influential in transforming Chinese business culture, and consequently, the relationship between the state and the private sector. In the early days of Chinese economic modernization, private capitalists were demonized and not trusted. However, because of shared cultural affinities and ethnic backgrounds, Taiwanese investors reduced Chinese apprehension against capitalism. As Taiwanese investors demonstrated how capitalism could work in a Chinese context, they reduced misconceptions of capitalism.

More significantly, they helped form a business culture increasingly toward the promotion of exports, crucial for economic modernization. The majority of Taiwanese investment projects were export platforms, and so, laid a foundation for the modern Chinese economy that is becoming the manufacturing hub for the world.

Despite positive contributions, the overwhelming cultural consequence of Taiwanese local engagement has been to expose the dark side of capitalism to China. To maximize efficiency and profits, the TBC have engaged in corrupt practices, such as abuse and mistreatment of female laborers (Chan 2001), which may have had a significant demonstration effect for their Chinese counterparts. As Taiwan's economic modernization was marked by extensive government-business collusion, so too did Taiwanese investors sought to replicate those government-business relationships in China by manipulating norms of *guanxi* (connections or relationships). The case of the President Enterprises Company is an example of Taiwanese attempts to create these government-business links in China. A relative latecomer to China, the President's Group did not invest in China until 1992. However, there were significant behind the scenes dealing and machinations as the Group's investment was one of the largest ever Taiwanese investments in China. These assumptions were proved when later in the year, "a snapshot immortalized a meeting between Jiang Zemin, and Kao Ching-yuan, head of the [President] group" (Mengin 2002, 238). It is no coincidence that Jiang and Kao's personal interactions were crucial in securing the sizable investment by the President Company, and as such, evidence that Taiwanese investors are leading the way in using *guanxi* with government officials to secure favorable incentives and manipulate governmental regulation of businesses. A more recent example revolves around the construction of a Taiwanese semiconductor plant near Shanghai. Leading the Taiwanese effort is Winston Wang, son of Wang Yung-ching, Taiwan's petrochemical tycoon while his Chinese counterpart is the son of Jiang Zemin, Jiang Mianheng (Roberts 2000). Such interactions are blurring the line between business and political elites; it is also perpetuating a business culture where state-business collusion is not only profitable, but also the norm.

On the local level, the TBC may also be facilitating the adoption of a corrupt business culture. Without a strong regulatory and legal framework, Taiwanese businesspeople have thrived by manipulating *guanxi* in circumventing regulations. This and other types of rent-seeking require at least tacit cooperation from local officials, and so, it is logical to assume that local Chinese authorities are learning from firsthand experience how to creatively subvert national regulations. Although the TBC did not have an active role in creating a lax regulatory environment, they certainly benefited from it and perpetuated its existence. Although direct evidence of collusion, corruption, and bribery is hard to come by, circumstantial evidence provides strong indication that the TBC participated in such activities. For example, Taiwanese investors often use local accounting agencies to audit their operations. Since business is competitive, Chinese accounting agencies "have competed with each other to offer looser auditing criteria" (La Croix and Xu 1995, 139), thereby increasing the space where corrupt business practices can be conducted. The increased autonomy of local bureaucrats to make economic concessions and incentives has also increased opportunities for corruption. The more one moves down the bureaucratic hierarchy, the more officials are susceptible to rent-seeking activities (Tian 2006, 131), so the opportunities for corruption grow at the local level. One clear example is how, working with local government officials, Taiwanese businesses have circumvented national Chinese law by postponing the implementation of the Labor Law (Mengin 2002, 240).

The willingness of the TBC to use corrupt business practices for economic gain is further reflected in Chinese perceptions of Taiwanese businesspeople. In place of concrete evidence of corruption, these societal perceptions serve as strong circumstantial evidence of corrupt practices. Increasingly, there is a stereotype of the TBC resorting to "person-to-person relations [as] corruption. Likewise, when the Taiwanese investor puts forward a comparative advantage in understanding the Chinese market, he is often compared to the exploiter capitalist, even to a Mafioso" (Ibid, 250). In interviewing local Fujian residents, another scholar found that "while the Taiwanese were perceived to be rich, open, and industrious, they were also perceived prone to 'going through the back door' [as] sneaky, backdoor goers" (Hsiao 2003, 158). Therefore, given the preponderance of illicit business activities related to Taiwanese businesses in China, real or perceived, one can conclude that the TBC plays a role in fostering a business culture of collusion and corruption.

However, while influencing state-business relations, the TBC has had a limited effect on the business practices and norms of Chinese businesses. While the TBC maintains extensive relations with Chinese government officials, both nationally and locally, it has had limited interactions with local Chinese business. Taiwanese firms have not integrated into the local Chinese economic networks, leading to low spillover effects on the normative practices and operation of the Chinese economy. As increasing numbers of Taiwanese firms are relocating to China, they have conglomerated around existing Taiwanese businesses. This concentration is not only in terms of geographical location, but also on how Taiwanese businesses operate. As two scholars note,

> Compared to Taiwanese subsidiaries in Southeast Asia, those in China are more closely tied to the other Taiwanese subsidiaries, with fewer ties

to local multinationals. Take, for example, Dongguan township of the Guangdong province where more than 3000 Taiwanese subsidiaries are located...According to some major electronics firms interviewed...they were able to procure up to 90 percent of the materials and parts (in terms of the items purchased) from local suppliers, mostly Taiwanese subsidiaries [and not local Chinese firms]. (Chen and Ku 2004, 164)

There is limited economic integration between the TBC and local Chinese firms because Taiwanese firms rely on other Taiwanese firms for inputs, product support, and managerial expertise. This is an unintended consequence of dedicated Taiwanese investment zones, where Chinese incentives have attracted both upstream and downstream suppliers to relocate in China. Therefore, "the effort to attract Taiwanese investment has combined with the natural clustering tendency of Taiwanese firms, resulting in many cases where companies up and down the supply chain are all Taiwanese" (Tian 2006, 142). When preferred Taiwanese suppliers have not relocated to China, many Taiwanese firms import their inputs directly from Taiwan. Based on surveys and interviews, one scholar concludes that "most Taiwanese manufacturers in China imported more than 80% of the inputs" (Hsing 1998, 128). While this is changing, as local Chinese companies have become more competitive, for much of the history of the TBC in China, it is true that their "production networks in China are almost distinctively Taiwanese [as] there is more duplication of Taiwan's networks than embeddedness in local networks" (Chen and Ku 2004, 165).

Beyond industrial and production capital, in seeking out human capital, Taiwanese firms also seem to rely more on Taiwanese skilled labor than local Chinese labor. One of the greatest economic benefits of the TBC in China has been employment creation, as many Taiwanese firms relocate to China to take advantage of significantly lower labor costs. But beyond low-skill workers, the TBC has not extensively recruited or integrated local Chinese talent beyond a few instances of semiconductor production facilities. Especially in high-skilled industries, "top and middle-level managerial personnel are normally sent from their parent corporations in Taiwan and control all aspects and stages of their operations [such that] these enclave operations have little linkage effect or demonstration effects on the local economy" (Luo and Howe 1993, 759). This type of managerial sourcing from Taiwan is further evident that "expatriate managers and engineers typically travel back across the straits quarterly [as Taiwanese] firms continue to rely on their Taiwanese headquarters for strategic decision-making and direction" (Smart and Hsu 2004, 559). The lack of significant interactions between Chinese and Taiwanese mid- to high-level management mean that Chinese firms have few opportunities to learn and emulate Taiwanese normative business practices and operations. This lack of normative convergence, or normative emulation, is reflected in the coexistence of well-managed Taiwanese firms and ill-managed Chinese firms. Instead of integration, there is parallel coexistence, as the positive spillovers of Taiwanese business practices and norms are relatively nonexistent. Therefore, while "some manufacturing activities once based in Taiwan are now being performed by Taiwanese firms in Mainland China. What we cannot say, however, is that new Chinese competitors have truly emerged. Shifting geography has, at least to date, failed to bring a comparable shift in control and capabilities" (Steinfeld 2005, 277).

The Taiwanese Business Community as an Actor in Chinese Society

Beyond an economic actor, the TBC is also emerging as an important social actor in Chinese society. Whereas early Taiwanese investments were small and relatively short-termed, Taiwanese investments are increasingly complex, requiring more management, and are more long-termed. As a result, Taiwanese businesspeople are staying in China longer, or have moved outright to China. In longer-term stays, these Taiwanese businesspeople have also brought their families, leading to the emergence of Taiwanese communities where Taiwanese businesses are concentrated. As Chen Liangyu, the then-secretary of Shanghai's Communist Party commented, "Many Taiwan compatriots work, study, and live in Shanghai all the year round, and have merged into urban Shanghai to become 'new Shanghainese'" (Xinhua April 24, 2006). An estimated 2 million Taiwanese work in China, while a quarter million live on a more permanent basis in China. As more and more Taiwanese investors move their families to China, the TBC "has gradually become an integral part of mainland local development [and] have created a social network closely connected with the prosperity of China's coastal areas" (Leng 1998, 505). This transition is facilitated by shared cultural affinities between the Taiwanese and the local Chinese populations. Taiwanese businesspeople, in interacting with their Chinese counterparts, are keen to reiterate the "the common grounds which united their two enterprises: they were all Chinese, in feelings and in language there were no barriers between them, [and] they could understand each other immediately" (Hertz 1998, 35).

It can be problematic to typify all of the Taiwanese investors and Taiwanese businesses operating in China as a single unitary actor. As one scholar puts it,

There are many cleavages within [the TBC]. Usually, they are not set in a conflicting mode. But they imply very diversified interests. The main one opposes large-sized firms to small- and medium-sized ones: they invest on the Mainland at different times, for different motives, and with different location strategies. The latter are the great majority of those 30,000 Taiwanese firms that relocated their production on the Mainland around 1986...On the contrary, large-sized enterprises gained a foothold on the Chinese market from 1992 onward. (Mengin 2002, 237)

Having different motivations and interests, however, does not preclude the TBC from being considered a Chinese actor. All actors simultaneously have different interests and motivations, but there is usually one overarching interest that dominates. For the TBC, the dominant interest, whether when referring to a small firm or a large firm, is to make a profit. United by a common focus on their bottom line, the cleavages and differentiations among the TBC can be minimized to allow for its grouping as a single actor. In most instances, variations among the types of firms operated by the TBC do not lead to differentiated actions.

However, despite the increased relocation of the TBC to China, the TBC has not integrated into local Chinese communities. Given limited depth and extent of social interactions between expatriate Taiwanese and local Chinese, the TBC only has an affect on Chinese social norms, the lowest and least internalized ideational structure. Far from being socially integrated, the TBC has settled into Taiwanese enclave communities in China. While leading businesspeople may cultivate *guanxi* with local government officials, the rest of the TBC remains largely separate from local Chinese communities. In Dongguan, for example, the children of Taiwanese investors and local Chinese children are segregated as "investors from Taiwan pooled 7 million yuan and set up a school [where] teachers come from Taiwan and their teaching methods are the same as those in Taiwan, [enabling] Taiwan investors to do business without misgivings now that the education of their children is being properly taken care of" (Jiang 2004, 165). Some of this informal segregation may also be caused by local Chinese governments. In seeking to attract Taiwanese investment, Chinese localities are increasingly offering greater social services and infrastructures so that Taiwanese investors can do business in China with fewer worries about how their families will adjust to life in China. This often results in the formation of exclusive Taiwanese enclave communities in Chinese suburbia. Even in instances where the TBC seems to be engaging the local Chinese community, it seems motivated more by economic reasons. This type of motivated and purposeful engagement is most often in the form of financial flows and does not reflect significant people-to-people interaction. In Xiamen for example, to maintain good relations with local authorities, the TBC frequently gives "monetary donations to educational systems and welfare institutions...to express their kindness and concerns for local 'compatriots'" (La Croix and Xu 1995, 140). Yet this type of impersonal financial gift hardly qualifies as societal integration or social exchange.

Nonetheless, there are signs that such enclave seclusion may be changing. Increasingly, there is intermarriage between Taiwanese and Chinese communities and Taiwanese families are sending their children to local Chinese schools. More significantly, as second and third generation Taiwanese entrepreneurs are growing up in China, and are even attending Chinese business schools, "a close schoolmate-based networking web between China and Taiwan's young business bloods is being established" (Leng 2002, 234). It will take time for these social networks to develop and mature. In the meantime, it is clear that though settling in China in large numbers, the TBC has not significantly integrated into local Chinese communities.

Given the limited interaction and integration of the TBC into Chinese society and social circles, their impact on the local population is limited to normative practices, and not deeply held identities or cultures. Although it is conceivable that the massive influx of an expatriate Taiwanese community to China could be instrumental in transforming Chinese identities and perhaps even instill a democratic culture, such sentiments are overstated given that Taiwanese enclaves are relatively segregated from local Chinese communities. The most significant normative affect that the TBC has on Chinese society has been to model a more materialistic lifestyle with higher conspicuous spending and personal indulgence. The very fact that the Taiwanese community congregates together reinforces their distinctiveness from the local Chinese. As "more cultured" and "more cosmopolitan," the lifestyles and relative extravagance is not demonized, but admired. This type of social influence is evident in the growing popularity of Taiwanese pop culture among younger Chinese generations. For many Chinese, the Taiwanese lifestyle is desirable because it "includes a whole new world of fashion, hairstyles, music, leisure, and desire for self-improvement" (Weidenbaum and Hughes 1996, 76). The Taiwanese influence on popular culture and society is perhaps most evident in Fujian. In Fujian, as the TBC grows in number, local communities are increasingly inundated with "pop songs, fiction, MTV, videos, and commercials for Taiwanese consumer goods and products, [representing], to many residents of Fujian . . . a model of the modernized version of Fujian's future, as nearly 70 percent of the Taiwanese are of Fujian origin" (Hsiao 2003, 158). From TV shows to Chinese pop music to the popularity of top-of-the-line electronics, Chinese society is integrating elements of Taiwanese pop culture, with Chinese characteristics. Though it may be increasingly difficult to isolate changing social norms as primarily caused by the TBC, especially as

Table 10.1   Comparison of provincial CCI against the national average CCI (1997–2005)

	Shanghai	Jiangsu	Fujian	Guangdong
Coefficient	56.98667	−3.536668	39.87111	79.07889
(standard error)	(49.44858)	(39.9456)	(45.52609)	(47.19257)
P-value	0.266	0.931	0.394	0.113

there are growing numbers of foreign investors and foreign communities in China, it is undeniable that the TBC, as one of the first communities to settle in China, remains a much-admired community whose lifestyle is imitated by growing numbers of Chinese.

To test the degree that the TBC has influenced the societal lifestyle norms, the conspicuous purchases of Chinese urbanites in Shanghai, Jiangsu, Fujian, and Guangdong can be examined. By compiling a conspicuous consumption index (CCI) comprising of the household purchase of four goods, cell phones, computers, DVD players, and health fitness machines (as sourced from the *China Statistical Yearbook*, 1998–2006), the growth in consumption of these goods by urban residents in the four main provinces where the TBC is active can be juxtaposed against the national average. Using a comparison-of-means test, results show that though not statistically significant, the TBC does affect social expenditure norms.

In table 10.1, the positive coefficients, except for the case of Jiangsu, suggest that in the majority of the urban areas where the TBC is present, conspicuous consumption has been higher that the national average. The CCI of these four provinces are equal, if not higher, than the national average. Though not conclusive evidence, as the coefficients are not statistically significant, this evidence does suggest changing social norms in Chinese localities where the TBC has a significant presence. As more in-depth data becomes available, it will be possible to construct more robust tests, though it is probable that those tests will reinforce the correlations found here.

Political Effects of the Taiwanese Business Community

Though the TBC has clear economic and social effects on local Chinese communities, its political effects are more ambiguous. In China, there is a defined dichotomy between economic, social, and political affairs. Existing logics of social change and normative convergence, then, require a reexamination in the Chinese context, as the transformation of economic and social norms and cultures does not result in subsequent effects on political identity. Two conventional hypotheses are that the TBC is empowering local provincial governments by fostering local economic growth while exacerbating pressures on the provincial governments as it has widened the economic inequality between rural and urban communities. In the first hypotheses, the TBC empowers local government, while the second hypothesis argues that the TBC undermines local government power.

Some scholars have hypothesized that the economic growth engendered by the TBC is strengthening the local governments vis-à-vis other regional rivals and even the central government. An oft-cited argument is that the TBC has empowered local provincial governments, winning for them greater political power and influence. Since most TBC firms are primarily export platforms, they have "provided the local government with direct linkages to the world market, which in turn strengthened their bargaining position with the central government" (Hsing 1998, 144). In the process, they have transformed local provincial governments, empowering them to become increasingly autonomous "commercial republics where rules can be bent and regulations ignored and laws are used only for reference" (Tian 2006, 128). Thus, the TBC is perceived to be a facilitator in expanding local Chinese linkages with the global economy, political autonomy, and self-awareness of assertive authority.

If such a hypothesis is to be validated, then one should observe the growing domestic power of Shanghai, Jiangsu, Fujian, and Guangdong. A viable, though by no means perfect, measure of domestic power in China is the fiscal share of the national budget. By measuring the change in provincial expenditures relative to the national average, (using data sourced from the *China Statistical Yearbook*, 1996–2006), some conclusions can be drawn on whether the TBC has empowered local governments.

As the data in table 10.2 shows, provinces with significant investment by the TBC have not significantly gained domestic power, where power is measured as the fiscal share of national expenditures. Only the Fujian test is statistically significant, and it shows that a decline of its fiscal share of local expenditures of nearly 5 percent. If factoring for the standard errors, the change in provincial expenditures are almost equal to the national average. Therefore, claims that the TBC have increased local provincial power cannot be substantiated, as at best, its empowerment effects have been cancelled out by other confounding factors.

Table 10.2 Comparison of increase in provincial fiscal expenditures against the national average (1995–2005)

	Shanghai	Jiangsu	Fujian	Guangdong
Coefficient	2.366058	2.82023	−4.774426	−2.076214
(standard error)	(2.242543)	(1.928933)	(1.70126)	(2.073651)
P-value	0.305	0.161	0.012	0.330

Table 10.3 Comparison of change in EDI by province against the national average (1991–2005)

	Shanghai	Jiangsu	Fujian	Guangdong
Coefficient	7.327134	2.555	−.3752789	−.842809
(standard error)	(10.96726)	(5.194887)	(3.326309)	(2.742589)
P-value	0.510	0.627	0.911	0.761

A second plausible hypothesis is that the TBC has increased the socio-economic inequalities of urban and rural areas. Since most Taiwanese firms locate their production in urban areas, its tremendous success in facilitating economic growth is hypothesized to have widened the intra-province income disparities. In the tradition that emphasizes the gap between winners and losers of economic development, it is argued that the TBC has perpetuated socioeconomic dualism where urban "families benefiting from Taiwanese investment have greatly improved their welfare [while] some outside this group have clearly lost" (Luo and Howe 1993, 760). If this is true, then the TBC would be a detriment to local authorities as it would increase social tensions and urban-rural disparities, potentially exacerbating local Chinese demands for political reform. The test for the empirical saliency of this hypothesis is to juxtapose the increase of the expenditures disparity index (EDI), which is defined as the ratio of the difference in intra-province urban and rural expenditures divided by rural expenditures (as reported in the *China Statistical Yearbook*, 1992–2006); a higher EDI implies greater income disparity.

As the table 10.3 shows, in each of the four provinces where Taiwanese investment has been focused, the increase in income disparities between urban and rural households, as measured by the EDI, is statistically equivalent to the national average. None of the four coefficients are statistically significant, and the standard error terms do not reveal a clear relationship, either higher than or lower than the national average, which means that provincial changes in the EDI are equivalent to the national average. Therefore, one can conclude that the TBC has not significantly increased intra-province income disparity.

The Taiwanese Business Community and Chinese Identity

Both hypotheses, either arguing that the TBC has strengthened or weakened local governmental authority, are not empirically salient. Although there are other factors that the statistical analysis did not control for, due to the lack of comprehensive Chinese data, the empirical evidence shows that both contradictory hypotheses are unfounded. This reflects a fundamental flaw in existing literature and political economy methodology that focuses only on economic measures of power. Instead, as suggested by the constructivist research agenda, the focus should be on the ideational structures that give meaning to determinants of economic power such as fiscal and household expenditures. As Wendt remarks, "The claim is not that ideas are more important than power and interests, or that they are autonomous from power or interest... The claim is rather that power and interest have the effects they do in virtue of the ideas that make them up" (1999, 135). In the Chinese context, the focus should be on how the TBC affects the constitutive determinants of power, and how it reinforces or undermines Chinese identity, which defines how power is used and understood. Though there are many Chinese identities, one that is salient in this context is the distinct dichotomy between politics and economics. On the macro level, it is manifested in the state's ability to pursue economic reform and modernization at the expense of political liberalization. Since identity is the ideational structure that priorities interests and values, such a Chinese identity has led to a "sequencing of reforms in China [where] liberalization of FDI vis-à-vis other reforms, has led to a delay in political change by enhancing the capacity of the CPC to implement difficult reforms while maintaining a political monopoly" (Gallagher 2005, 28). On a microlevel, the Chinese identity shapes actors such that their economic and political interests are clearly demarcated, to the point that economic interests almost always trump political interests.

Given that the Chinese identity is predicated on this dichotomy between economic concerns and political concerns, the manner and engagement, or the lack thereof, of the TBC in local communities reinforce this status quo identity. Though the TBC has the capacity to have political influence, it has chosen not to exercise it. In the limited interactions that Taiwanese businesspeople have had with their Chinese counterparts, the relationship and dialogue has focused strictly on business. The TBC has kept an extremely low political profile, guided by the belief that the best strategy is to "protect one's own business with private efforts and interpersonal connections and without engaging in any collective action" (Hsiao 2003, 150). There is also virtually nonexistent interaction with local Chinese grassroots advocacy or activism groups. The TBC perceives that any form of activism would be interpreted as political activity, potentially upsetting the *laissez-faire* attitude that local officials afford to the TBC. Even in Fujian, where local participation might not be inconceivable because many Taiwanese investors have Fujian ancestry, there seems to be no willingness of the TBC to be engaged or even associated with local Chinese grassroots organizations. Indeed, the TBC are "hesitant in expressing views on Fujian's social reform issues [and] there is no clear evidence that [Taiwanese] capital in

Fujian has ever made a conscious attempt to develop direct or close contact with Fujian's various intellectuals, professionals, and other intermediary institutions" (Hsiao 2003, 153).

The Taiwanese taboo of political participation extends to their shying away from active participation in governmental institutions established to provide a forum to facilitate constructive engagement with local authorities. Since 1990, local provincial and city governments have established so-called Taiwanese business associations. As membership can be a means by which Taiwanese businesspeople gain access to local officials and officials from the Taiwan Affairs Office to solve problems, these business associations seem relatively apolitical. However, even here, the TBC has maintained only minimal participation. A survey conducted by a private consulting firm in Taipei found that based on their interviews, "78 percent of Taiwanese investors find 'their own way' to solve problems in China, 13 percent contact Chinese officials, and only 6 percent solve problems through the Taiwanese business associations" (Leng 1996, 115). The fact that less than one in five Taiwanese investors go to local authorities to resolve problems reflects a low desire for direct political participation by the TBC. It seems that there is a Taiwanese desire to maintain relationships with Chinese politicians only to the extent necessary to reduce administrative red tape and ensure that they do not intervene in business operations. Again, in Fujian, where it would not be unexpected if the TBC shows some willingness to become active locally, the TBC has "not yet become involved in any substantial way in the organization and the activities of the horizontal enterprise associations which held organizations with the local state [as] the Taiwanese businessmen in Fujian have been more or less acting as 'outsiders' to many of the local chambers of commerce" (Hsiao 2003, 150).

The TBC's demonstration effect of nonparticipation in politics reinforces the dominant Chinese identity predicated on a defined dichotomy between politics and economics. Contrary to neoliberal expectations, the expansion of economic ties in China has not led to political consolidation as Chinese exposure to international markets and foreign influences has not increased desires for political liberalization. The TBC, almost religiously maintaining that they are not a political actor, sets a precedent that potentially hinders Chinese political liberalization. Just as the TBC's interactions with local Chinese communities led to changes in the business culture and lifestyle norms, so the TBC's self-imposed exclusion from the political realm signals to Chinese localities that economic prosperity comes when economic priorities are given precedence over political concerns. Though the TBC may have private misgivings about Chinese politics, behavior and attitudes perceivable to Chinese communities are marked by political apathy. More significantly, their unwillingness to use their economic influence and potential capacity to effectuate political reform dashes hope that the TBC can emerge as a friendly catalyst for political liberalization. If one takes the position that political liberalization is essential for China's development, then the TBC represents a great missed opportunity, as it would represent the most unimposing Chinese actor capable of initiating reform from within. Therefore, given the growingly influence and level to which the TBC is admired by local Chinese, their silence in political matters speaks volumes in affirming the status quo sociopolitical landscape in China.

Conclusion

In analyzing the role of the TBC in China, many paradoxes emerge. While sharing great cultural affinities with the local Chinese population, the TBC is not thoroughly integrated, choosing instead to aggregate and live together in enclave communities. Also, while reducing fears of capitalism, the TBC may have also exposed local Chinese government officials and entrepreneurs how profit maximization drives companies toward collusion and corruption. Nonetheless, it is undeniable that the TBC is more than merely an economic actor in China, but a social and political actor whose actions are transforming Chinese norms, cultures, and identities. A close examination of TBC interactions with local Chinese communities reveal that the TBC is fostering a culture of state-business collusion, introducing a new normative lifestyle, and reinforcing the status quo Chinese identity. However, its effects on state-society relations in China are less clear. Although its actions perpetuate the political status quo, the social and cultural consequences of its continued economic engagement may plant the seeds for a new popular discontent that could threaten the state's authority. It is not unforeseeable for the close state-business cooperation engendered by the Taiwanese model to descend into unacceptable levels of corruption and collusion. Similarly, their fostering of a new individualistic and more materialistic lifestyle may threaten Chinese social harmony as the wealth generated by a few may increase social tensions over socioeconomic inequalities. Only further analysis and study will be able to answer these questions. For now, the economic benefits brought by the TBC trump any negative social or cultural side effects, and the TBC is welcomed as an implicit ally of the state. The TBC, at least in the foreseeable future, should remain an actor whose innovative and financial capital will be welcomed with open arms. Prediction, especially about the future, is difficult; what is relatively certain, amid an ever changing Chinese landscape marked by uncertainty, is that the TBC is an increasingly important Chinese actor that has significant economic, social, and political influences in China's domestic landscape.

References

Bowring, P. 2003. China 2002: The geopolitical context. In *China: Enabling a new era of changes,* ed. P. C. M. Mar and F. J. Richter, 119–144. Singapore: John Wiley and Sons.

Chan, A. 2001. *China workers under assault: The exploitation of labor in a globalizing economy.* Armonk: M. E. Sharpe.

Chen, T. J. and Y. H. Ku. 2004. Networking strategies of Taiwanese firms in Southeast Asia and China. In *Chinese Enterprise, Transnationalism, and Identity,* ed. E. T. Gomez and H. H. M. Hsiao, 151–171. New York: Routledge.

Gallagher, M. E. 2005. *Contagious capitalism: Globalization and the politics of labor in China.* Princeton, NJ: Princeton University Press.

Hertz, E. 1998. *The trading crowd: An ethnography of the Shanghai stock market.* New York: Cambridge University Press.

Hsiao, H. H. M. 2003. Social transformations, civil society, and Taiwanese business in Fujian. In *China's Developmental Miracle: Origins, Transformations, and Challenges,* ed. A. Y. So, 136–160. Armonk: M.E. Sharpe.

Hsing, Y. T. 1998. *Making capitalism in China: The Taiwan connection.* New York: Oxford University Press.

Jiang, X. J. 2004. *FDI in China: Contributing to growth, restructuring and competitiveness.* New York: Nova Science Publishing.

La Croix, S. and Y. B. Xu. 1995. Political uncertainty and Taiwan's investment in Xiamen's Special Economic Zone. In *Emerging Patterns of East Asian Investment in China From Korea, Taiwan, and Hong Kong,* ed. S. J. La Croix, M. Plummer, and K. Lee, 123–141. Armonk: M. E. Sharpe.

Leng, T. K. 1996. *The Taiwan-China connection: Democracy and development across the Taiwan Strait.* Boulder, CO: Westview Press.

———. 1998. Dynamics of Taiwan-Mainland China economic relations: The role of private firms. *Asian Survey* 38: 494–509.

———. 2002. Economic globalization and IT talent flows across the Taiwan Strait: The Taipei/Shanghai/ Silicon Valley Triangle. *Asian Survey* 42: 230–250.

Luo, Q. and C. Howe. 1993. Direct investment and economic integration in the Asia Pacific: The case of Taiwanese investment in Xiamen. *China Quarterly* 136: 746–769.

Mainland Affairs Council. 2007. *Cross-Strait Economic Statistics Monthly No.175.*

Mengin, F. 2002. Taiwanese politics and the Chinese market: Business's part in the formation of a state, or the border as a stake of negotiations. In *Politics in China: Moving Frontiers,* ed. F. Mengin and J. L. Rocca, 232–257. New York: Palgrave Macmillan.

Roberts, D. 2000. Uneasy collaborators. *Business Week* Issue 3694, August 14. Available at http://www.businessweek.com/2000/00_33/b3694012.htm.

Smart, A. and J. Y. Hsu. 2004. The Chinese diaspora, foreign investment and economic development in China. *Review of International Affairs* 3: 544–566.

Standing Committee of the Fifth National People's Congress. 1979. "Message to Compatriots in Taiwan." January 1.

Steinfeld, E. S. 2005. Cross Strait integration and industrial catch-up: How vulnerable is the Taiwan miracle to an ascending mainland. In *Global Taiwan: Building competitive strengths in a new international economy,* ed. S. Berger and R. Lester, 228–280. Armonk: M. E. Sharpe.

Tian, J. Q. 2006. *Government, business, and the politics of interdependence and conflict across the Taiwan Strait.* New York: Palgrave Macmillan.

Weidenbaum, M. and S. Hughes. 1996. *The bamboo network: How expatriate Chinese entrepreneurs are creating a new Economic superpower in Asia.* New York: Martin Kessler Books.

Wendt, A. 1995. Constructing international politics. *International Security* 20: 71–81.

———. 1999. *Social theory of international politics.* New York: Cambridge University Press.

Xinhua. 2006. Chen Liangyu meets Lien Chan and his party. April 24.

Yu, X. T. 2003. Outlook for economic relations between the Chinese mainland and Taiwan after joining the World Trade Organization. In *Breaking the China-Taiwan impasse,* ed. D. S. Zagoria, 135–142. Westport, CT: Praeger.

CHAPTER ELEVEN

CHINA'S CYBER FORUMS AND THEIR INFLUENCE ON FOREIGN POLICYMAKING

Junhao Hong

The development of the Internet in China has occurred at a geometric rate during the last fifteen years. Cyber forums in particular have created a profound influence on the many aspects of China's societal structure and political system, an area that has long inhibited the participation of ordinary people. Now, an increasing number of people are using the Internet to express their views on economic, political, and social issues in the attempt to generate changes, despite the fact that public participation in online forums is unbalanced across the nation due to various limitations (Hong and Huang 2005).

This chapter examines how cyber forums in China have become a new social force and have affected the Chinese authorities' handling of foreign relations. The main purpose of this chapter is to explore the following issues: (1) the main trends and characteristics of China's cyber forums on foreign relations and international issues; (2) the attitudes of the Communist Party of China (CPC) and the Chinese government toward online public opinions and its influence toward the authorities' handling of foreign relations; and (3) the factors that have contributed to the formation of this new social force and its implications.

A variety of methods have been deployed to study the influence of online public opinions on policymaking (Yin 1994). This research uses three indicators as reflections of the influence of online opinions on China's foreign relations. The first concerns the change in the authorities' attitude toward public online discussions of China's foreign relations and international issues—an attitude that has shifted from prohibition of discussion to a willingness to listen. The second indicator is the change in the decision-making process. In particular, the government has to an extent started treating online forums as a public voice in the policymaking process. The third looks at the actual change in foreign relations due to public pressure. The use of these three indicators can, to a certain degree, collectively demonstrate the influence of online public opinions on the authorities' handling of foreign relations.

This study is based on the primary research materials and data gathered through an extensive examination of hundreds of Chinese language Web sites, chat rooms, and bulletin board sites (BBSs). Content related to foreign relations and international issues from selected sample Web sites, cyber forums, and online public opinions are analyzed. In addition, some of the research materials and data used in this study were obtained through recent field research in China and interviews with relevant Chinese government officials, scholars, and researchers, Web site and online forum producers, and Internet café owners.

This chapter consists of three parts. The first part reviews the rapid development of the Internet in China, especially the emergence of the cyber public forums, including BBSs, news discussion groups, and personal blogs. The second part discusses the trends and characteristics of online public opinions on China's foreign relations and international issues and the interactions between public and foreign-relations-oriented cyber opinions. Finally, the third part analyzes the implications, problems, and prospects of China's online public opinions as a new social force and its influence on foreign relations and international issues.

Rapid Growth of the Internet and the Explosive Emergence of Cyber Forums

China established its first domestic Internet e-mail node in September 1987. Similar to other countries across the world, the Internet has been at the forefront of the information revolution in China, but compared to many countries, the Internet in China in the last two decades has had the highest growth in the world. According to the most recent figures on China's Internet released by the Chinese Academy of Social Sciences in *The 21st Statistical Survey Report on the Internet Development in China*, the total number of Internet users in mainland China has reached 210 million, second highest in the world after the United States with 215 million users, as of December 2007. Also at this time, the number of computers that can access the Internet reached 78 million, and the number of Web sites at 1.5 million (China Internet Network Information Center 2008). Compared to the figures of each of the three categories in 1997 when China began developing the Internet, in ten years Internet users, online computers, and Web sites have increased by 339 times, 262 times, and 1,001 times, respectively.

Considering China's social and political contexts where the state controls the media, ideology, and public opinions (see Chu 1986 and 1994; Hong 1998, 2005a, and 2005b; Lee 1990, 1994, and 2003; Zhao 1998), probably the most significant part of Internet development in the country is the emergence of cyber forums that provide the public with a variety of ways for online expression. Functions of cyber forums include online chatting, instant messaging, BBSs, and other online discussion forms, such as blogs, Wikis, and SMSs. The three most popular online activities in China are reading news, online chatting/cyber forum discussion, and downloading information. Together they constitute more than 60 percent of total online activities. Among them, online chatting is the sixth most frequently used online activity by 40.2 percent of total Internet users, and BBS posting is the seventh by 21.3 percent of total users (State Information Office of China 2006). These figures indicate that online discussion and opinion-exchange are becoming a major online activity of Internet users in China.

The cyber forums are effective and functional especially for public participation or civic involvement in sociopolitical activities, as postings and news text on the forums can be read by any visitor. Moreover, the information posted on cyber forums can be instantly shared with any online community regardless of national borders. Furthermore, online information and comments can elicit further responses, promote discussions, and encourage exchanges of various kinds of views from the public, thus putting public participation on a much larger scale, beyond the capacity of any other mediums. More importantly, cyber forums can pose as platforms for organizing off-line campaigns and social movements (Chase and Mulvenon 2004). In addition to the above-mentioned functions, cyber forums in China have an even more significant and unique function: in a society that has a tightly controlled, closed social and political system, the availability of cyber forums inevitably becomes a new social force that yields an unprecedented impact on the country's social structure and political system.

The growth of cyber forums can be considered as phenomenal despite the brevity of its existence. For instance, while there were very few cyber forums within the Chinese domain before 2003, by the end of 2003 in mainland China there were 2,536 Chinese language chat room Web sites and 12,592 cyber BBS columns, favorite places for "netizens" to speak their minds and engage in discussions of public affairs (China Education and Research Center 2003). Online individuals are usually involved in cyber forum discussions by subject, though many are often multisubject participants.

In the last few years, the government has taken great effort to promote Internet development, despite the political risks of the new technology, such as the difficulty of information control. The chief motivation of Chinese authorities' encouragement is for economic and technological development. As noted by Zhao Qizheng, former minister of the Chinese State Council's Information Office, "We (the government) missed a lot of the industrial revolution, but we do not want to miss the information revolution. We are determined not to be left behind this time" (Ming 2007). Consequently, China's information technology sector has grown at a rate faster than any other industry, and it is three times as fast as the country's overall economic growth rate (Hachigian 2001).

Nonetheless, the other motivating factor is political. The party and the government have realized that providing the public with some freedom to surf the Web and to chat on the Internet may give citizens fewer incentives to challenge the ruling authorities. The party and the government leaders thus appear to be willing to tolerate a certain amount of frankness in online public opinions that would be stamped out in the traditional media. The *People's Daily*, the most important state-owned national newspaper and the political organ and mouthpiece of the CPC, runs a very poplar online BBS, *Strong Nation Forum*, offering a cyber platform for the public to vent their emotions and express their voices on social and political issues. Many of the issues are politically sensitive and would have been forbidden in the past. The *Strong Nation Forum*, for instance, has more than 280,000 registered users and more than 12,000 postings per day (Zhu 2005). Although China is moving toward a more open society, the party and government either willingly or unwillingly wants to know how the public react to certain issues. As a result, the ease of collecting public opinions and views via the Internet has prompted the government's commitment to the e-government plan. Such plan intends to use advanced information technologies to improve communications and relations between the government and its citizens. One goal of the e-government project is to establish the online opinion collection system, through which the party and government can draw public views from the Internet effectively and efficiently.

According to a survey of ten large Chinese cities conducted in 2003, 63.95 percent of Internet users surveyed go to online forums regularly. Although hobbies is the most popular topic of the Web forums, political affairs ranks a very close second, followed by academic issues in third (China Internet Network Information Center 2003). Despite the fact that most chat rooms and other cyber forums are mainly used to discuss people's daily life, many of the discussions do contain outbursts of frustration with the political system, party and government policies, and other contentious matters. For example, regarding China's foreign relations and international issues, including incidents such as the U.S. bombing of the

Chinese Embassy in Yugoslavia in 1999, the collision of a U.S. spy plane with a Chinese fighter plane in 2001, the assault of Chinese businesswoman Zhao Yan by a U.S. immigration officer in 2004, or the Sino-Japanese row over the Diaoyu Islands, have all led to heated discussions and fierce criticisms in online chat rooms and other types of cyber forums.

During the last several years, the development of cyber forums in China has been accompanied by the proliferation of the online community. The cyber community, or virtual community, is composed of social aggregations that emerge from the Internet when enough people carry online discussions long enough to form webs of personal relationships in cyberspace (Rheingold 2000). To a certain degree, this is the basis and precondition for the formation of a public sphere. In today's China, these "virtual communities" or "public spheres," are becoming a new burgeoning citizen-based social force, which has started to gradually affect many aspects of society, ranging from people's behaviors, social structure to the political system and ruling ideology.

Since the mid-1990s, the public has been using the Internet to express their views and criticisms on various social and political issues despite the many restrictions and tight controls. Cyber forums are now being used by millions of individuals. Although the users are always monitored closely by the authorities, the cyber forums can at least serve as an outlet for popular discontent and criticism. Whether it is on domestic issues or on foreign relations and international issues, the influence of the online community's involvement in public and political affairs can no longer be ignored by authorities. For instance, the public's online discussions of the incident of Sun Zhigang, who was arrested for not carrying his city resident certificate and then beaten to death by the police during his custody in 2003, quickly led to the government's elimination of the city resident certificates across the nation due to the enormous pressure from online public opinions. Just two hours after Sun Zhigang's incident was placed online, 4,000 comments were posted expressing outrage and anger. Almost immediately, it became a national political topic among almost all cyber forums, including e-mail groups, commercial Web sites, personal blogs, and even government-run official Web sites. The government reacted by executing a prison officer responsible for Sun Zhigang's death and announced the abolition of city resident certificates, which were required for hundreds of millions of migrant peasants working in cities. For the first time in Chinese history, public opinions formed a new societal force that yielded a strong and enormous impact on the authorities' decision-making process.

Cyber forums have thus begun to play a noticeable role in China's political reform and social transformation. While most online discussions have been dealing with general public policies, corruption and power abuse of party/government officials, and social justice issues, a noticeable new area has been focused on China's foreign relations and international issues. Especially since 2003, a growing number of cyber forums focusing on foreign relations and international issues have emerged. Although not every online event has resulted in a significant change in party and government policies as the Sun Zhigang case, together online public opinions have begun to form a new type of public pressure and influence. The public's unprecedented political participation, so far still confined mostly through cyberspace is nevertheless an impressive phenomenon in the country's history.

Trends and Characteristics of
Foreign-Relations-Oriented Online Public Opinions

In the last several years, there have been an increasing number of Chinese cyber groups focusing on foreign relations and international issues, especially on China's relations with the West or nations that are considered or perceived by the Chinese public as the country's historical or present enemies.

Several trends of China's online public opinions on foreign relations and international issues have been displayed. The first trend is that the public's online opinions have increasingly received government attention and sometimes have been taken into consideration in foreign policy making. Partly to be "politically correct," the authorities have begun to listen to the public one of the regular procedures of their work, regardless of how much is actually absorbed from public opinions. To a certain extent, cyber forums are factors affecting the government's decision-making procedure, and handling of foreign relations. For example, a number of state-owned official Web sites have established cyber forums that are exclusively used for discussions on foreign relations and international issues, such as the Development Forum and Reunification Forum on the Xinhua News Agency Web site, or the China Diplomacy Forum on the Ministry of Foreign Affairs Web site. Apart from these cyber forums, many other online BBSs, chat rooms, and Web site voting systems have also become channels for the authorities to collect public opinions. The party and government have started using cyber forums to gauge public opinions on a broad range of foreign relations and international issues.

In early April 2003, the Ministry of Foreign Affairs posted a notice on its Web site inviting online interactions between viewers at the China Diplomacy Forum, the official Web site of Ministry of Foreign Affairs and the Directors of the Asia-Africa Department and International

Department of China's Foreign Affairs Ministry. On April 8 from 3:00 p.m. to 4:30 p.m., Internet users and government officials exchanged views and opinions regarding the situation in Iraq and China's relevant foreign policies (Fan 2005). Later in the same year, on December 23, China's then Foreign Minister Li Zhaoxing participated in a scheduled online chat session on the Xinhua News Agency's Web site. Li chatted online with the public, leading the country's mass media to declare it as an effective new channel for Chinese leaders to learn the public's views and was regarded as a step forward in China's political democracy. In this two-hour-long online interaction, the then foreign minister was bombarded with 2,000 queries from more than 40,000 participants. The content ranged from the overall foreign policy, Sino-U.S. and Sino-Japanese relations, to China's role in the reconstruction of Iraq (Ibid 2005). Without cyber forums, it would have been impossible for such interactions to occur between individuals and the government. The government's interactive online chatting with the public demonstrates that the authorities have begun to recognize the role of the public opinion on social and political activities.

The second trend of China's online public opinions on foreign relations and international issues is that Sino-U.S. and Sino-Japanese relations have been the most discussed topics on the foreign-relations-oriented cyber forums, and most of these online opinions contain a very strong anti-U.S. or anti-Japan sentiment.

In the aftermath of the September 11, 2001, Internet users throughout China flooded BBSs and chat rooms with postings. The majority of online postings viewed the incident as a result of U.S. "imperialistic hegemony." In the week following the 9/11 attack, the Strong Country Forum hosted as many as 25,000 visitors a day simultaneously during its peak time, but many of the postings overtly praised the terrorist attack. Some wrote that the 9/11 event is the "just desserts" to the Americans for being a hegemonic power that bombed the Chinese Embassy in Belgrade in 1999 and downed a Chinese fighter plane in the South China Sea in 2001 (Guo 2005). These online opinions posed a tough situation for China's leaders to handle the country's official reactions toward the attack and its relations with the United States. As a result, not only was China's official condemnation of the terrorist attack announced later than many other nations, but its reactions toward the attack were milder than many others, including Arabic and Muslin countries. Realizing that supportive online opinions about the terrorist attack might have affected Sino-U.S. relations and caused a negative image of China in the world, the government had to quickly censor extreme anti-U.S. postings in the cyber forums.

A more recent example is the public online reactions to the case of Zhao Yan, a Chinese businesswoman. On July 22, 2004, Zhao Yan was seriously assaulted by a U.S. immigration officer during her trip to Niagara Falls in the United States. This incident was reported only as a local news story in the U.S. media, but the incident elicited very strong and emotional concern from the Chinese public and authorities. Zhao Yan's case immediately became a new hot spot in Sino-U.S. relations for the Chinese government and the Chinese people as well (Liu 2005). The Chinese public called this incident another representation of the American imperialistic hegemony, and a most serious violation of human rights and thus formed a strong online anti-U.S. sentiment. Although there were discrepancies regarding the incident in cyber space, the overwhelming majority of online comments vented anger toward the United States, and some explicitly stated that "the United States is the world's real terrorist" (Liu 2005). On September 8, 2005, the same day after Robert Rhodes III, the U.S. Homeland Security official who was charged with severely beating Zhao Yan, was found not guilty in the U.S. Federal Court, the news was immediately posted on thousands of Chinese Web sites, shocking and upsetting the nation. Within 24 hours, more than 11,000 people went online to vent their outrage, criticisms, and protests about the acquittal. Almost all of the postings strongly condemned the verdict, believing it displayed American discrimination toward people of other countries. There was widespread perception both online and offline in China that the judgment was unfair, the punishment did not fit the crime, and for whatever reasons the wheels of justice did not move correctly (Burton 2005).

Many of the online public opinions on foreign relations and international issues have also focused on the change in China's relations with Japan. In the last several years, friction concerning the long-standing Sino-Japanese dispute over the Diaoyu Islands has become one of the hottest political issues on China's cyber forums. According to China, the Diaoyu Island and its affiliated islands lying in the East China Sea (Senkaku Islands for the Japanese) have long been the inherent territory of China, which has historically viewed the Diaoyu Islands as part of its Taiwan province. Yet, in recent years disputes over the sovereignty of the Diaoyu Islands have occurred from time to time between Japan and China, which stimulated an outpouring of very strong anti-Japan and nationalistic sentiment in China motivating a series of unofficial public "Diaoyu Islands Defense Actions" among many Chinese netizens. On March 24, 2004, a group of fifteen people from China and Hong Kong reached the Diaoyu Islands by a fishing boat, hanging a vast Chinese flag and proclaiming that the islands belonged to China. Japanese police detained seven Chinese landing activists and the event triggered a large scale online protest across China. This online action was aimed at supporting the Chinese government's claim of indisputable sovereignty over the Diaoyu Islands.

Meanwhile, the Chinese government kept the official media away from discussions and comments in an attempt to silence the public's growing anti-Japanese sentiment. Zhao Qizheng, former minister of the State Council's Information Office, openly admitted Chinese authorities' intervention in news reporting on Japan and indicated that the government had no hesitations to improve ties with Japan (*The Strait Times* October 4, 2004). The Chinese government is committed to improving its relations with Japan as it is a major trading partner. Chinese authorities therefore insisted that the dispute between China and Japan should be resolved through government negotiations. As a result, on April 3, 2004, the then Chinese Foreign Minister Li Zhaoxing engaged in dialogue with his Japanese counterpart Yoriko Kawaguchi, who was on her two-day visit to China to improve bilateral relations.

Despite these attempts, China's online chat rooms and BBSs were still full of fierce anti-Japanese sentiments. Such online opinions included: (1) fully supporting the Diaoyu Islands defense action by saluting those activists as "national heroes" and "the pride of the nation" and to organize new actions to protest against Japan; (2) calling for a boycott of Japanese products, especially cars and Japanese investment; and (3) demanding military action against Japan. The anti-Japanese sentiment is especially evident in the following online postings: "It is humiliating to use Japanese products, and it is the time to exterminate Japanese"; "My fellows, please boycott Japan, please love your country more"; and "Our country should garrison on the Diaoyu Islands to show our military power" (Comments collected from various Chinese Web sites). After the Diaoyu Islands incident, the number of anti-Japanese Web sites in China increased dramatically from a dozen to more than seventy. Presently, there are approximately 100,000 regular bloggers on anti-Japanese online forums, a voice that have to an extent impacted directly and indirectly on the Chinese government's stance on Japan (Ming 2007).

Pressures from online public opinions have put the Chinese government in a dilemma. On the one hand, in the view of the authorities, an anti-Japanese attitude is not in China's best interest due to the importance of Japan as an investor and trading partner. On the other, if the authorities continue to remain silent to the public's anti-Japanese sentiment and maintain a pro-Japan policy, the anger of the general public may inevitably transform into an anti-Chinese government sentiment. For instance, some online visitors stated, "The Diaoyu issue once again unveils the corruption and weakness of the CPC and the central government... It is so difficult for them to do good deeds to our citizens. The reason why the Japanese are so insatiable is that Japanese see the decay of the CPC" (Zhu 2005). Some cyber forums thus had online petitions to urge the Chinese government to intervene in the Diaoyu Islands incident. Facing this dilemma and public pressures, the authorities responded by strictly monitoring BBSs and chat rooms with an attempt to prevent them from becoming breeding grounds for anti-Japanese turning into antigovernment sentiments. Under the pressures of growing anti-Japanese opinions from both the online forums and the general public, the Chinese government finally demanded on March 26, 2005 that Japan clearly recognize the severity of the situation and unconditionally release the seven detained Chinese citizens; if not released, the issue would jeopardize Sino-Japanese relations. The Chinese government's change in tone toward Japan reflects the influence of online public opinions as a new social force. Such a response to the Diaoyu Islands situation is in part attributable to the potential threat of online opinions to the legitimacy of CPC's rule. It also demonstrates that online public opinions have the possibility of influencing the government's foreign relations. As a result of Japan's denial and ambiguity toward its role in China during the 1940s, hundreds of cyber forums specializing in Sino-Japanese relations and almost all displaying strong anti-Japanese sentiment have emerged in the last few years (Song 2005). Meanwhile, the stance of the Chinese government on Japan is becoming tougher, and China recently decided to suspend the regular meetings of top-ranking officials between the two countries.

One of the reasons for the rising nationalism along with the anti-U.S. and anti-Japanese sentiments in the foreign-relations-oriented cyber forums is China's fast economic growth and the regaining of Chinese cultural confidence. Significantly, nationalism in China is often used by leaders and elites to hold the society together and to enhance the communist ruling. In recent years, the authorities have often used online forums to mobilize the wave of nationalistic responses to certain international events.

The third trend of China's online public opinions on foreign relations is that of cyber-forums acting as platforms for mobilizing and organizing mass campaigns and/or demonstrations (Wu 2003). The massive online petition for opposing the importing of Japan's *shinkansen* for the high-speed train to operate between Beijing and Shanghai is a very successful example of online mobilization. The high-speed railway between Beijing and Shanghai is a mega project with a budget of $23 billion Chinese yuan (US$3 billion). The project is part of preparations for the 2008 Beijing Olympic Games. News that Japan's Shinkansen Bullet Train Operator was tipped as the favorite bidder to win the contract triggered an outpouring of anti-Japanese sentiment on Chinese Internet. On July 19, 2003, the cyber forum Patriots Alliance launched an online petition against Japan's Shinkansen for the Beijing–Shanghai railway project. In ten days, the petition collected more than 80,000 online signatures (Fan 2005). This was the largest-ever online petition that forced Chinese authorities to listen seriously to the public. The bid was reconsidered, thus abandoning the decision to import the Japanese Shinkansen. A month later, the Patriots Alliance Forum launched another massive online petition appealing to the Japanese government to compensate for the victims in China's northeastern city of Qiqihar who died or were injured due to unearthed chemical weapons containing deadly toxins dropped by the Japanese army during World War II. Within one month, the online petition collected 1,119,248 signatures and became the then largest petition in China's cyber-protest history (Ibid 2005).

During the same time, online public opinions in China have also transformed into several large social actions. The demonstrations against the U.S. bombing of China's Embassy in Yugoslavia in May 1999 is a typical example of actions initiated by the cyber community. With the U.S. government repeatedly claiming that it was a mistake, the Chinese government believed it as a deliberate action of aggression. Although China's official media used an angry but somewhat diplomatic tone to report the bombing, the netizens launched a strong anti-U.S. storm in cyberspace. Just one day after the bombing, there were 50,000 visitors to the Protest Forum (previously known as Strong Nation Forum). The number of visitors to the forum reached half a million within the week (Ibid 2005). They not only criticized the "American hegemony," but also initiated and organized street demonstrations.

The student-led anti-U.S. demonstrations were initiated and organized by the cyber community, but they were encouraged and facilitated by authorities as an attempt to send a political message to the United States and to stave off possible intra-elite criticism as well. Through online organizing, many large crowds, especially nationalistic college students, protested outside the U.S. Embassy in Beijing and all U.S. Consulates across China. The street demonstrations turned violent with students pelting the U.S. Embassy and consulates with rocks and water bottles and damaging property. Tens of thousands of students streamed into the center of Beijing and were joined by tens of thousands of sympathetic onlookers. The protest swelled to an estimated 100,000 people, becoming the largest street demonstration in China since the 1989 June Fourth Tiananmen Square pro-democracy movement (Zhang and Sun 2003). Again the protests generated deep concern for Chinese authorities, fearing that the protesters would eventually turn on the government. The government realized that "riding the tiger" of online nationalism could carry serious risks, thus swiftly halted the demonstrations and restore order on college campuses and streets through all means possible. Although the CPC and the government may be able to use online public opinions to serve a certain political purpose, extreme nationalistic opinions from the public may also put authorities in a difficult situation when they have to balance the public's views and the interests of the nation.

The Implications and Prospect of Online Opinions' Influence

The concepts of online public opinion and discourse have a complex genealogy (Crossley and Roberts 2004). The association between the public's political participation with democratization heavily depends on the creation of various forms of public debate and discussion. Such discussion and debates provides the space for a public sphere, but must occur outside of the realm of official government channels. In the information age, the Internet is thought to herald new possibilities of political participation for the public. Unlike traditional mass media such as newspapers and television, online networks allow people to interact directly with the information with which they are presented with. Consequently, the public can have real time conversations with authorities and voice their opinions. Claims that the Internet can lead to a greater democratization or political modernization of a society is founded on the tenets of (1) the public's uncontrolled and unlimited access to information and (2) the public's equal participation in various kinds of political and cultural discourse (Crossley and Roberts 2004). Bass (1996) similarly believes that cyberspace is and should be a discursive arena that is home to citizen debate, deliberation, agreement, and action. Here, individuals are supposed to and should be able to freely share their views with one another in a process that closely resembles true participatory democracy.

In the last few years, due to the emergence and development of the Internet in China, especially that of cyber forums, an embryonic force of public opinions mostly within cyberspace is gradually becoming a social force. Although most people, including most netizens, are not aware of the growing importance of this new social mechanism in China's transformation toward a democratic and civic society, they have nevertheless started to feel and agree that the emergence and development of the Internet and cyber forums has provided them with more opportunities to participate in public affairs. A survey on Internet usage and impact conducted in China's twelve largest cities in 2003 shows that Internet users and nonusers alike have confidence and optimism for expressing opinions on the Internet (State Information Office of China 2003). For instance, 71.8 percent of Internet users surveyed, agreed or strongly agreed that the Internet gave them more opportunities to express their political views. Similarly, 68.8 percent of Internet users surveyed also agreed or strongly agreed that the Internet allowed greater opportunities for people to criticize government policies. This corroborates with 79.2 percent of Internet users surveyed agreeing or strongly agreeing that the Internet was a tool for becoming more knowledgeable on politics. Lastly, 72.3 percent of Internet users surveyed agreed or strongly agreed that through the Internet highly ranked officials will be better acquainted with public opinion. These findings display that many now believe that at the very least, cyberspace gives them more opportunities to publicly express their views.

However, China still faces a number of serious obstacles in making the Internet and cyberspace a truly workable social mechanism. Political, economic, and cultural distortions all impede the Internet and cyber forums in China from becoming a truly powerful public force. First, there is an economic and technological obstacle; an obvious digital divide exists in China (Wilson, Wallin, and Reiser 2003).[1] Internet usage in China continues to be dominated by an extremely narrow sliver of the national demographic, primarily young, highly educated urban group. Despite the booming growth, China's Internet population is only 16 percent of the country's total population, and this percentage is lower than the world's average of 19 percent (Internet World Statistics 2007). Internet users are concentrated in a few economically and politically "developed" cities, 54.1 percent of the country's total netizens are in Beijing, Shanghai, Guangzhou, and several coastal provinces, compared to 6.4 percent of the online population from China's vast western area, the poorest part of the country (China Internet Network Information Center 2008). Moreover, only 15 percent of China's total population, mostly college students and highly educated elites, receive news information primarily through the Internet (People's Daily September 25, 2007). The remaining 85 percent of the total population still receive their news information mainly through reading the 2,100 party and government newspapers, and 98 percent of total households do so through watching programs broadcasted from 1,600 state-owned television stations (Ding 2005; Fang 2004). Thus, the majority of people in China today still rely on the official media for news information. Of the total 210 million Chinese Internet users, only 24.7 percent are those residing in rural areas, which represent just 4.3 percent of the total rural population in China (China Internet Network Information Center 2008). This clearly suggests that in China the present situation of Internet development and use cannot represent an accurate reflection of the public's opinions.

Second, there is a cultural and emotional obstacle. The recent trends in China's cyber forums show that the current Internet-using cohort is highly radical and nationalistic in outlook, particularly in the discussion forums on China's relations with the United States, Japan, Taiwan, and Hong Kong. Overall, China's cyber forums have displayed two noticeable characteristics: liberalism and radicalism, which are more apparent in the forums on foreign relations and related issues. In the Chinese context, liberalism has many positive values and is reflected in the use of liberal words, personalism, and antitradition trends on the Internet. Meanwhile, radicalism is reflected through strongly expressed responsibility to social problems and national/international politics. Although radicalism is not the dominant characteristic of online opinions, it has a stronger impact than liberalism. Radicalism in China's cyber forums may also be categorized into two types that of pro-democracy, which have a great concern for domestic political problems and advocates radical political reforms; and the other being nationalism, which is a great concern for China's foreign relations. Particularly, they advocate a radical approach to the various foreign relations. Especially in recent years, these nationalistic opinions insist that China must be treated differently in world affairs, and must reassert its "proper" world standing as a modern, advanced, and powerful nation. Opinions of this type have a strong historical, political, or cultural sentiment toward Western countries in general. The radical nature of online opinions and nationalism is not a true representation of broad public opinions as it is dominated by a small number of netzines belonging to certain social, political, or cultural groups (Wang 2004).

Third, there is a political obstacle; the authorities continue to control the Internet by filtering online content. China has the tightest regulatory and policy control of the Internet and also the best online content filtering devices in the world, despite the fact that enforcement has become increasingly difficult because more and more netizens have learned how to circumvent the filters. Nevertheless, the authorities keep trying to crush attempts to use the Internet to spread antigovernment sentiment and criticism on communist rule. If online public opinions are perceived to be too critical or politically oversensitive, they are blocked by the government's censors. Presently, various levels of government are employing different high technologies and administrative regulations to control information on the Internet and cyber forums, including content filters, voice-recognition software, surveillance cameras with the assistance of 40,000 well-trained cyber specialists acting as "web police" conducting online surveillance 24 hours a day (United Press International February 29, 2004). Technologically advanced countermeasures, such as the "Great Fire Wall," are used to block certain political Web sites to reduce the potential risks of disseminating antigovernment ideas. Although these barriers often have proven unreliable, they do have the ability to successfully block the majority of "unwanted" information and opinions on the Internet (U.S. Embassy in China 2001). According to the founders of BlogDriver, they are under pressure from authorities to censor online content that the government does not like, but because "there are so many bloggers posting and it is distributed so quickly, it is very hard to censor" (Dong 2005; Feng 2005). Thus, self-censorship has become another important method for Internet control (Harwit and Clark 2001). The government has imposed self-censorship on private Internet providers and among individual users. In fact self-censorship of Internet providers is now the primary regulating and control method over cyberspace.

Certainly, there are legitimate reasons for the CPC and the government to be very concerned with potential political risks brought on by the Internet. Most Web sites of political nature are hosted overseas and/or by unsanctioned groups inside China for "subversive" purposes. The essential problem is that there is no clear line between tolerated free speech and the politically subversive conduct that the authorities will not tolerate. Thus, the existing censorship mechanism of both government censorship and the self-censorship seriously impedes the formation of a true force of online public opinions in China. According to Hass (2004), a true force of public opinion must adhere to certain rules, such as no speaker may be prevented by internal or external coercion, from exercising their right of speaking, acting, and questioning freely. This rule reflects the emancipatory potential of the autonomous individual since government and business institutions cannot affect what any person posits or questions. The openness of expression that the "ideal speech situation" demands and requires that the rapid exchange of dialogue and production of information online take place unchecked. Therefore, censorship of electronic communication, regardless of format raises enormous outcries from those who claim that free speech is the essential component of democracy and civic society.

Conclusion

Benefiting from the rapid development of the Internet in China in recent years, cyber forums are exerting more influence on society, lifestyle, social structure, and political system. More importantly, increasing Internet users in China are trying to enhance their efforts by articulating their views on economic, political, and social issues with an attempt to change policies. This chapter suggests that online opinions in China are beginning to have an influence on China's foreign relations, despite the fact that the CPC and the government are the ultimate decision makers on foreign policy. Owing to the participation of ordinary citizens, the cyber community in China has begun to influence and challenge the authorities' monopoly of communication channels and has started to revitalize a citizen-based democracy. Today, mass media communication technology in China is still largely obedient to the state. China's traditional mass media is tightly controlled by the CPC and has immense power to determine what information people can receive. Public discussions were impossible based on traditional mass media, particularly those discussions with a political substance including opinions on foreign relations. For decades, China has had no systematic channels for the public to express themselves and participate in political and public affairs. Therefore, cyber forums have become the new and only venue for the public to voice their views and opinions, particularly on political topics. In doing so, as a whole the Internet has started providing the public with a certain degree of freedom to disseminate information, express opinions, and publish criticisms on political issues and public affairs. The Internet and cyber forums have enabled the public to break through the state's control on information, thus gradually changing the political landscape. Online opinions are not only affecting China's foreign policy and relations, but are also becoming a new social force that has started influencing many aspects of society.

It is worth noting that nationalistic sentiments reflected on Chinese cyber forums have had a strong impact on China's foreign relations, especially with its relations with the United States, Japan, Taiwan, and Hong Kong. In the last few years, while the Chinese authorities have been trying to improve ties with the United States and Japan for economic and political reasons, the public's online opinions have tended to be against such a "soft" approach. Although cyber forums in China do provide a freer space for the public to voice their opinions than before, the emergence and existence of online opinions alone cannot represent the formation of genuine public opinions. These forums do not offer the "ideal speech situation," which demand the equal participation and truly free expression from the public, due to the economic/technological, cultural/emotional, and political/ideological constraints. In other words, the unbalanced participation of the online community, the radical trend of online opinions, and the state's heavy control are seriously hampering cyberspace in China from becoming a real force of public opinions. Nonetheless, online communities are proliferating in China and have started to play a role in influencing the country's social structure and political system. The Internet has given the public a place to gather, debate, communicate, publish, receive information, and amplify its voice on political affairs. With the increasing availability of the Internet, the public's growing online political participation, and the formation of a vast virtual community, online public opinions will only become stronger, and the online civic groups will become increasingly influential. Despite the state's persistent efforts of Internet censorship, the rising tide of online opinions has become an indispensable part of the public's political life and is expanding its impact on social change.

The Internet has already set China on an irreversible course toward openness, democracy, and political modernization. With the continuing development of the Internet and continuing online political participation and with China's growing efforts to play a more important role in world affairs, online public opinions in China will become a stronger and more salient force that influences China's foreign policy and relations.

Note

1. Digital divide is a concept developed to describe the gap between those sections of the population with computers or access to computers and the Internet and those without (Liff and Steward 2001).

References

Bass, R. 1996. *Habermas' public sphere.* ERIC Lesson Plan, Publics.

Burton, J. 2005. Border officer acquitted of assault on Chinese tourist. *The Spectrum,* September 12.

Chase, M. S. and J. C. Mulvenon, 2004. Political use of the Internet in China. In *You've got dissent! Chinese dissident use of the Internet and Beijing's counterstrategies,* 1–43. RAND: National Security Research Division Books and Publications.

China Education and Research Center. 2003. *The fourth investigative report on China's outstanding cultural websites.* Available at: http://www.chinaculture.org (accessed June 18, 2008).

China Internet Network Information Center. 2003. *The internet timeline of China.* Beijing: Ministry of Information Industry.

———. 2008. *The 21st CNNIC Report.* Beijing: Ministry of Information Industry.

Chu, L. 1986. Mass communication theory: The Chinese perspective. *Media Asia* 13: 14–19.

———. 1994. Continuity and change in China's media reform. *Journal of Communication* 44: 4–21.

Crossley, N. and M. Roberts. 2004. *After Habermas: New perspective on the public sphere.* Oxford: Blackwell.

Ding, H. 2005. Interview, an official of China's Ministry of Information Industry. Beijing, China.

Dong, D. 2005. Interview, an Internet café owner. Beijing, China.

Fan, W. 2005. Interview, Professor of Foreign Affairs Institute. Beijing, China.

Fang, D. 2004. China: No comment, just facts in state media reports. *South China Morning Post* March 26.

Feng, Q. 2005. Interview, an Internet café owner. Shanghai, China.

Guo, Z. 2005. Interview, Professor of China University of Communication. Beijing, China.

Haas, T. 2004. The pubic sphere as a sphere of publics: Rethinking Habermas's theory of the public sphere. *International Communication Association Bulletin* 2: 8–10.

Hachigian, N. 2001. China's cyber-strategy. *Foreign Affairs* 80: 118–133.

Harwit, E. and D. Clark. 2001. Shaping the Internet in China: Evolution of political control over network infrastructure and content. *Asian Survey* 41: 405–407.

Hong, J. 1998. *The internationalization of television in China: The evolution of ideology, society, and media since the reform.* London: Praeger.

——. 2005a. Media reform in China. In *Chinese civilization encyclopedia,* ed. J. Luo, 389–392. Westport, CT: Greenwood.

——. 2005b. Press freedom in China. In *Chinese civilization encyclopedia,* ed. J. Luo, 481–484. Westport, CT: Greenwood.

Hong, J. and L. Huang. 2005. A split and swaying approach to building information society: The case of Internet cafes in China. *Telematics and Informatics* 22: 377–393.

Internet World Statistics. 2007. *Internet world statistics newsletter,* November 2007.

Lee, C. 1990. *Voice of China: The interplay of politics and journalism.* New York: Guilford Press.

——. 1994. *China's media, media's China.* Boulder, CO: Westview Press.

——. 2003. *Chinese media, global context.* London: Routledge.

Liff, S. and F. Steward. 2001. Community e-gateways: Locating networks and learning for social inclusion. *Information, Communication and Society* 3: 317–340.

Liu, X. 2005. Interview, Research Fellow of China Foreign Relations Institute. Beijing, China.

Ming, D. 2007. Interview, Research Fellow of China's Academy of Social Science Research. Beijing, China.

People's Daily. 2007. China Internet Congress. September 25.

Rheingold, H. 2000. *The virtual community: Homesteading on the electronic frontier.* Revised Edition. Cambridge, MA: MIT Press.

Song, X. 2005. Interview, Professor of Remin University of China. Beijing, China.

State Information Office of China. 2003. *The survey on internet usage and impact in Beijing, Shanghai, Guangzhou, Chengdu and Changsha.* Beijing, China: State Information Office.

——. 2006. *The investigative report on internet use and its impact.* Beijing, China: State Information Office.

The Straits Times. 2004. China: Beijing tightens controls on domestic reporting on Japan. October 4.

United Press International. 2004. China's Internet policy is criticized. February 29.

U.S. Embassy in China. 2001. *China's internet information skirmish.* Available at: http://www.usembassy-china.org.cn (accessed June 18, 2008).

Wang, Y. 2004. The Diaoyu Islands event: Both sides leave the difficult problem for China and Japan. *Phoenix Weekly* 143: 25–29.

Wilson, R., S. Wallin, and C. Reiser. 2003. Social stratification and the digital divide. *Social Science Computer Review* 2: 133–143.

Wu, M. 2003. *The Internet and civic protest in China: Emerging online petition.* Paper presented at Aoir Conference, Toronto, October 16–19.

Yin, K. 1994. *Case study research: Design and method.* 2nd edition. Thousand Oaks: Sage.

Zhang, D. and L. Sun. 2003. *A closer look at China.* Beijing: China Intercontinental Press.

Zhao, Y. 1998. Media, market, and democracy in China: Between the party line and the bottom Line. Champaign: University of Illinois Press.

Zhu, W. 2005. Interview, Professor of Fudan University. Shanghai, China.

Contributors

Editors

Reza Hasmath is a Sociologist at the University of Cambridge. He has published articles on topics ranging from social development practices, good governance, and the management of ethnic difference in the Americas and East Asia. He has recently completed the monograph, *The Ethnic Penalty* and the edited collection *Multiculturalism: The Great Marketing Strategy? An International Perspective.*

Jennifer Hsu is a specialist in development studies at the University of Cambridge. She has published research looking at the development of civil society organizations in China, including HIV/AIDS, and the changing nature of Chinese state-society relationship in an era of socioeconomic reforms. Her current research examines the development of migrant non-governmental organizations in China.

Authors

Carrie Liu Currier is an Assistant Professor at Texas Christian University. She has published several articles on the gendered effects of market reforms.

Xiaogang Deng is an Associate Professor of Sociology in the Department of Sociology at the University of Massachusetts, Boston. He is the Director of Criminal Justice Program. His teaching and research interests include statistics, criminology, deterrence, research methods, and deviance.

Junhao Hong is an Associate Professor at the Department of Communication, State University of New York at Buffalo. He is also a Research Associate of the Fairbank Center for East Asian Research at Harvard University. His main research interests include media and society, communication and development, and new information technology and its impact, with a focus on China and East Asian countries.

Jennifer Hubbert is based in the Department of Anthropology, Lewis and Clark College. Her most recent work has been on historical memory and public culture in China. She is currently studying the 2008 Olympics in Beijing and is working on a book about generational narratives of nationalism among Chinese intellectuals and on a paper addressing the recent growth of Chinese historical theme parks.

Andrea Leverentz is based in the Department of Sociology at the University of Massachusetts, Boston.

Ian Morley is based in the Department of History at the Chinese University of Hong Kong and is author of numerous papers on urbanism and civic design.

Paul Thiers is an Associate Professor of Political Science at Washington State University where he teaches international political economy, comparative politics, and environmental policy in the program in public affairs. His research focuses on the political, economic, and environmental consequences of interaction between global forces and local political economy in China.

Joshua Su-Ya Wu is based in the Department of Political Science at the Ohio State University. His research focuses are East Asia, a culturally sound and contextually relevant approach to study Asia's international relations and Asia's strategic balance.

Jing Yang is a Postdoctoral Fellow in the Department of Sociology, National University of Singapore.

Lening Zhang is an Associate Professor of Sociology/Criminal Justice in the Department of Behavioral Sciences at Saint Francis University. He has published approximately 50 articles and a coedited book, *Crime and Social Control in a Changing China*.

Li Zhang is a Professor in the School of Social Development and Public Policies at Fudan University. His research areas include migration, urban, and regional development in China. He has published a number of articles in academic journals, such as *China Quarterly, International Journal of Urban and Regional Research, Regional Studies, Urban Studies, Geoforum, Habitat International, International Regional Science Review, Asian Survey,* and *China Economic Review.*

INDEX

Note: Page numbers in **bold** indicate tables and figures.